THE CONVERSION OF THE IMAGINATION

The Conversion of the Imagination

Paul as Interpreter of Israel's Scripture

RICHARD B. HAYS

William B. Eerdmans Publishing Company
Grand Rapids, Michigan / Cambridge, U.K.

© 2005 Wm. B. Eerdmans Publishing Co.

Wm. B. Eerdmans Publishing Co.
255 Jefferson Ave. S.E., Grand Rapids, Michigan 49503 /
P.O. Box 163, Cambridge CB3 9PU U.K.

Printed in the United States of America

10 09 08 07 06 05   7 6 5 4 3 2 1

Library of Congress Cataloging-in-Publication Data

Hays, Richard B.
      The conversion of the imagination: Paul as interpreter of Israel's Scripture /
   Richard B. Hays.
            p.   cm.
      Includes bibliographical references.
      ISBN 0-8028-1262-7 (pbk.: alk. paper)
      1. Bible. N.T. Epistles of Paul — Relation to the Old Testament.   2. Bible. O.T.
   — Relation to the Epistles of Paul.   3. Bible. N.T. Epistles of Paul — Criticism,
   Interpretation, etc.   4. Bible. O.T. — Quotations in the New Testament.   5. Bible.
   O.T. — Criticism, interpretation, etc. — History —Early church, ca. 30-600.
   I. Title.

   BS2655.R32H38   2005
   227'.06 — dc22

                                                                    2005045111

www.eerdmans.com

Contents

Acknowledgments

I would like to acknowledge the assistance of several people who have contributed materially to the completion of this book. Jon Pott of Eerdmans encouraged publication of the book and then patiently waited more than two years for me to complete the process of assembling and revising the essays. At an early stage of the project, my research assistant David Moffitt graciously undertook the task of reading through the essays, checking the Greek and Hebrew texts, and making helpful editorial suggestions. Mary Ann Andrus provided administrative support and helped to secure permissions for reprinting of the essays. Carole Baker, Research Associate at Duke Divinity School, cheerfully and capably undertook the painstaking work of reading page proofs and compiling the indexes. Thanks are due also to Duke Divinity School for a sabbatical leave during the Fall semester of 2004, during which the process of editing and reworking was brought to completion. The editorial staff of Eerdmans has been unfailingly professional and helpful in the complex task of assembling this group of disparate essays into a coherent volume.

Most of all, my wife Judy took time from her own professional work to help with necessary correspondence in conceptualizing and launching the project, provided encouragement at every turn, and listened to more thinking out loud than could reasonably have been anticipated when we took our marriage vows. I offer her inadequate but heartfelt thanks.

Grateful acknowledgment is made for permission to reprint the following material, some of which has been revised and expanded for inclusion in the present volume.

"The Conversion of the Imagination: Scripture and Eschatology in 1 Corinthians," *New Testament Studies* 45 (1999) 391-412. Reprinted with permission of Cambridge University Press.

"'Who Has Believed Our Message?' Paul's Reading of Isaiah," *SBL Seminar Papers* 1998, 205-25. Reprinted with permission. This essay has also appeared in John M. Court, *New Testament Writers in the Old Testament: An Introduction* (London: SPCK, 2002), pp. 46-70.

"Psalm 143 and the Logic of Romans 3," *Journal of Biblical Literature* 99 (1980) 107-15. Reprinted with permission of the Society of Biblical Literature.

"'Have We Found Abraham to Be Our Forefather according to the Flesh?' A Reconsideration of Rom 4:1," *Novum Testamentum* 27 (1985) 76-98. Reprinted with permission of Brill Academic Publishers.

"Three Dramatic Roles: The Law in Romans 3–4," pp. 151-64 in J. D. G. Dunn (ed.), *Paul and the Mosaic Law*. Wissenschaftliche Untersuchungen zum Neuen Testament 89. Tübingen: J. C. B. Mohr, 1996. Reprinted with permission.

"Christ Prays the Psalms: Paul's Use of Early Christian Exegetical Convention." Reprinted by permission from *The Future of Christology*, edited by Abraham J. Malherbe and Wayne A. Meeks, copyright 1993 Augsburg Fortress, pp. 122-36.

"'The Righteous One' as Eschatological Deliverer: Hermeneutics at the Turn of the Ages," pp. 191-215 in J. Marcus and M. L. Soards (eds.), *The New Testament and Apocalyptic*. Sheffield: JSOT Press, 1988. Reprinted with permission of Sheffield Academic Press.

"The Role of Scripture in Paul's Ethics," pp. 30-47 in E. H. Lovering, Jr. and J. L. Sumney (eds.), *Theology and Ethics in Paul and His Interpreters*. Nashville: Abingdon Press, 1996. Used by permission.

"On the Rebound: A Response to Critiques of Echoes of Scripture in the Letters of Paul," pp. 70-96 in C. A. Evans and J. A. Sanders (eds.), *Paul and the Scriptures of Israel*. JSNT Supplements 83. Sheffield: JSOT, 1993. Reprinted with permission of Sheffield Academic Press.

"Salvation by Trust? Reading the Bible Faithfully," Copyright 1997 Christian Century Foundation. Reprinted by permission from the Feb. 26, 1997, issue of the *Christian Century*. Subscriptions from P.O. Box 378, Mt. Morris, IL 61054. 1-800-208-4097. This essay has also appeared in Richard Lischer (ed.), *The Company of Preachers: Wisdom on Preaching, Augustine to the Present* (Grand Rapids: Eerdmans, 2002), pp. 265-74.

INTRODUCTION:

Learning from Paul
How to Read Israel's Scripture

This book advances three theses: (1) the interpretation of Israel's Scripture was central to the apostle Paul's thought; (2) we can learn from Paul's example how to read Scripture faithfully; (3) if we do follow his example, the church's imagination will be converted to see both Scripture and the world in a radically new way.

These claims are hardly novel: they go back at least to Origen, who declared that Paul "taught the church which he had gathered from among the Gentiles how to understand the books of the Law" (*Homilies on Exodus* 5.1). As a Christian interpreter living in a pagan world, Origen was able to see clearly that Gentile converts to the faith needed to have their minds remade, and that instruction in how to read Scripture was at the heart of Paul's pastoral practice: Gentiles needed to be initiated into reading practices that enabled them to receive Israel's Scripture as their own.[1] Thus, Origen, the greatest biblical interpreter of his era, saw in Paul a precursor and mentor. In modernity, however, this aspect of Paul's teaching has tended to recede from view. Most interpreters in the nineteenth and twentieth centuries gave little attention to scriptural interpretation as a constitutive element of Pauline theology — or, to the extent that they did take note of Paul's scriptural interpretation, they regarded it as aberrant and embarrassing, heedless of the literal sense of the Old Testament texts.

Within the past twenty years there has been a resurgence of interest in

---

1. For a helpful introduction to Origen as scriptural interpreter, see L. T. Johnson, "Origen and the Transformation of the Mind," in L. T. Johnson and W. S. Kurz, S.J., *The Future of Catholic Biblical Scholarship: A Constructive Conversation* (Grand Rapids: Eerdmans, 2002), 64-90.

and appreciation for Paul as a reader of Scripture. My own work, particularly *Echoes of Scripture in the Letters of Paul*,[2] has played some role in encouraging this renewed interest, but I suspect several factors have converged to make Paul's biblical interpretation a matter for lively attention at the end of the twentieth century and the beginning of the twenty-first. These factors include: the post-Holocaust reassessment of Judaism and the Jewish roots of Christianity; renewed dialogue between Jewish and Christian interpreters; the demise of modernist historicism as a dominant hermeneutical paradigm; the emergence of "intertextuality" as a vital perspective in literary-critical studies;[3] growing interest in the biblical canon as a significant context for theological hermeneutics; and the concern within "postliberal" theology to reconnect with the particular ways of reasoning that are integral to the classic Christian confessional tradition. In my judgment all these developments are to be welcomed, and all will promote the theological health of the church.

Within the framework of these wider cultural developments, the essays in this volume constitute a series of engagements with Paul as an interpreter of Scripture. I was drawn to this topic early in my scholarly career not merely by intellectual curiosity — though the issues are fascinating in their own right — but by a persistent sense that the church was in great need of a better way of approaching the Bible.[4] The usual options on offer were (to paint with a very broad brush) some version of liberal demythologizing on one hand and conservative literalism on the other. Each option was, in its own way, rigid and unimaginative, and neither was life-giving for the community of faith. (Indeed, as I now see it, each was simply a different permutation of an epistemologically cramped modernism.) Most tellingly, neither approach seemed able to account adequately for the ways in which *Paul* actually read the biblical texts. In contrast to the demythologizing hermeneutic, Paul celebrated Scripture's witness to the real and radical apocalyptic action of God in the world; in contrast to the literalist hermeneutic, Paul engaged Scripture with great imaginative freedom, without the characteristic modernist anxiety about factuality and authorial intention. And so I began to investigate

2. R. B. Hays, *Echoes of Scripture in the Letters of Paul* (New Haven: Yale University Press, 1989).

3. For an assessment of this development, see S. Alkier and R. B. Hays, eds., *Die Bibel im Dialog der Schriften: Konzepte Intertextuelle Bibellektüre* (Tübingen: Francke, 2005).

4. On this topic see now E. F. Davis and R. B. Hays, eds., *The Art of Reading Scripture* (Grand Rapids: Eerdmans, 2003).

Paul more closely to see if I could understand what he was doing as a reader of the Bible that he knew (which was, of course, that collection of sacred writings that Christians later came to call the Old Testament).

The underlying purpose of all the essays collected here, then, is to explore what Scripture looks like from within Paul's imaginative narrative world. The result of the exploration — carried out through a series of admittedly tentative probes — is to discover a way of reading that summons the reader to an epistemological transformation, a *conversion of the imagination*. The fruit of such a conversion is described in this book's culminating essay, "A Hermeneutic of Trust."

The essays appeared in various journals, Festschriften, and essay collections during the period 1980-1999. Some of them preceded the publication of *Echoes of Scripture in the Letters of Paul* and represented my early attempts to think through these problems. The greater number of them followed the publication of *Echoes,* seeking to work out the fuller implications of the reading of Paul that I set forth in that book. Although these pieces were written discretely for various occasions, taken together they represent a sustained attempt, over a period of twenty years, to wrestle with Paul as a hermeneutical model, an exemplar of how we might learn anew to read Scripture.[5]

The first chapter in the book, "The Conversion of the Imagination: Scripture and Eschatology in 1 Corinthians," was actually the last one written, and it therefore represents a capstone to my work on these questions. I have placed it first in the present volume because it most clearly articulates the conceptual framework within which the other essays are to be read. An earlier form of the essay was originally presented as an invited main paper at the meeting of the Studiorum Novi Testamenti Societas in Copenhagen in 1998.[6] This essay, which draws together insights I gained while writing a

5. The essays included here have been reprinted substantially in their original form, though they have been edited stylistically, and in a few places I have made brief but substantive revisions or additions, along with selected bibliographic updates. The pieces still bear some telltale marks of their original settings (as I shall explain below), and I have not sought to eliminate all overlaps between them. This results in a few redundancies, but in these cases readers may be interested to see how an idea that originally surfaced in one context is redeployed and developed in a subsequent argument.

6. I profited significantly from the responses and suggestions of several colleagues at that international gathering, and the piece was subsequently revised and published in *NTS* 45 (1999): 391-412.

commentary on 1 Corinthians,[7] seeks to link two dimensions of Paul's thought that are often set in artificial antithesis to one another: narrative continuity with Israel's story and radical apocalyptic transformation. In 1 Corinthians both elements are grounded in Paul's reading of Israel's Scripture. I contend that Paul's pastoral strategy for reshaping the consciousness of his pagan converts was to narrate them into Israel's story through metaphorical appropriation of Scripture — and precisely by so doing to teach them to think apocalyptically.

The second chapter, "'Who Has Believed Our Message?' Paul's Reading of Isaiah," was first presented as an invited paper for the Formation of Isaiah Group at the Annual Meeting of the Society of Biblical Literature in Orlando, Florida, in 1998.[8] This piece is placed near the beginning of the present volume because it articulates a literary-theological approach to intertextuality and offers a more fully developed discussion of the seven criteria for discerning the presence of Old Testament echoes in Paul that I originally set forth in *Echoes*.[9] Thus, the essay provides a significant methodological foundation for the other studies that follow. I would like to acknowledge the particular help and stimulation provided by J. Ross Wagner, now associate professor of New Testament at Princeton Theological Seminary, who was at the time I composed this article in the midst of writing his Duke dissertation on Paul's reading of Isaiah in Rom 9–11.[10] Many of the ideas set forth in this article emerged in the course of our lively ongoing conversations about Paul and Isaiah, and my way of seeing the issues owes much to his insights.

The next four chapters focus in various ways on Paul's use of Scripture in the argument of his letter to the Romans. The first of these, "Psalm 143 as Testimony to the Righteousness of God," is the oldest piece in this book. It was originally written for Leander Keck's seminar on Paul at Emory University, during my graduate student days.[11] This short essay may be seen as the

---

7. R. B. Hays, *First Corinthians*, Interpretation (Louisville: John Knox, 1997).

8. This essay was published in the *SBL 1998 Seminar Papers*, 205-24, and subsequently reprinted in J. M. Court, ed., *New Testament Writers and the Old Testament: An Introduction* (London: SPCK, 2002), 46-70.

9. Hays, *Echoes*, 29-33.

10. See J. R. Wagner, *Heralds of the Good News: Isaiah and Paul "In Concert" in the Letter to the Romans*, NovTSup 101 (Leiden: Brill, 2002).

11. The essay was published under the title "Psalm 143 and the Logic of Romans 3," *JBL* 99 (1980): 107-15.

seed from which my subsequent work on Paul's interpretation of Scripture grew. It was here, in a close reading of Rom 3, that I first realized how crucial it is to understand the wider literary context of Paul's OT citations and allusions: Ps 143 provides the intertextual matrix within which Paul's argument in Rom 3 finds its coherence. Though John Hollander had not yet published *The Figure of Echo*,[12] and I was therefore not yet acquainted with his exposition of the term "metalepsis," I was already describing in this essay the *phenomenon* of metalepsis, the sort of semantically resonant intertextual interaction I was later to explore more fully in *Echoes*. I also realized, in the course of working on this piece, that the famous debate between Ernst Käsemann and Rudolf Bultmann over the meaning of δικαιοσύνη θεοῦ had been misconceived. Käsemann was right to challenge Bultmann's neo-Lutheran interpretation of "the righteousness of God" but wrong to think he needed to find some special history-of-religions background for this idea outside the biblical canon. In fact, Paul finds δικαιοσύνη θεοῦ right before his eyes in the Psalter, specifically in the very psalm to which he alludes in Rom 3:20. The fact that this key source for Paul's theological reflection was overlooked by exegetes as insightful as Bultmann and Käsemann was, to say the least, thought-provoking. I began to wonder how much more of Paul's argumentation might presuppose biblical contexts that had been insufficiently appreciated by modern interpreters.

Chapter 4, "Abraham as Father of Jews and Gentiles," investigates Paul's revisionary rereading of the Abraham story in Rom 4.[13] This essay, written during my early years of teaching at Yale Divinity School, reflects my attempts to help students grasp the unfolding logic of Paul's letter to the Romans. (And I am therefore grateful to my Yale students in the early 1980s for their helpful questions and comments on early versions of this argument.) Though the article initially takes off from the springboard of a fresh proposal about the translation of the notoriously vexing Greek text of Rom 4:1, the heart of its argument is to show that all of Rom 4 must be read as Paul's demonstration that his gospel *confirms*, rather than negates, the Law, as he claims in Rom 3:31. Paul's argument works only if Abraham is understood as a narrative prototype whose faith prefigures the faithful-

---

12. John Hollander, *The Figure of Echo: A Mode of Allusion in Milton and After* (Berkeley: University of California Press, 1981).

13. Originally published as "'Have We Found Abraham to Be Our Forefather according to the Flesh?' A Reconsideration of Rom 4:1," *NovT* 27 (1985): 76-98.

ness of Christ, through whom many are blessed. The point has often been missed by interpretations that focus on Abraham's faith as a precursor of the Christian's subjective faith in Christ. In fact, "faith in Christ" plays no role in Rom 4. My essay seeks to explore how Rom 4 offers a thoroughly Jewish reading of the Genesis story; Paul is seeking to persuade his readers that the gospel of inclusion of Gentiles in the promised blessing is already present, at least proleptically, in the scriptural text.

Chapter 5, "Three Dramatic Roles: The Law in Romans 3–4," was originally presented in 1994 in Durham, England, at the Durham-Tübingen Research Symposium on Earliest Christianity and Judaism.[14] My assignment for that conference was to offer an account of Paul's treatment of Law in Rom 3–4. This essay develops the proposal that Paul's diverse statements about the Law, which have caused so much difficulty for interpreters who seek systematic uniformity in Paul's thought, are best understood as narratively ordered within an unfolding dramatic plot, so that the role of the Law changes at different stages of the story. This approach allows for the exploration of several themes not developed in the previous chapters of this book: the identity-marking function of Scripture, the role of the Law in pronouncing condemnation on all humanity, and the *oracular* function of the Law as a witness giving mysteriously coded testimony to the gospel. If Paul can employ Scripture for such different purposes, we would be ill-advised to seek a reductive or homogenizing account of these varying uses. The imaginative range of Paul's uses of Scripture corresponds to a range of voices present within Scripture itself.

The final essay in this group of studies on Romans, "Christ Prays the Psalms: Israel's Psalter as Matrix of Early Christology," focuses on Rom 15. This chapter, originally written for a Festschrift in honor of Leander Keck[15] and expanded somewhat in the present volume, marks something of a turning point in my own thought about Paul's use of Scripture. My earlier work had emphasized the ecclesiocentric character of Paul's interpretations: he read the OT as being chiefly "about" the church. In this essay, however, I explore a passage in which Paul surprisingly represents Christ as the praying voice of Ps 69. This passage turns out to be an impor-

14. It was subsequently published in J. D. G. Dunn, ed., *Paul and the Mosaic Law*, WUNT 89 (Tübingen: Mohr Siebeck, 1996), 151-64.

15. "Christ Prays the Psalms: Paul's Use of an Early Christian Exegetical Convention," in *The Future of Christology: Essays in Honor of Leander E. Keck*, ed. A. J. Malherbe and W. A. Meeks (Minneapolis: Fortress, 1993), 122-36.

tant clue about the key role of Israel's lament psalms in the formation of the earliest church's understanding of Jesus' identity. The revised form of the essay that appears in this book adds some concluding reflections about the broader implications of Rom 15:1-13 for understanding the way in which the converted imagination of the church produced revisionary interpretations of the Psalter — and vice versa.

Chapter 7, "Apocalyptic Hermeneutics: Habakkuk Proclaims 'The Righteous One,'" originally appeared in a Festschrift for J. Louis Martyn.[16] The emphasis on apocalyptic, suggested by Martyn's important work on Paul, proved illuminating when applied to the analysis of Paul's scriptural hermeneutics. My essay argues that Paul's reading of Scripture leads us into apocalyptic perceptions not only of the biblical text but also of the reality in which we find ourselves. The main burden of the essay is to advocate an apocalyptic-messianic interpretation of ὁ δίκαιος ("the Righteous One") in Paul's reading of Hab 2:4; however, this interpretation has larger implications for the apocalyptic character of Pauline hermeneutics as a whole. As I would now put the matter, Paul rereads Scripture with an imagination converted by the death and resurrection of Jesus.

An imagination so converted will necessarily see the moral world in which we live and move through new eyes. That is the theme of chapter 8, an essay originally contributed to a Festschrift for Victor Furnish.[17] This chapter aims to show that despite the relative paucity of appeals to Scripture as a source of laws or moral rules, Paul nonetheless employs Scripture as the source of the world story in which the community of Christ's people is to find its identity. This scripturally grounded identity then shapes the community's action in highly specific ways. More than some of the other essays in this book, this chapter emphasizes the community-forming dimensions of Paul's hermeneutical practices. Readers will note the significant thematic connections between this essay and the book's opening chapter, "The Conversion of the Imagination."

As explained at the beginning of chapter 9, this essay ("On the Rebound: A Response to Critiques of *Echoes of Scripture in the Letters of*

16. "'The Righteous One' as Eschatological Deliverer: A Case Study in Paul's Apocalyptic Hermeneutics," in *The New Testament and Apocalyptic*, ed. J. Marcus and M. L. Soards, JSNTSup 24 (Sheffield: JSOT Press, 1989).

17. "The Role of Scripture in Paul's Ethics," in *Theology and Ethics in Paul and His Interpreters: Essays in Honor of Victor Paul Furnish*, ed. E. H. Lovering, Jr., and J. L. Sumney (Nashville: Abingdon, 1996), 30-47.

Paul") has a somewhat different character from the other chapters in this volume. The essay originated in a Society of Biblical Literature program unit (Scripture in Early Judaism and Christianity) that organized a special session in 1990 focused on critical responses to my book. The piece that appears here is my reply to these critiques, now edited in a way to make the reply intelligible as a freestanding essay. Thus, while most of the other chapters in this book are exegetical in character, chapter 9 focuses on methodological issues. Some of the questions posed by my respondents (Craig Evans, James Sanders, William Scott Green, and the late J. Christiaan Beker) have continued to surface in various ways in the ongoing critical conversation about Pauline scriptural interpretation; therefore, I hope readers will find this chapter of value. Those who are less interested in questions of method may skip this essay and go on to the last chapter.

Chapter 10, "A Hermeneutic of Trust," was originally presented in the Bible and Christian Theology section of the SBL meeting in 1996, where it elicited strong approbation from some and expressions of dismay from others.[18] In this respect the essay found a reception not unlike the reception accorded to the apostle who was its inspiration. More than the other essays in this book, "A Hermeneutic of Trust" seeks to articulate constructively the implications of learning from Paul how to read Scripture. For that reason it provides an appropriate conclusion to this volume. The key contention of this essay is that Paul's hermeneutic of trust (πίστις) offers a dramatic and life-giving alternative to the corrosive hermeneutic of suspicion that has come to dominate the modern academy.

When these ten essays are viewed together, certain key themes surface repeatedly. A brief summary of these themes may help readers keep the larger landscape in view as they pick their way amongst the trees.

First, Paul's interpretation of Scripture is always a pastoral, community-forming activity. His readings are not merely flights of imaginative virtuosity; rather, they seek to shape the identity and actions of a community called by God to be the bearers of grace. The conversion of the imagination that Paul seeks is not merely the spiritual enlightenment of

---

18. It subsequently appeared as "Salvation by Trust? Reading the Bible Faithfully," *Christian Century* 114, no. 7 (February 26, 1997): 218-23; it was later anthologized, under the present title, in R. Lischer, ed., *The Company of Preachers: Wisdom on Preaching, Augustine to the Present* (Grand Rapids: Eerdmans, 2002), 265-74.

individuals but rather the transformed consciousness of the community of the faithful.

Second, Paul's readings of Scripture are *poetic* in character. He finds in Scripture a rich source of image and metaphor that enables him to declare with power what God is doing in the world in his own time. He reads the Bible neither as a historian nor as a systematic theologian but as a poetic preacher who discerns analogical correspondences between the scriptural story and the gospel that he proclaims.

Third, as the previous observation suggests, Paul reads Scripture *narratively.* It is not for him merely a repository of isolated proof texts; rather, it is the saga of God's election, judgment, and redemption of a people through time.[19] Paul sees the church that has come into being in his own day as the heir of that vast ancient story and as the remarkable fulfillment of the promises made to Israel.

Fourth, the fulfillment of those promises has taken an entirely unexpected turn because of the world-shattering apocalyptic event of the crucifixion and resurrection of the Messiah, Jesus. When he rereads Israel's Scripture retrospectively, Paul finds numerous prefigurations[20] of this revelatory event — which nevertheless came as a total surprise to Israel and continues to function as a stumbling block for those who do not believe. Once the Scriptures are grasped in light of this hermeneutical key, their pervasively eschatological character comes into focus; therefore, Paul seeks to teach his readers to read Scripture *eschatologically,* mindful of God's final judgment of every human thought and action, while also looking forward in hope to God's final reconciliation of all things to himself.

Finally, Paul reads Scripture *trustingly.* He believes that Scripture discloses a God who loves us and can be trusted, in his righteousness, to keep his promises and to save us. Thus, he always comes to the reading of Israel's Scripture with the expectation that what he will find there is a word of deep grace.

Taken together, the essays in this volume invite the reader to come to grips with one of the most brilliant and provocative readers of Scripture that Is-

---

19. In support of the claim that Paul reads scriptural texts with a view to their contextual narrative sense, see now also Francis Watson, *Paul and the Hermeneutics of Faith* (London: T. & T. Clark, 2004).

20. Especially in the Psalms.

rael's tradition has ever produced. Despite the many objections that may fairly be raised about Paul's intertextual interpretations, his powerful imaginative readings continue to generate new communities of readers who are transformed by the renewing of their minds and thereby summoned to lives of self-critical humility and self-giving service. They are sustained in that self-criticism and self-giving precisely by reading Scripture in the imaginative way Paul modeled. It is my hope that this collection of studies may enable such readers to gain a more penetrating understanding of the conversion of the imagination to which Paul's construal of Scripture calls us.

Abbreviations

AB	Anchor Bible
ABD	*The Anchor Bible Dictionary* (ed. Freedman)
AGJU	Arbeiten zur Geschichte des antiken Judentums und des Urchristentums
AnBib	Analecta biblica
ANTC	Abingdon New Testament Commentaries
BAGD	Bauer, Arndt, Gingrich, and Danker, *Greek-English Lexicon of the NT*
BDF	Blass, Debrunner, and Funk, *A Greek Grammar of the NT*
BETL	Bibliotheca ephemeridum theologicarum lovaniensium
BevT	Beiträge zur evangelischen Theologie
BFCT	Beiträge zur Förderung christlicher Theologie
BHT	Beiträge zur historischen Theologie
Bib	*Biblica*
BZNW	Beihefte zur *ZNW*
CBQ	*Catholic Biblical Quarterly*
CRINT	Compendia rerum iudaicarum ad novum testamentum
EKKNT	Evangelisch-katholischer Kommentar zum Neuen Testament
ET	English translation
EvT	*Evangelische Theologie*
ExpTim	*Expository Times*
FRLANT	Forschungen zur Religion und Literatur des Alten und Neuen Testaments
HBT	*Horizons in Biblical Theology*

xviii

HeyJ	*Heythrop Journal*
HNT	Handbuch zum Neuen Testament
HNTC	Harper's NT Commentaries
HTKNT	Herders theologischer Kommentar zum Neuen Testament
HTR	*Harvard Theological Review*
HUT	Hermeneutische Untersuchungen zur Theologie
ICC	International Critical Commentary
IDBSup	Supplementary volume to *Interpreter's Dictionary of the Bible*
Int	*Interpretation*
JAAR	*Journal of the American Academy of Religion*
JBL	*Journal of Biblical Literature*
JRE	*Journal of Religious Ethics*
JSNT	*Journal for the Study of the New Testament*
JSNTSup	Journal for the Study of the New Testament — Supplement Series
JSOTSup	Journal for the Study of the Old Testament — Supplement Series
JSS	*Journal of Semitic Studies*
JTS	*Journal of Theological Studies*
KJV	King James Version
LXX	Septuagint
MeyerK	H. A. W. Meyer, Kritisch-exegetischer Kommentar über das Neue Testament
MNTC	Moffatt NT Commentary
MT	Masoretic Text
MTZ	*Münchener theologische Zeitschrift*
NCB	New Century Bible
NICNT	New International Commentary on the New Testament
NovT	*Novum Testamentum*
NovTSup	Novum Testamentum, Supplements
NRSV	New Revised Standard Version
NTD	Das Neue Testament Deutsch
NTS	*New Testament Studies*
OTP	*Old Testament Pseudepigrapha* (ed. Charlesworth)
ResQ	*Restoration Quarterly*

RSV	Revised Standard Version
SBLDS	SBL Dissertation Series
SBLSP	SBL Seminar Papers
SBS	Stuttgarter Bibelstudien
SEÅ	*Svensk exegetisk årsbok*
SNTSMS	Society for New Testament Studies Monograph Series
SVTP	Studia in Veteris Testamenti pseudepigrapha
TDNT	*Theological Dictionary of the New Testament* (ed. Kittel and Friedrich)
TLZ	*Theologische Literaturzeitung*
TS	*Theological Studies*
TSK	*Theologische Studien und Kritiken*
VT	*Vetus Testamentum*
WBC	Word Biblical Commentary
WTJ	*Westminster Theological Journal*
WUNT	Wissenschaftliche Untersuchungen zum Neuen Testament
ZNW	*Zeitschrift für die neutestamentliche Wissenschaft*
ZTK	*Zeitschrift für Theologie und Kirche*

The Conversion of the Imagination:
Scripture and Eschatology in 1 Corinthians

Were the Corinthians Performing Isaiah's Script (1 Cor 14:25)?

At the conclusion of a long argument urging the Corinthians to practice intelligible prophecy rather than unintelligible speech in tongues, Paul asks them to consider the effects of their speech on outsiders who may be present in their worship assembly. "If, therefore, the whole church comes together and all speak in tongues, and outsiders or unbelievers enter, will they not say that you are out of your mind? But if all prophesy, and an unbeliever or outsider enters, he is reproved by all, called to account by all. The hidden things of his heart are disclosed, and thus, he will fall on his face and worship God, declaring, 'Truly, God is among you'" (1 Cor 14:23-25). Although there is no explicit citation formula here signaling an Old Testament quotation, it has been widely recognized that Paul's imagined description of the unbeliever's reaction alludes to at least two passages from the prophets, Isa 45:14 and Zech 8:23. Nestle-Aland[27], in fact, treats the words ὁ θεὸς ἐν ὑμῖν ἐστιν as a direct quotation of the Isaiah passage,[1] with a marginal notation indicating an allusion to Zechariah. The possible significance of these intertextual connections, however, has rarely received sustained consideration.[2] The two most comprehensive recent studies of

---

1. Nestle-Aland also italicizes ὄντως as part of the quotation, although this word is lacking in the LXX. See, however, the MT of 45:15, in which אכן is the first word.

2. Commentators who briefly note the OT reference include H.-D. Wendland, *Die Briefe an die Korinther*, NTD 7 (Göttingen: Vandenhoeck & Ruprecht, 1954), 113; C. K. Barrett, *The First Epistle to the Corinthians*, HNTC (New York: Harper and Row, 1968), 327; H. Conzelmann, *1 Corinthians*, Hermeneia (Philadelphia: Fortress, 1975), 244 n. 35; G. D. Fee, *The First Epistle to the Corinthians*, NICNT (Grand Rapids: Eerdmans, 1987), 687; A. Linde-

Paul's citation technique, those of Dietrich-Alex Koch and Christopher D. Stanley, explicitly decline to treat 1 Cor 14:25c as an OT quotation and offer no discussion of the passage.[3]

In the absence of a citation formula, some scholars remain skeptical that Paul intends to remind his readers of any OT passage.[4] Allusions and echoes are for those who have ears to hear. Nonetheless, as a heuristic exercise, let us pose the following question: *If* in fact 1 Cor 14:25 does echo the language of Israel's prophets, how would this echo affect our interpretation of the text?

In *Echoes of Scripture in the Letters of Paul* I sought to show that Paul's OT allusions and echoes frequently exemplify the literary trope of metalepsis. Metalepsis is a rhetorical and poetic device in which one text alludes to an earlier text in a way that evokes resonances of the earlier text *beyond those explicitly cited.* The result is that the interpretation of a metalepsis requires the reader to recover unstated or suppressed correspondences between the two texts.[5] If Paul's phrasing in 1 Cor 14:25 is, as I

---

mann, "Die Schrift als Tradition: Beobachtungen zu den biblischen Zitaten im Ersten Korintherbrief," in *Schrift und Tradition: Festschrift für Josef Ernst zum 70. Geburtstag,* ed. K. Backhaus and F. G. Untergassmair (Paderborn, Munich, Vienna, and Zürich: Schöningh, 1996), 219-20; R. B. Hays, *First Corinthians,* Interpretation (Louisville: John Knox, 1997), 239. A. Robertson and A. Plummer (*A Critical and Exegetical Commentary on the First Epistle of St. Paul to the Corinthians,* 2nd ed., ICC [Edinburgh: T. & T. Clark, 1914], 319) cite a distant parallel from Plato's *Symposium* but overlook the OT quotation. The most extensive treatment known to me is the recently published study of Florian Wilk, *Die Bedeutung des Jesajabuches für Paulus,* FRLANT 179 (Göttingen: Vandenhoeck & Ruprecht, 1998), 331-33.

3. Koch does not discuss the passage, commenting that the relation of Paul's formulation to the alleged OT source is "wesentlich lockerer" than other cases where he does acknowledge an unmarked quotation (*Die Schrift als Zeuge des Evangeliums: Untersuchungen zur Verwendung und zum Verständnis der Schrift bei Paulus,* BHT 69 [Tübingen: J. C. B. Mohr (Paul Siebeck), 1986], 18). Stanley excludes the passage from consideration because he is following "strict guidelines that limit the investigation to passages that offer explicit indication to the reader that a citation is being offered" (*Paul and the Language of Scripture: Citation Technique in the Pauline Epistles and Contemporary Literature,* SNTSMS 69 [Cambridge: Cambridge University Press, 1992], 206 n. 85).

4. Everyone acknowledges that within the same paragraph, at 1 Cor 14:21, Paul explicitly quotes Isa 28:11-12. His interpretation of this passage is so obscure that most critical attention has focused on the explicit quotation. On 14:21 see Hays, *First Corinthians,* 238-40. The presence of an explicit Isaiah quotation in the paragraph enhances the likelihood that Paul is alluding to another passage from Isaiah in 14:25.

5. For fuller explanation of this approach to reading Paul's intertextual echoes, see R. B. Hays, *Echoes of Scripture in the Letters of Paul* (New Haven and London: Yale University

believe, an instance of metalepsis, we must go back and examine the wider contexts in the scriptural precursors to understand the figurative effects produced by the intertextual connections.

Isa 45 is part of Deutero-Isaiah's prophecy concerning the end of Israel's exile and the restoration of Jerusalem. As a result of this dramatic turn in Israel's fortunes, the Gentile nations will be moved to recognize the glory of Israel's God (cf. Isa 49:23; 60:1-16). "And they shall bow down (προσκυνήσουσιν) before you and pray to you, because God is among you (ἐν σοὶ ὁ θεός ἐστιν), and they shall say, 'There is no God besides you; for you are God, and we did not know it, the God of Israel, the Savior'" (Isa 45:14b-15 LXX). Paul echoes the verb προσκυνήσουσιν, changing it to the singular προσκυνήσει since he is talking about a single Gentile unbeliever, and he repeats the quotation "God is among you," changing the pronoun from singular σοὶ to plural ὑμῖν because he is referring not to Israel as a nation but to the assembled community of worshipers in Corinth.[6] Thus, Paul subtly pictures the conversion of Gentile unbelievers through the prophetic activity of Corinthian Christians as a fulfillment of Isaiah's eschatological vision: the Gentiles will recognize the presence of God in the midst of God's people.

Similar motifs appear in Zech 8:20-23 and in Dan 2:46-47.[7] The strongest verbal connection, however, is to Isa 45:14. In all three of these OT subtexts we see a common pattern: through the mediating witness of the people of God, the Gentile outsider is brought to offer worship to Israel's God. This way of formulating the matter, however, immediately exposes

---

Press, 1989), 14-21. For a full discussion of the trope in literature ancient and modern, see J. Hollander, *The Figure of Echo: A Mode of Allusion in Milton and After* (Berkeley: University of California Press, 1981). A similar literary phenomenon has been traced within the Hebrew Bible by Michael Fishbane, *Biblical Interpretation in Ancient Israel* (Oxford: Clarendon, 1985). For important reviews and critiques of the methodology of *Echoes*, see H. Hübner, "Intertextualität — die hermeneutische Strategie des Paulus," *TLZ* 116 (1991): 881-98; C. A. Evans and J. A. Sanders, eds., *Paul and the Scriptures of Israel*, JSNTSup 83 (Sheffield: JSOT Press, 1993), 42-96.

6. As Koch and Stanley have shown, adaptations of this sort are a standard feature of Paul's quotation practice: he tailors the grammar and syntax of the quotation to fit the application he is giving it.

7. The Daniel passage, though overlooked by Nestle-Aland, is noted by Wendland, *Briefe an die Korinther*, 113; Barrett, *First Epistle*, 327; H. Hübner, *Biblische Theologie des Neuen Testaments*, vol. 2 (Göttingen: Vandenhoeck & Ruprecht, 1993), 197; Wilk, *Bedeutung des Jesajabuches*, 331.

the novelty of Paul's metaleptic evocation of Isaiah in 1 Cor 14:25. In Paul's scenario it is *the church* — itself a predominantly Gentile community — through which God will accomplish the eschatological conversion of outsiders. The Gentile Christian "understudies" seem now to have stepped into the role originally assigned to Israel in Isaiah's eschatological drama. Using the scriptural imagery in a metaphorical manner, Paul has clothed his depiction of the conversion of "outsiders" in language that originally had been used by Isaiah to portray the response of Gentiles to an eschatologically restored *Israel*.

Theses concerning Apocalyptic Eschatology and Scripture in 1 Corinthians

I offer these preliminary remarks about 1 Cor 14:25 as a "teaser," a way of reopening the question of Scripture and eschatology in 1 Corinthians. We have become so thoroughly accustomed to thinking of Paul as "Apostle to the Gentiles" that we may be in danger of overlooking what this self-designation suggests: Paul understood himself as a Jew sent by the God of Israel to the world of Gentile "outsiders" for the purpose of declaring to them the message of eschatological salvation promised in Israel's Scriptures — preeminently Isaiah — to the whole world.

In Gal 1:15-16 Paul describes his own call to this apostolic ministry in language that echoes the vocation of the "servant" of Isa 49, whom God sends as "a light to the nations, that my salvation may reach to the end of the earth" (Isa 49:6; see the parallel between Gal 1:15 and Isa 49:1). This means that Paul understands his apostolic vocation to be inseparable from his *apocalyptic interpretation of certain biblical texts* that prefigure the events of the end time. His gospel proclaims that through the death and resurrection of Jesus this end time has broken in upon the world. It is no accident that in 2 Cor 6:2 Paul articulates his λόγος τῆς καταλλαγῆς by first quoting from Isa 49:8 ("At an acceptable time I have listened to you, and on a day of salvation I have helped you"), and then declaring, "Behold, now is the well-favored time; behold, now is the day of salvation!" This passage nicely illustrates the way in which Paul's apostolic self-understanding as Christ's ambassador (2 Cor 5:20) is woven together with an eschatological hermeneutic that produces startling new readings of Israel's Scripture.

The integral connection between Paul's gospel and an apocalyptic worldview has been widely recognized. This insight was championed in different ways by Albert Schweitzer[8] and Ernst Käsemann,[9] and it has been developed in the English-speaking world — again in interestingly different ways — by J. Christiaan Beker[10] and J. Louis Martyn.[11] What has not always been equally clear, however, is how Paul's missionary strategy in his confrontation with pagan culture repeatedly draws upon eschatologically interpreted Scripture texts to clarify the identity of the church and to remake the minds of his congregations. This essay will examine Paul's use of Scripture in 1 Corinthians as a test case.

In 1 Corinthians we find Paul calling his readers and hearers to a *conversion of the imagination*. He was calling Gentiles to understand their identity anew in light of the gospel of Jesus Christ — a gospel message comprehensible only in relation to the larger narrative of God's dealing with Israel. Terence L. Donaldson has recently argued that "the shape of Paul's rhetoric concerning Gentile salvation can best be accounted for in terms of an underlying pattern of convictions in which Gentiles are thought of as proselytes to an Israel reconfigured around Christ."[12] This seems to me to be exactly correct. We must emphasize, as Donaldson does, the word "*re*configured" in order to make it clear that Paul was not promulgating a linear *Heilsgeschichte* in which Gentiles were simply absorbed into a Torah-observant Jewish Christianity. Rather, the "Israel" into which Paul's Corinthian converts were embraced was an Israel whose story had been hermeneutically reconfigured by the cross and resurrection. The result was that Jew and Gentile alike found themselves summoned by the gospel story to a sweeping reevaluation of their identities, an imaginative paradigm shift so comprehensive that it can only be described as a "con-

---

8. A. Schweitzer, *Die Mystik des Apostels Paulus* (Tübingen: Mohr [Siebeck], 1930).

9. The seminal essays by Käsemann are "Zum Thema der urchristlichen Apokalyptik" and "Gottesgerechtigkeit bei Paulus," in *Exegetische Versuche und Besinnungen*, vol. 2 (Göttingen: Vandenhoeck & Ruprecht, 1964), 105-31, 181-93.

10. J. C. Beker, *Paul the Apostle: The Triumph of God in Life and Thought* (Philadelphia: Fortress, 1980).

11. J. L. Martyn, *Theological Issues in the Letters of Paul* (Edinburgh: T. & T. Clark; Nashville: Abingdon, 1997); see also the extended note "Apocalyptic Theology in Galatians" in J. L. Martyn, *Galatians*, AB 33A (New York: Doubleday, 1997), 97-105.

12. T. L. Donaldson, *Paul and the Gentiles: Remapping the Apostle's Convictional World* (Minneapolis: Fortress, 1997), 236.

version of the imagination."[13] Such a thoroughgoing conversion could be fostered and sustained only by a continuous process of bringing the community's beliefs and practices into critical confrontation with the gospel story.

This hermeneutical confrontation is nowhere more visible than in 1 Corinthians. A careful consideration of this letter leads to the formulation of two major theses:

1. Paul was trying to teach the Corinthian church to think eschatologically.
2. Paul was trying to teach the Corinthian church to reshape its identity in light of Israel's Scripture.

These two theses are necessarily intertwined: Paul reads Scripture through the lens of an eschatological hermeneutic, and conversely, he "reads" the identity of the eschatological community through the lens of Scripture.

The critical cutting edge of these two theses may be clarified if I state polemically two negative corollaries.

1. The Corinthians did not have an "overrealized eschatology." Instead, they employed categories of self-understanding derived from a decidedly noneschatological Greco-Roman cultural environment. Their particular form of "enthusiasm" seems to have been a hybrid of Stoic and Cynic philosophical influences, popular sophistic rhetoric, and charismatic spiritual fervor. Paul keeps injecting future apocalyptic language[14] into his argument to gain critical leverage against various problematical practices of the Corinthians; this in no way demonstrates, however, that the source of the Corinthian errors was a premature eschatological timetable.

2. Adolf von Harnack was badly mistaken about Paul's use of Scripture

---

13. Wayne Meeks and other social historians of the Pauline communities have used the term "resocialization" to point to social dimensions of the phenomenon I am describing here. See, e.g., W. A. Meeks, *The Moral World of the First Christians* (Philadelphia: Westminster, 1986), 13-14, 126, 129.

14. For thorough studies of Paul's pastoral use of such language, see D. W. Kuck, *Judgment and Community Conflict: Paul's Use of Apocalyptic Judgment Language in 1 Corinthians 3:5–4:5*, NovTSup 66 (Leiden: Brill, 1992); M. Konradt, *Gericht und Gemeinde: Eine Studie zur Bedeutung und Funktion von Gerichtsaussagen im Rahmen der paulinischen Ekklesiologie und Ethik im 1 Thess und 1 Kor*, BZNW 117 (Berlin: De Gruyter, 2003).

in his mission to the Gentiles. Harnack, as is well known, contended that "Paulus das A.T. nicht als das christliche Quellen- und Erbauungsbuch von vornherein den jungen Gemeinden gegeben . . . hat," and that he engaged with them in arguments about the interpretation of the OT "nur . . . wenn sie in Gefahr standen, dem judaistischen Irrtum zu verfallen," i.e., only when his hand was forced by Judaizing opponents.[15] This account simply fails to do justice to Paul's varied and rich uses of Scripture in 1 Corinthians, where the problems have nothing to do with "Judaizing"[16] or with outside opponents. This letter gives evidence that Origen was right when he wrote, in his *Homilies on Exodus* 5.1, that the apostle Paul, "'teacher of the Gentiles,' taught the church which he had gathered from among the Gentiles, how to understand the books of the Law."

Recent scholarship has shown, from many angles, how problematical are both the "overrealized eschatology" hypothesis and the view that Paul did not teach Scripture to his churches. Yet, one continues to find such views in print.[17] Therefore, a fresh examination of these issues is necessary.

One final word of preliminary clarification: I am by no means suggest-

---

15. A. von Harnack, "Das Alte Testament in den Paulinischen Briefen und in den Paulinischen Gemeinden," *Sitzungsberichte der Preussischen Akademie der Wissenschaften, Philosophisch-historische Klasse* (1928), 124-41; the passages quoted here are from 137, 130. By way of contrast, see the findings of A. Lindemann ("Schrift als Tradition," 225), who concludes that "Paulus selbst im Zuge der Heidenmission die jüdische Bibel als die authoritative Tradition des Christentums eingeführt hat."

16. I would insist on this point, despite the ingenious efforts of Michael Goulder to rehabilitate a classic "Tübingen" view of the conflict in Corinth as a dispute between a Pauline faction and a Judaizing Petrine faction whose "wisdom" consisted of a body of halakic rulings on the application of the Law (M. D. Goulder, "ΣΟΦΙΑ in 1 Corinthians," *NTS* 37 [1991]: 516-34). The weakness of Goulder's reconstruction appears when, in order to accommodate his hypothesis, he has to treat major portions of the letter (chaps. 5–6, 8–10, and perhaps 11) as Paul's diplomatic criticisms of his own Pauline faction (534).

17. The most thorough and nuanced recent defense of the "overrealized eschatology" hypothesis is to be found in C. M. Tuckett, "The Corinthians Who Say 'There Is No Resurrection of the Dead' (1 Cor 15,12)," in *The Corinthian Correspondence,* ed. R. Bieringer, BETL 125 (Leuven: Leuven University Press, 1996), 247-75; Tuckett's notes offer a survey of the literature on this question. The view that Paul did not teach Scripture in his churches is perhaps less widely held, but see, e.g., the carefully formulated comments of J. L. Martyn: "How extensively . . . did [Paul] function as a teacher of the Scriptures? Specifically, did he take it as one of his tasks to offer lengthy and detailed exegetical discourses to his congregations? His letters suggest no such thing" (*Theological Issues,* 159). More common is the view that Paul's use of Scripture is simply "proof texting," without regard for original context.

ing that Scripture and Jewish apocalyptic eschatology were the only tools
Paul used in his efforts to reshape the minds of his congregations. Paul
drew on a wide range of resources to accomplish his pastoral ends, appealing at times to the conventions of Greco-Roman moral philosophy[18] and
pervasively to Christology and early Christian confessional and liturgical
traditions — many of which were also strongly eschatological in character.
I do not presume in this short essay to give a comprehensive account of the
strategies Paul employed in seeking to transform the thinking of his readers; rather, I aim to concentrate attention on the two themes I have identified and to trace their outworking in selected passages of a single letter.

"Written for Our Instruction, upon Whom the Ends of the Ages Have Met" (1 Cor 10:1-22)

In 1 Cor 10 Paul sets forth an extended typological correspondence between Israel in the wilderness and the situation of the Corinthian church
as it confronts the issue of eating meat sacrificed to idols. Even though
Paul explicitly quotes just one biblical verse (Exod 32:6, in 1 Cor 10:7), his
argument alludes to several episodes narrated in Exodus and Numbers[19]
and presupposes that his Corinthian readers are familiar with the story.[20]
Indeed, the people's central act of infidelity, the worship of the golden calf
in Exod 32, is not explicitly described at all; instead, it is suggestively
evoked by the oblique quotation of Exod 32:6, which connects idolatry
with sitting down to "eat and drink" — a connection that has considerable
rhetorical force in Paul's argument against *eating* and *drinking* in pagan
temples. This is a wonderful example of the figurative device of metalepsis:
the full force of the quotation is apparent only to a reader who recognizes
its original narrative context. Paul is arguing *from* the story, not narrating
it as something new to his audience. The thing that is new here is the way
he brings the narrative of Israel into metaphorical conjunction with the issues the Corinthians face.[21]

18. See, e.g., A. J. Malherbe, *Paul and the Popular Philosophers* (Philadelphia: Fortress,
1989); H.-D. Betz, *Der Apostel Paulus und die sokratische Tradition*, BHT 45 (Tübingen: Mohr
[Siebeck], 1972).

19. See, e.g., Num 14:26-35; 25:1-9; 26:62; 21:5-9; and 16:41-50.

20. As rightly observed by Lindemann, "Schrift als Tradition," 215.

21. See my *Echoes*, 91-104. See also R. B. Hays, "The Role of Scripture in Paul's Ethics," in

Paul's first important hermeneutical move is to introduce the Israel of the wilderness generation as "our fathers" (οἱ πατέρες ἡμῶν, 10:1). For the predominantly Gentile Corinthian church, this is already an important gesture. Israel's story is not somebody else's history;[22] rather, Paul addresses the Gentile Corinthians as though they have become part of Israel.[23] They are invited to understand themselves now as descendants of the characters who appear in the pages of Scripture.

This interpretation is confirmed by Paul's passing reference to the Corinthians' past life as idol worshipers in 1 Cor 12:2. "You know," he writes, "that when you used to be Gentiles (ὅτε ἔθνη ἦτε), you were carried away to dumb idols." This formulation implies that he considers them ἔθνη no longer. Within Paul's symbolic world, they are no longer among the *goyim*, because they have been taken up into the story of Israel.[24] It should be noted that Paul is not trying to convince his Gentile readers to accept this identity description as a novel claim; rather, he assumes their identification with Israel as a given and tries to reshape their behavior in light of this identification.

In this case Paul's concern is that the "strong" Corinthians were participating in festive meals held in the temples of pagan gods (8:10) and thereby dangerously "partaking of the table of demons" (10:21). Within the discipline of New Testament studies there has been a long history of speculative reconstructions of the Corinthians as proto-Gnostic sacramentalists.[25]

Theology and Ethics in Paul and His Interpreters: Essays in Honor of Victor Paul Furnish, ed. E. H. Lovering, Jr., and J. L. Sumney (Nashville: Abingdon, 1996), 30-47; reprinted in the present volume, 143-62.

22. By contrast, we might recall the notorious remarks of Rudolf Bultmann: "For the person who stands within the Church the history of Israel is a closed chapter. . . . Israel's history is not our history, and in so far as God has shown grace in that history, such grace is not meant for us. . . . The events which meant something for Israel, which were God's Word, mean nothing more to us" ("The Significance of the Old Testament for Christian Faith," in *The Old Testament and Christian Faith,* ed. B. W. Anderson [New York: Harper and Row, 1963], 8-35, here 14).

23. Cf. Rom 11:17-24.

24. Thus, Paul's offhand expressions in 10:1 and 12:2 support Donaldson's thesis (n. 12, above) that Paul thinks of his converts as proselytes to an eschatologically reconfigured Israel.

25. This theory was articulated in an influential essay by H. von Soden, "Sakrament und Ethik bei Paulus: Zur Frage der literarischen und theologischen Einheitlichkeit von 1 Kor 8-10," in *Urchristentum und Geschichte: Gesammelte Aufsätze und Vorträge,* vol. 1 (Tübingen: Mohr [Siebeck], 1951), 239-75. For a recent summary of various reconstructions

There is, however, no clear evidence in the text that the "strong" Corinthians justified their behavior on the basis of some sort of realized eschatology or magical sacramentalism.[26] In the immediate context, the more obvious basis for their behavior is the simple slogan πάντα ἔξεστιν (10:23). As many commentators have noted, the closest parallels to this language are to be found in Stoic/Cynic thought.[27] The slogan claims that the σοφός is free to do whatever he chooses because he possesses the knowledge (cf. 8:1) that sets him above the petty taboos of social convention; he possesses ἐξουσία — philosophically informed inner freedom.

Against this line of thought, Paul poses several arguments in 8:1–11:1; in 10:1-22 he urges the Corinthians to understand themselves as standing in typological relationship to Israel.[28] He is calling for a conversion of the imagination — an imaginative projection of their lives into the framework of the Pentateuchal narrative. The Pentateuchal imagery is not confined to verses 1-13; Paul sustains it through verse 22. The phrase "they sacrificed to demons and not to God" (10:20) is taken directly from the Song of Moses in Deut 32:17 (and thus it refers, contrary to many English translations, not

---

and proposals, see W. Schrage, *Der Erste Brief an die Korinther*, 2. Teilband, EKKNT 7/2 (Solothurn and Düsseldorf: Benziger; Neukirchen-Vluyn: Neukirchener, 1995), 385-86.

26. For a recent challenge to the "sacramentalist" interpretation, see K.-G. Sandelin, "Does Paul Argue against Sacramentalism and Over-Confidence in 1 Cor 10.1-14?" in *The New Testament and Hellenistic Judaism*, ed. P. Borgen and S. Giversen (Aarhus: Aarhus University Press, 1995), 165-82.

27. Conzelmann (*1 Corinthians*, 108) remarks that "only the Stoics and Cynics provide material for comparison." For references see J. Weiss, *Der erste Korintherbrief*, MeyerK 5 (Göttingen: Vandenhoeck & Ruprecht, 1925), 157-58; R. M. Grant, "The Wisdom of the Corinthians," in *The Joy of Study: Papers on New Testament and Related Subjects Presented to Honor Frederick Clifton Grant*, ed. S. E. Johnson (New York: Macmillan, 1951), 51-55; J. Dupont, *Gnosis: La Connaissance Religieuse dans les Epitres de Saint Paul* (Louvain: Nauwelaerts; Paris: Gabalda, 1949), 298-308; Kuck, *Judgment and Community Conflict*, 217 n. 348.

28. The suggestion that Paul is here drawing upon a preformulated Jewish Christian midrash continues to find defenders (e.g., W. A. Meeks, "'And Rose Up to Play': Midrash and Parenesis in 1 Cor 10:1-22," *JSNT* 16 [1982]: 64-78; Koch, *Schrift als Zeuge*, 214-16). Richard Horsley, while regarding the passage as a Pauline composition, has suggested that Paul is "echoing the language of the Corinthian spirituals" and seeking to counteract interpretations of the Exodus narrative that they had learned from Alexandrian traditions of allegorical exegesis introduced into the community by Apollos (R. A. Horsley, *1 Corinthians*, ANTC [Nashville: Abingdon, 1998], 134-37). In my judgment this hypothesis goes beyond the evidence of the passage. Paul gives no indication that he is rebutting any other interpretation of the story; he is simply alluding to the biblical narrative for his own parenetic purposes.

to "pagans" but to unfaithful Israel), and Paul's rhetorical question in 10:22 loudly echoes the language of Deut 32:21: "Or shall we provoke the Lord to jealousy (παραζηλοῦμεν)?"[29] Paul picks up this language in 1 Cor 10:14-22 to warn the Corinthians not to recapitulate Israel's error, not to provoke God's jealousy as the wilderness generation did by their idolatry. His hortatory point depends upon the reader's act of imaginative identification with Israel.

In the course of the argument Paul provides an explicit hermeneutical warrant for this act of imaginative identification: "These things happened to them τυπικῶς, and they were written for our instruction, on whom the ends of the ages have met" (10:11). Here we see how Paul's eschatological hermeneutic informs his reading and application of Scripture. He calls his converts to understand that they live at the turning point of the ages, so that all the scriptural narratives and promises must be understood to point forward to the crucial eschatological moment in which he and his churches now find themselves. His eschatological reasoning calls upon the Corinthians to perform a complex imaginative act. On the one hand, they are to see in their own experience the typological fulfillment of the biblical narrative. The events narrated in Scripture "happened as τύποι ἡμῶν" (10:6). The phrase does not mean — despite many translations — "warnings for us." It means "types of us," prefigurations of the *ekklēsia*. For Paul Scripture, rightly read, prefigures the formation of the eschatological community of the church. This is what I sought to emphasize in *Echoes of Scripture in the Letters of Paul* by speaking of Paul's "ecclesiocentric hermeneutics."

But this is only the first half of the complex imaginative act to which Paul summons his readers. The Corinthians are not only to see how Scripture points to its fulfillment in their own community, but also to see that God's final judgment stands over their present experience. The prospect of future apocalyptic judgment, symbolized by the destruction that came upon the idolatrous Israelites in the wilderness, hovers over the entire passage. If the "strong" persist in provoking God's jealousy, they will suffer loss and destruction (cf. 3:10-17; 4:1-5; 5:1-5; 6:9-10; 11:27-32). Because Paul and his readers stand at the turn of the ages, they must envision their present experience both as the fulfillment of the scriptural figures and, at the

---

29. On the importance of Deut 32 in 1 Cor 10:14-22, see Hays, *Echoes*, 93-94. See also R. H. Bell, *Provoked to Jealousy: The Origin and Purpose of the Jealousy Motif in Romans 9–11*, WUNT 2, ser. 63 (Tübingen: Mohr [Siebeck], 1994).

same time, as a hint of the eschatological consummation that is still to come. Thus, Paul's reading of Scripture is "bifocal," corresponding to the dialectical ("already/not yet") character of his eschatology.

Paul does not deal with the idol meat problem in halakic fashion[30] by finding a pertinent rule or commandment in the OT. For example, he does not quote commandments against idol worship (e.g., Exod 20:4-6; Deut 17:2-7). This is the correct insight underlying Harnack's observation that Paul did not treat the OT as an *Erbauungsbuch* for his Gentile churches: he did not treat it as a rule book. Instead, he sketches a broad narrative and invites his readers to undertake the metaphorical leap of finding their own circumstances figured in the narrative.[31]

By offering explicit reflection about how to read Scripture as an eschatological community-forming word for a Gentile congregation grafted into Israel, 1 Cor 10 lays bare the hermeneutical assumptions that govern Paul's references to Scripture throughout the letter. Thus, we can employ this passage as a lens to bring several other texts more sharply into focus. Since a single essay cannot survey all the passages in 1 Corinthians where we see the interplay of Scripture and apocalyptic eschatology, let us consider two significant blocks of the text in which we see these motifs at work: the opening attack on "wisdom" (1:18-31) and Paul's first specific response to Corinthian misbehavior, the case of the incestuous man (5:1-13).

"I Will Destroy the Wisdom of the Wise" (1 Cor 1:18-31)

After the opening appeal for unity in the church (1:10-17), Paul launches into a long deliberative argument against factionalism.[32] The first major unit of the letter (1:18–4:21) is directed, as recent studies have convincingly

---

30. *Pace* P. Tomson, *Paul and the Jewish Law: Halakha in the Letters of the Apostle to the Gentiles*, CRINT III/1 (Assen and Maastricht: Van Gorcum; Minneapolis: Fortress, 1990), 187-220.

31. See Hays, "Role of Scripture," 39-42. For a broader discussion of the metaphorical use of scriptural narrative in moral judgment, see Hays, *The Moral Vision of the New Testament* (San Francisco: HarperSanFrancisco; Edinburgh: T. & T. Clark, 1997), 298-304.

32. Margaret M. Mitchell (*Paul and the Rhetoric of Reconciliation: An Exegetical Investigation of the Language and Composition of 1 Corinthians*, HUT 28 [Tübingen: Mohr (Siebeck), 1991]) has shown definitively that 1 Corinthians should be read as a unified deliberative composition appealing for concord.

demonstrated, against the Corinthians' infatuation with popular sophistic rhetoric and against their resultant arrogance and competitiveness.[33] The expression σοφία λόγου in 1:17 refers to the eloquent rhetorical presentation of wisdom (cf. 2:4). Against slickly packaged philosophical rhetoric, Paul sets in stark antithesis ὁ λόγος ὁ τοῦ σταυροῦ, which is "foolishness to those who are perishing but, to us who are being saved, the power of God" (1:18). Already in this antithesis Paul has introduced an apocalyptic motif, the division of all humanity into two groups: those who are to be destroyed along with the present evil age and those who are rescued by God's intervention. Those who are being saved are called to live in the light of another wisdom — defined precisely by the shocking form of the cross — that subverts everything the Corinthians had previously counted as σοφία. Paul is seeking to reshape their consciousness into this apocalyptic mode so that they will find their primary identification with fellow believers rather than seeking legitimacy according to the status-defining standards of their native civic culture.

The backbone of the discussion in 1:18–3:23 is a series of six OT quotations (1:19; 1:31; 2:9; 2:16; 3:19; 3:20), all taken from passages that depict God as one who acts to judge and save his people in ways that defy human imagination. Paul thus links his gospel of the cross to the older message of judgment and grace proclaimed in Israel's Scripture, and he challenges the boastful pretensions of his readers.

The first quotation (1:19), taken from Isa 29:14, declares God's eschatological annihilation of human wisdom. Clearly, Paul has selected this quotation because it pronounces God's sentence of judgment on σοφία. The impact of Paul's intertextual link becomes clearer when we listen to the oracle of Isa 29:13-14 in its entirety.

---

33. See especially P. Marshall, *Enmity in Corinth: Social Conventions and Paul's Relations with the Corinthians,* WUNT 2, ser. 23 (Tübingen: Mohr [Siebeck], 1987); T. H. Lim, "Not in Persuasive Words of Wisdom, but in the Demonstration of the Spirit and Power," *NovT* 29 (1987): 137-49; S. M. Pogoloff, *Logos and Sophia: The Rhetorical Situation of 1 Corinthians,* SBLDS 134 (Atlanta: Scholars, 1992); D. Litfin, *St. Paul's Theology of Proclamation: 1 Corinthians 1–4 and Greco-Roman Rhetoric,* SNTSMS 79 (Cambridge: Cambridge University Press, 1994); B. W. Witherington III, *Conflict and Community in Corinth: A Socio-Rhetorical Commentary on 1 and 2 Corinthians* (Grand Rapids: Eerdmans; Carlisle: Paternoster, 1995); B. W. Winter, *Philo and Paul among the Sophists,* SNTSMS 96 (Cambridge: Cambridge University Press, 1997). This interpretation was advocated earlier by J. Munck, "The Church without Factions: Studies in 1 Corinthians 1–4," in *Paul and the Salvation of Mankind* (Atlanta: John Knox; London: SCM, 1959); L. Hartman, "Some Remarks on 1 Cor 2:1-5," *SEÅ,* 1974, 109-20.

The Lord said:
Because these people draw near *with their mouths*
and honor me *with their lips,*
while their hearts are far from me,
and their worship of me is a human commandment learned by rote;
so I will again do
amazing things with this people,
shocking and amazing.
The wisdom of their wise shall perish
and the discernment of the discerning shall be hidden.[34]

The Isaiah text pointedly associates σοφία with "lip service," a purely verbal show of piety — the very thing for which Paul will chastise the Corinthians, not only in 1:18-31 but throughout the letter. Furthermore, Isa
29:14a suggests that God will do away with "the wisdom of the wise" by doing "shocking and amazing" things, precisely as Paul now declares God has
done through using the ignominious death of Jesus on a cross to overturn
human wisdom. Even Paul's choice of the expression τοῖς ἀπολλυμένοις in
1 Cor 1:18 anticipates the strong verb ἀπολῶ in the Isaiah quotation. For
this reason we should perhaps read the participle as a true passive voice
construction: those who regard the cross as foolishness are not just "perishing" but actually "being destroyed" *by God.* God's eschatological judgment is taking effect precisely in their incomprehension of God's saving
action. (See Rom 1:18-32 for a close parallel.)

Here again we see Paul trying to teach the Corinthians to perceive reality within the framework of a dialectical "already/not yet" eschatology.
God has already put the wise to shame through the foolishness of the
cross, the apocalyptic event that has shattered the old order of human
wisdom. The σοφός and the γραμματεύς and the rhetorician *of this age*
have all been effectively brought to nothing (1 Cor 1:20; cf. 1:28:
καταργήσῃ) by the cross; therefore, "this age" no longer has power or pertinence. The Corinthians who still prize σοφία λόγου are oblivious to
God's apocalyptic delegitimation of their symbolic world. On the other

---

34. Isa 29:13-14 NRSV, emphasis added. Paul's citation of 29:14b follows the LXX precisely except for the last word, where he substitutes ἀθετήσω for κρύψω. As Stanley notes
(*Paul,* 186), this is a Pauline modification to strengthen the description of God's scandalous
action.

hand, the present participles ἀπολλυμένοις and σῳζομένοις in 1:18 show that Paul regards the unfolding of the eschatological scenario as still in progress, not yet complete.

Can it be merely fortuitous that Paul introduces his exposition of the "word of the cross" with a Scripture quotation (1:19)? The conversion of the imagination that Paul demands is fostered by placing σοφία in a *scriptural* framework of God's judgment; in light of Scripture, Paul is calling on the Corinthians to reevaluate their prizing of rhetoric. Paul does not read Isa 29:14 merely as a general maxim about how God always regards human wisdom. Rather, the argument takes its particular force from Paul's conviction that the transforming action of God prophesied by Isaiah *has now taken place* in the crucifixion of Jesus. Consequently, Paul and his readers now stand in the new eschatological situation where Isaiah's words must be read not merely as a judgment on ancient Judean leaders but also as an indictment of the rhetorical affectations of the Corinthians — and simultaneously as a warning of the destruction that is coming on "the day of our Lord Jesus Christ" (1 Cor 1:8) for those who do not live according to the word of the cross.

This call for scriptural reevaluation is made even more explicit in 1:26-31, as Paul shifts the focus from Isa 29 to another biblical passage: "Let the one who boasts boast in the Lord." The text is usually identified as Jer 9:24 (= Jer 9:23 LXX), but J. Ross Wagner has recently argued that an equally good case can be made for finding the source of the quotation in the closely parallel passage 1 Kgdms 2:10 LXX (= 1 Sam 2:10).[35] Happily, we are not forced to choose between these two OT passages as the background for 1 Cor 1:26-31. Significant writing often mingles the echoes of multiple precursors. Both passages provide rich subtexts for Paul's argument.

The threefold reference in 1 Cor 1:26 to the Corinthians' lowly status before their calling ("not many were wise [σοφοί] . . . , not many were powerful [δυνατοί], not many were of noble birth [εὐγενεῖς]") mirrors the threefold warning against boasting in Jer 9:22 LXX: "Let the wise man (σοφός) not boast in his wisdom, let the strong man (ἰσχυρός) not boast in his strength, and let the rich man (πλούσιος) not boast in his

---

35. J. R. Wagner, "'Not beyond the Things Which Are Written': A Call to Boast Only in the Lord (1 Cor 4.6)," *NTS* 44 (1998): 279-87. This possibility is noted by Koch (*Schrift als Zeuge,* 35-36) and Schrage (*Der Erste Brief an die Korinther,* 1. Teilband, EKKNT 7/1 [Solothurn and Düsseldorf: Benziger; Neukirchen-Vluyn: Neukirchener, 1991], 205) but overlooked by Stanley (*Paul,* 186-88).

riches."[36] In Jeremiah this warning occurs in the context of a series of judgment oracles: because the people are caught up in lies, iniquity, oppression, and idolatry, God's judgment is coming upon Jerusalem and Judah (Jer 8:3–9:26). A repeated theme of this unit is that people who claim to be "wise" will soon incur God's judgment (for example, 8:9: "The wise shall be put to shame, they shall be dismayed and taken; since they have rejected the word of the Lord, what wisdom is in them?"). Jer 9:23-24 brings this section to a climax by warning against all boasting and reaffirming that God will act with "steadfast love, justice, and righteousness in the earth." If Paul is thinking of this passage, he has elaborated Jeremiah's admonitions in his proclamation that God has now shamed the wise and the strong (τοὺς σοφούς and τὰ ἰσχυρά, 1 Cor 1:27), and he has condensed Jer 9:24 into a pithy maxim: "Let the one who boasts boast in the Lord."[37] The scriptural quotation — as Paul has hermeneutically reformulated it — is primarily a warning of eschatological judgment.

If Paul is thinking of 1 Kgdms 2:10, on the other hand, he is alluding to Hannah's song of praise, a song that extols God for having reversed the fortunes of the poor and the downtrodden. The theme of eschatological judgment is still present, but the emphasis lies more on the startling reversal brought about by God's gracious power. This motif resonates with Paul's exposition of paradoxical status reversal through the foolishness of the cross, the fundamental theme of 1 Cor 1:18-31. The entire Song of Hannah leaves lingering echoes as we listen to Paul's critique of the Corinthian fascination with rhetoric. Consider the following admonition in 1 Kgdms 2:3: "Do not boast (μὴ καυχᾶσθε), and do not speak lofty things; do not let grandiloquence (μεγαλορρημοσύνη) come out of your mouth, because the Lord is a God of knowledge, and God prepares his own designs." The pertinence of this passage to Paul's epistolary purposes hardly requires comment. Finally, the climactic admonition to boast in the Lord

---

36. See G. R. O'Day, "Jeremiah 9:22-23 and 1 Corinthians 1:26-31: A Study in Intertextuality," *JBL* 109 (1990): 259-67.

37. The same shortened quotation shows up in identical form in 2 Cor 10:17 without a citation formula. Rather than showing that Paul does not regard the sentence as a scriptural quotation, this shows that he regards it — by the time he wrote 2 Cor 10–13 — as thoroughly familiar to his readers. If I quote or paraphrase "Blessed are the meek, for they shall inherit the earth" in a sermon, I do not need to insert a citation formula to explain to the congregation that I am quoting a saying of Jesus.

in 1 Kgdms 2:10 is virtually identical to the parallel in Jer 9:24: ἀλλ' ἢ ἐν τούτῳ καυχάσθω ὁ καυχώμενος, συνιεῖν καὶ γινώσκειν τὸν κύριον.

Some critics have contended that in 1 Cor 1:31 Paul is merely quoting a common early Christian maxim without direct awareness of any scriptural context. Otherwise, so the argument goes, how could he have passed up the chance to quote Jer 9:22 (LXX) explicitly (μὴ καυχάσθω ὁ σοφὸς ἐν τῇ σοφίᾳ αὐτοῦ)?[38] I am afraid that this line of reasoning merely illustrates our guild's characteristic resistance to the rhetorical effect of literary allusion. Allusions are often most powerful when least explicit. This remains true even if some readers are slow of heart to discern the metalepsis. Paul's argument is perfectly intelligible at the surface level with or without the OT echoes,[39] but the reader who overhears the original context of these citations will be all the more deeply affected by the hearing.

In either case we see that Paul is once again drawing upon Scripture in an effort to reshape the identity of the Corinthian community. He has imaginatively projected the σοφοί at Corinth into the role of the "wise" and boastful leaders of Israel and Judah who were admonished by the prophetic oracles of Isaiah and Jeremiah. Like those leaders, the Corinthians stand under a warning of God's coming judgment and a summons to change their ways. They can respond appropriately to Paul's letter only if they hear God's word to Israel as a word spoken directly to them. Furthermore, when Scripture says ὁ καυχώμενος ἐν κυρίῳ καυχάσθω, Paul understands the κύριος to be the κύριος Ἰησοῦς Χριστός. Consequently, when he tells them to "boast in the Lord," he is summoning the Corinthians to reconfigure their self-understanding and conduct in light of Jesus Christ crucified (2:2), the figure to whom Scripture points.

If we are correct that Paul's argument aims fundamentally at calling the contentious Corinthians to reevaluate themselves by the standard of Scripture, then it follows that there really should be no further dispute about the meaning of the slogan in 1 Cor 4:6: μὴ ὑπὲρ ἃ γέγραπται. It means that Paul is trying to teach the puffed-up Corinthians not to transgress these specific scriptural warnings against arrogance. He has conducted the extended *synkrisis* of himself and Apollos (3:5–4:5) with this

---

38. Koch, *Schrift als Zeuge*, 36; T. Holtz, "Zum Selbstverständnis des Apostels Paulus," *TLZ* 91 (1966): 326.

39. Lindemann ("Schrift als Tradition," 205) comments: "[D]ie Tatsache, dass es sich um ein Schriftwort handelt, hat für den Inhalt der Aussage von 1,31 kein grundsätzlich entscheidendes Gewicht."

goal in mind. Wagner has shown how the entire argument of 1:18–4:21 focuses on the biblical admonition against boasting, which is explicitly repeated in 3:21 after two more biblical quotations (Job 5:13 and Ps 93:11 LXX) that reinforce the same lesson.[40] A more thoroughgoing examination of the OT quotations in 1 Cor 2:9, 2:16, 3:19, and 3:20 would only underscore the point: Paul is trying to remake the minds of his readers by teaching them to interpret their lives in light of an eschatologically interpreted Scripture.

This leads to one further observation. If Paul was trying to teach the Corinthians to think in eschatological terms, it hardly makes sense to suppose that they had an "overrealized eschatology."[41] The overrealized escha-

---

40. Wagner, "Not Beyond," 283-85. Wagner's argument fills out and supports the interpretation set forth by Morna Hooker, "'Beyond the Things Which Are Written': An Examination of 1 Cor. IV.6," *NTS* 10 (1963): 127-32. Virtually simultaneously with Wagner's essay, two other journal articles on 1 Cor 4:6 appeared in print. One of these (R. L. Tyler, "First Corinthians 4:6 and Hellenistic Pedagogy," *CBQ* 60 [1998]: 97-103) reiterates the hypothesis (following B. Fiore and J. Fitzgerald) that the slogan quoted by Paul refers to the practice whereby children were taught to write the alphabet by tracing over letters written by their teacher: μὴ ὑπὲρ ἃ γέγραπται means "stay within the lines, follow the teacher's example exactly." This interpretation makes some sense in context, but it fails to reckon with the fact that there is no other extant evidence for this particular slogan in antique pedagogical practice; more tellingly, it fails to take sufficiently into account the fact that Paul elsewhere, without exception, uses γέγραπται to refer to what is written in *Scripture*. (Goulder's translation, "The Bible and nothing but the Bible" ["ΣΟΦΙΑ in 1 Corinthians," 519], correctly identifies the semantic field of the verb, even though his interpretation of the historical situation remains unpersuasive.) The other coincident article (J. C. Hanges, "1 Corinthians 4:6 and the Possibility of Written Bylaws in the Corinthian Church," *JBL* 117 [1998]: 275-98) advances the speculation that Paul is referring to a body of written rules that were supposed to govern the congregational life of the church. This is unpersuasive in the extreme: If such "church bylaws" existed, why are there no other references to them in this letter or anywhere else in Paul's correspondence? In view of Wagner's demonstration that the warning against violating the scriptural prohibition of boasting makes perfect sense in context, and in view of the centrality of biblical quotations in Paul's argument throughout this section of the letter, I regard the argument as settled.

41. The origin of this idea in modern scholarship appears to be von Soden's essay "Sakrament und Ethik bei Paulus" (n. 25, above), originally published in 1931. Whatever one may make of von Soden's proposal to understand the Corinthians as "überspannte Enthusiasten des Pneumaglaubens," the exegetical basis for the proposal that their enthusiasm was rooted in realized eschatology was exceedingly slender. For instance, von Soden's suggestion that 15:12 should be interpreted to mean that some Corinthians believed the resurrection was already past — quoted repeatedly by subsequent scholars — appears in a sin-

tology hypothesis rests on only the scantiest evidence in the letter. One bit of purported evidence is 1 Cor 15:12, interpreted to mean that some Corinthians, whom Paul describes as denying the resurrection, were in fact claiming that they had already experienced it (on the analogy of 2 Tim 2:17-18). This tortuous interpretation, which requires us to suppose that Paul misunderstands or misrepresents the Corinthians' actual opinions, has been decisively undermined by more recent studies.[42] An apparently stronger textual basis for the overrealized eschatology hypothesis is 1 Cor 4:8, where Paul flings at the Corinthians an ironic word of reproach: "Already you are filled! Already you are rich! Apart from us you have become

---

gle footnote (259-60 n. 28) as a bare assertion with no exegetical argumentation. The case was more fully argued by J. Schniewind ("Die Leugner der Auferstehung in Korinth," in *Nachgelassene Reden und Aufsätze* [Berlin: Töpelmann, 1952], 110-39), who argued for continuity between the Corinthian position and later Gnostic sources. The depiction of the Corinthians as "Gnostics" with a realized eschatology was "canonized" in Bultmann's *Theologie des Neuen Testaments* (Tübingen: Mohr [Siebeck], 1953), 168. In the English-speaking world this hypothesis became influential through the translation of Bultmann, through the translated essays of Käsemann (especially "On the Subject of Primitive Christian Apocalyptic," in *New Testament Questions of Today* [Philadelphia: Fortress, 1969], 108-37), through C. K. Barrett's commentary (e.g., 109), and through J. M. Robinson and H. Koester, *Trajectories through Early Christianity* (Philadelphia: Fortress, 1971), 30-40, 148-52. The most systematic attempt to defend the hypothesis exegetically was made by A. C. Thiselton, "Realized Eschatology at Corinth," *NTS* 24 (1977/78): 510-26. In fact, however, Thiselton's argument depends on showing repeatedly that *Paul* appeals to future eschatology in his arguments to correct the Corinthians' behavior; but this does not prove that the Corinthians had a *realized* eschatology! It merely shows that Paul was trying, with some difficulty, to teach them to think in eschatological categories. More recent commentators, recognizing that the hypothesis rests on an improbable construction about Gnosticism in Corinth, have backed away cautiously from the full-blown hypothesis and speak more cautiously about the Corinthians as having a "spiritualized eschatology" (Fee, *First Epistle*, 12 and passim); see also Schrage, *Der erste Brief an die Korinther*, 1:38-63. For helpful surveys of the history of the debate over this hypothesis, see Kuck, *Judgment and Community Conflict*, 16-31; G. Sellin, *Der Streit um die Auferstehung der Toten: Eine religionsgeschichtliche und exegetische Untersuchung von 1 Korinther 15*, FRLANT 138 (Göttingen: Vandenhoeck & Ruprecht, 1986), 15-37.

42. Particularly noteworthy are the following: B. Pearson, *The Pneumatikos-Psychikos Terminology in I Corinthians*, SBLDS 12 (Missoula, Mont.: Scholars, 1973); Sellin, *Der Streit um die Auferstehung*; A. J. M. Wedderburn, *Baptism and Resurrection*, WUNT 44 (Tübingen: Mohr [Siebeck], 1987); M. C. De Boer, *The Defeat of Death: Apocalyptic Eschatology in 1 Corinthians 15 and Romans 5*, JSNTSup 22 (Sheffield: Sheffield Academic Press, 1988); and Kuck, *Judgment and Community Conflict*, especially 214-20.

kings!" As many scholars have pointed out, however, while these status attributions no doubt reflect the Corinthians' self-description, the temporal framework supplied by the adverb ἤδη represents Paul's own perspective, not theirs, just as the phrase χωρὶς ἡμῶν also represents Paul's own ironic commentary on the Corinthians' boasting.[43]

The evidence is overwhelming that the claim to possess all things and to be self-sufficient and kingly was a distinguishing mark of Stoic and Cynic thought. Two familiar examples will suffice: According to Epictetus, the true Cynic can say, "Who, when he lays eyes upon me, does not feel that he is seeing his king and master?" (*Dissertationes* 3.22.49). Or again, Plutarch comments wryly, "But some think the Stoics are jesting when they hear that in their sect the σοφός is termed not only prudent and just and brave, but also *an orator,* a poet, a general, *a rich man,* and *a king;* and then they count themselves worthy of all these titles, and if they fail to get them, are vexed" (*De tranquillitate animi* 472A, emphasis added). Of course, neither Stoics nor Cynics were led to such views because of an excess of eschatological enthusiasm! Instead, they claimed a superior philosophical knowledge and personal discipline. There is no reason to think that the Corinthians were any different; they were simply absorbing such attitudes from the popular philosophers and rhetoricians around them and "baptizing" them into Christian discourse. Paul, horrified at their posturing, responds by appealing again and again to apocalyptic warrants to get theological leverage against such boastful claims.

Their boasting is wrong not because it prematurely claims eschatological fulfillment but because it leaves eschatology out of consideration altogether. It foolishly ignores that all human actions stand under the final

43. R. A. Horsley, "'How Can Some of You Say That There Is No Resurrection of the Dead?' Spiritual Elitism in Corinth," *NovT* 20 (1978): 203-5; Sellin, *Der Streit um die Auferstehung,* 24-25; D. Doughty, "The Presence and Future of Salvation in Corinth," *ZNW* 66 (1975): 61-90; M. A. Plunkett, "Sexual Ethics and the Christian Life: A Study of 1 Corinthians 6:12–7:7" (Ph.D. diss., Princeton Theological Seminary; Ann Arbor: University Microfilms, 1988), 116-18. See especially the convincing discussion of Kuck (*Judgment and Community Conflict,* 214-20), who, following Horsley, argues that the words of 4:8 are "Paul's own *reductio ad absurdum* of the Corinthian way of thinking." These expressions "do not mean that they think they have already experienced the eschaton which Paul still awaits, but rather that they think they have advanced to maturity on a faster track than Paul. Paul is sarcastically accusing them of thinking that they have advanced spiritually and ethically beyond their teacher" (216). This explains why Paul moves into a discussion of his own suffering in vv. 9-13; see especially the ironic *synkrisis* in v. 10.

judgment of the Lord, "who will bring to light the things now hidden in darkness and disclose the purposes of the heart" (4:5). It is God alone who retains the power to judge and to render rewards. In the present time, however, Christian existence is to be lived under the sign of the cross, as exemplified by Paul's own apostolic suffering (4:9-13).

If Paul was seeking to correct the Corinthians' overrealized eschatology, he committed a colossal pastoral blunder when he wrote to them later, in 2 Cor 6:2, "Now is the day of salvation." We gain far more insight into the issues driving 1 Corinthians when we recognize that Paul is seeking to redefine their identity — which has been shaped by noneschatological ideas indigenous to their culture — within an apocalyptic narrative that locates present existence in the interval between cross and parousia (cf. 1 Cor 11:26). Within that interval he calls the Gentile Corinthians to shape their behavior in accordance with Scripture's admonitions, to act like the eschatological Israel he believes them to be.

"Clean Out the Old Leaven" (1 Cor 5:1-13)

Finally, a brief glance at 1 Cor 5 will illustrate how Paul's appeals to Scripture and eschatology operate in shaping his specific behavioral directives to the church.

When Paul begins to scold the Corinthian church for failing to discipline a man involved in an incestuous relationship, he complains that this kind of πορνεία is not to be found even ἐν τοῖς ἔθνεσιν (5:1). Once again, as in 12:2, this formulation implies that he considers his Gentile Corinthian converts to belong no longer to the category of the ἔθνη. While Paul regards the offending behavior as a violation even of pagan morality, it is also, more specifically, a violation of Jewish law. The most immediately pertinent text is Deut 27:20: "Cursed be anyone who lies with his father's wife" (see also Deut 23:1[22:30]; Lev 18:8; 20:11). Probably, Paul does not cite the OT warrant because he sees no need to argue the point; he thinks such conduct should be self-evidently abhorrent to his Gentile converts. Nonetheless, the fact that the offender has violated Israel's covenant law turns out to be highly relevant for understanding Paul's response. His directive to the congregation (1 Cor 5:13) is a quotation of the formula used repeatedly in Deuteronomy to prescribe the death penalty for offenses that lead the community into idolatry or flagrant impurity: ἐξάρατε τὸν πονηρὸν ἐξ ὑμῶν αὐτῶν.[44] Most commentaries, following the notation in the Nestle-Aland margin, list this as a citation of Deut 17:7, a passage that prescribes the stoning of idolaters. Because this seems unrelated to the situation Paul is addressing, few commentators see the OT quotation as having any particular significance for Paul's argument.[45]

Once we recognize, however, that the same formula appears in other contexts in Deuteronomy, we can hardly overlook the fact that one of the offenses requiring the death penalty is adultery. In Deut 22:22, 24 Moses prescribes capital punishment for adulterers and then invokes the purgation formula: ἐξαρεῖς τὸν πονηρὸν ἐξ Ἰσραηλ/ἐξ ὑμῶν αὐτῶν. Precisely within this immediate context, we also find a commandment forbidding a man to "take" his father's wife (23:1).[46] The inference lies readily at hand that Paul, who knows the Torah inside and out, has categorized the case of Corinthian incest as a violation of the law articulated in Deut 27:20 and 23:1. Having so categorized the offense, he calls for the punishment associated with it in Deut 22, and he cites the Deuteronomic formula as a direct command to the church. This helps to explain why he feels it necessary to call for the drastic punishment of "destruction of the flesh" of the offender (5:5). Thus, rather than regarding 1 Cor 5:13 as a quotation of Deut 17:7, we should see the subtext as Deut 22:22–23:1.[47]

44. The formula appears, with minor variations, in Deut 13:5; 17:7, 12; 19:19; 21:21; 22:21, 22, 24; 24:7. In 17:12 and 22:22 it reads ἐξαρεῖς τὸν πονηρὸν ἐξ Ἰσραηλ. In Paul's citation he tailors the verb to address the Corinthian situation by changing LXX's ἐξαρεῖς to ἐξάρατε. It should be emphasized that Paul does not envision the church actually executing capital punishment on the offender; he reinterprets the formula to require exclusion of the offender from the community, in this respect paralleling the common interpretation of these texts in Second Temple Judaism (see W. Horbury, "Extirpation and Excommunication," *VT* 35 [1985]: 13-38).

45. Once again, Stanley does not treat the passage, because Paul does not introduce the quotation with a citation formula. In *Echoes* (97), I also followed the convention of treating 1 Cor 5:13 as a quotation of Deut 17:7. For reasons explained here, I now regard this identification as imprecise; the more relevant textual precursor is Deut 22:22–23:1.

46. Many translations, recognizing the connection of Deut 23:1 to the preceding context, number it as Deut 22:30.

47. This analysis follows B. S. Rosner, *Paul, Scripture, and Ethics: A Study of 1 Corinthians 5-7*, AGJU 22 (Leiden: Brill, 1994), 82-83. (Rosner [61-93] offers a wide-ranging discussion of other possible scriptural backgrounds to 1 Cor 5.) The fact that Paul cites the formula as "Remove the evil person ἐξ ὑμῶν αὐτῶν" rather than "ἐξ Ἰσραηλ" (Deut 22:22), is of no special significance. He is merely quoting the formula as it appears in seven of its nine occurrences in Deuteronomy, including in 22:24, the instance in closest proximity to 23:1. The

This analysis demonstrates once again that Paul thinks of his Gentile Corinthian readers as having been taken up into Israel in such a way that they now share in Israel's covenant privileges and obligations. The unmarked quotation in 1 Cor 5:13 functions as a metaphor that figuratively transfers the Corinthians into the shoes of the Israel to whom Moses proclaimed, "Hear, O Israel, the statutes and ordinances that I am addressing to you today" (Deut 5:1). Paul does not regard the whole Torah as binding on these Gentiles (that is a topic for another day),[48] but he does, nonetheless, address them as participants in the covenant community, using the language of Scripture. He is trying to reshape their consciousness so that they take corporate responsibility for the holiness of their community; he does this by using Scripture to address them as Israel.

Is this rhetorical device too subtle? Might the Corinthians have been oblivious to the original context of the OT quotation? One feature of this passage suggests that Paul's invocation of the Torah might not have been totally wasted on his Corinthian readers. In verses 6-8 he once again castigates the community for boasting and restates the demand for community discipline by using the story of Passover as a metaphor. Because Christ has already been slain as the Passover lamb, he says, it is time to purify the lump of dough, time to celebrate the festival of unleavened bread rightly by removing all leaven from the house (Exod 12:14-15).

The extraordinary thing about Paul's use of this metaphor is how little he explains. He does not quote Exod 12, he does not explain his striking christological typology that links Jesus with the Passover lamb, and he does not explain the Jewish custom of removing all leaven from the home in preparation for the feast. Yet he seems to expect his readers to understand the argument. How are we to assess this? Is this simply a rhetorical miscalculation, a failed act of communication? Or did Paul expect that his emissaries, such as Timothy (1 Cor 4:17), would explain this passage to the Corinthians? Or, alternatively, should we infer that the implied readers of this letter have been taught more about Scripture than we might suppose? Paul treats them as readers able to discern the allusion to Exod 12 (or Deut 16:1-8), to recover the original context, and to interpret the figurative link-

---

two formulations are synonymous, a point of some importance for understanding Paul's metaphorical transference of this language to the Corinthian congregation.

48. On this topic see Markus Bockmuehl, *Jewish Law in Gentile Churches: Halakhah and the Beginning of Christian Public Ethics* (Edinburgh: T. & T. Clark, 2000).

age between Israel and the Corinthian congregation. The text makes sense if and only if the readers of the letter embrace the typological identification between themselves and Israel.

For readers who do make the link, the metaphor is complex and illuminating. Sexual immorality, like leaven, can spread and contaminate the whole community; therefore, the evil influence must be purged. The result is that the community itself will be like the unleavened bread prepared for the feast. Christ's death as Passover lamb marks the community's deliverance from bondage and passage to freedom. The community, then, is metaphorically portrayed not only as the unleavened bread but also as the journeying people of the exodus, called to celebrate the feast and to live in ways appropriate to their identity as a people rescued by God from the power of evil and death. The incestuous man, on the other hand, is to be excluded from the household whose door is marked by the blood of Jesus, the Passover lamb; thus, he is left outside, exposed to the power of the destroyer (1 Cor 5:5; cf. Exod 12:12-13).

The Passover imagery, in this typological reading, is interpreted eschatologically. The death of Jesus as paschal lamb rescues the community from the wrath that is coming, and the community is called to maintain its purity and integrity, leaving God to deal with outsiders in the eschatological judgment (1 Cor 5:12-13).

All of this is only suggested, not explained, by Paul's allusion to Passover tradition. His metaphorical evocation of that tradition leaves much to the imagination of the readers. Precisely for that reason, 1 Cor 5 exemplifies the way Paul employs Scripture to foster the conversion of the imagination.

"Who Has Believed Our Message?"
Paul's Reading of Isaiah

How did Paul read Isaiah? The question has usually not been posed in just this way. Most NT scholars have tended to assume that Paul merely exploited the OT as a collection of oracular proof texts, without regard for original context; thus, the idea that Paul read any individual OT book as a literary or theological unity has seldom been entertained.[1] A careful examination of the evidence, however, might lead to different, and interesting, conclusions.

Paul seems to have had a special interest in Isaiah. In the seven letters generally acknowledged as authentic, Paul quotes Isaiah 31 times (out of approximately 89 OT quotations overall).[2] Furthermore, in his letter to the Romans he cites Isaiah explicitly by name 5 times (Rom 9:27, 29; 10:16, 20; 15:12). It is noteworthy that, while the 31 quotations are taken from throughout the book of Isaiah, there are significant clusters of citations from some sections, notably chapters 28–29 (6 quotations) and 49–55 (10 quotations). The evidence is even more impressive if we count allusions as well as explicit quotations. Allusions are more difficult to quantify precisely, but the list given in the 27th edition of Nestle-Aland can serve as a rough indicator:

---

1. Since I wrote this essay in 1998, two important technical studies have appeared that do precisely what I said was not being done — focusing on Paul as a reader of Isaiah: F. Wilk, *Die Bedeutung des Jesajabuches für Paulus*, FRLANT 179 (Göttingen: Vandenhoeck & Ruprecht, 1998); J. R. Wagner, *Heralds of the Good News: Isaiah and Paul "In Concert" in the Letter to the Romans*, NovTSup 101 (Leiden: Brill, 2002).

2. The total of 89 OT quotations is taken from D.-A. Koch, *Die Schrift als Zeuge des Evangeliums: Untersuchungen zur Verwendung und zum Verständnis der Schrift bei Paulus*, BHT 69 (Tübingen: Mohr Siebeck, 1986), 21-24. The tabulation of 31 quotations of Isaiah is my own, based on the list of "Loci Citati vel Allegati" in Nestle-Aland[27], 789-93. According to Koch's tally (p. 33), there are 28 citations of Isaiah in the authentic letters.

out of 50 allusions to Isaiah in the seven-letter corpus, 21 point to Isaiah 49–55. Paul was of course innocent of the modern critical division of Isaiah into three parts, but he seems to have been drawn particularly to the section of the book that modern scholarship has designated Deutero-Isaiah.

This rough statistical evidence suggests — at the very least — that Paul attributed particular significance to the prophecies of Isaiah, and that he found some portions of this prophetic book to be particularly useful in his interpretation and defense of the gospel. The reasons for this are not difficult to fathom. Isaiah, more clearly than any other OT book, links the promise of the redemption and restoration of Israel to the hope that Israel's God will also reveal his mercy to the Gentiles and establish sovereignty over the whole earth. Thus, Paul finds in Isaiah — particularly the prophecies of Deutero-Isaiah — a prefiguration of his own distinctive apostolic ministry to the Gentiles.[3]

Christian interpreters of the NT have sometimes focused on the depiction of the "Suffering Servant" of Isa 53 as a key to Pauline Christology (although this approach was dealt a severe blow by Morna Hooker's monograph of forty years ago, *Jesus and the Servant*).[4] Paul may have read Isa 53 as a prophecy of Christ's vicarious suffering, but it is hard to substantiate this claim. I believe, however, that Paul's explicit use of Isaiah is uncontestably "ecclesiocentric," as is his use of Scripture more generally.[5] His reading of Isaiah points primarily toward the formation of an eschatological people of God in which Gentiles are to be included. Indeed, he seems to find in Isaiah not only a *warrant* for his apostolic ministry to Gentiles but also a direct prophetic *prediction* of it, closely analogous to the way the Qumran covenanters read scriptural texts as prophecies of their own communal life and vocation.

---

3. These themes are discussed in J. R. Wagner, "The Heralds of Isaiah and the Mission of Paul," in *Jesus and the Suffering Servant: Isaiah 53 and Christian Origins*, ed. W. H. Bellinger, Jr., and W. R. Farmer (Harrisburg, Pa.: Trinity, 1998), 193-222. See also Wagner, *Heralds of the Good News*.

4. "In the writings of the theologians of the early church, we found little evidence that the identification of Jesus with the Servant played any great part in the thinking of St Paul, St John, or the author of the Epistle to the Hebrews, and no *proof* that it was known to them at all" (M. Hooker, *Jesus and the Servant: The Influence of the Servant Concept of Deutero-Isaiah in the New Testament* [London: SPCK, 1959], 127).

5. For explanation of my use of this term, see R. B. Hays, *Echoes of Scripture in the Letters of Paul* (New Haven: Yale University Press, 1989), 84-87.

Once this insight is established through attention to Paul's explicit quotations of Isaiah, I believe we may discern the broader outlines of Paul's overall reading of the book. The explicit citations are merely the tip of the iceberg; they point to a larger mass just under the surface, Paul's comprehensive construal of Isaiah as a coherent witness to the gospel.[6] I believe that Paul had read and pondered the scroll of Isaiah as a whole, over the years of his apostolic ministry, and developed a sustained reading of it as God's revelation of "the mystery that was kept secret for long ages but is now disclosed, and through the prophetic writings is made known to all the Gentiles, according to the command of the eternal God, to bring about the obedience of faith" (Rom 16:25-26).[7]

To make this claim credible, however, we must digress to examine the model of reading that we bring to our task. Paul's reading of Isaiah is just one instance of the larger phenomenon of intertextual reading and writing by early Christian authors. Thus, some slightly broader methodological reflection is required.

Reading Intertextually: A Literary-Theological Paradigm

If we want to understand what the New Testament writers were doing theologically — particularly how they interpreted the relation of the gospel to the more ancient story of God's covenant relationship to Israel — we cannot avoid tracing and understanding their appropriation of Israel's Scriptures. This is so a fortiori for Paul, the self-described Hebrew of Hebrews who, by his own account, surpassed all his contemporaries in zeal for the traditions of his fathers. He received and passed on — indeed, in-

---

6. For purposes of comparison, see J. Marcus, *The Way of the Lord: Christological Exegesis in the Gospel of Mark* (Louisville: Westminster/John Knox, 1992); R. Watts, *Isaiah's New Exodus and Mark*, WUNT 2, ser. 88 (Tübingen: Mohr Siebeck, 1997).

7. For text-critical reasons, the majority of commentators regard Rom 16:25-27 as an interpolation rather than a part of the original text of Romans. For discussion and further references, see, e.g., J. D. G. Dunn, *Romans 9–16*, WBC 38B (Dallas: Word, 1988), 912-13; J. A. Fitzmyer, *Romans*, AB 33 (New York: Doubleday, 1993), 753-56. Even if these verses are secondary, the relation they describe between gospel, Scripture, and proclamation to the Gentiles is an apt summary of Paul's argument in Romans; thus, at the very least, these words represent a well-informed reading of Pauline theology by an early editor of the Pauline corpus. My own inclination is to regard Rom 16:25-27 as Paul's own original and rather elegant conclusion to the letter, not least because the passage provides, along with Rom 1:1-7, a satisfying *inclusio*.

sisted upon — the tradition that the death and resurrection of Jesus had happened κατὰ τὰς γραφάς (1 Cor 15:3), and he persistently developed his theological arguments in relation to the stories and oracles he found in those Scriptures. His letter to the Romans opens with the affirmation that "the gospel of God" was "promised ahead of time through his prophets in holy writings" (Rom 1:2),[8] and in the course of his argument in this letter he quotes Scripture more than sixty times.[9] Despite the puzzling resistance of some NT scholarship to acknowledging the formative role of the OT in Paul's theology,[10] it must be affirmed that Paul was a hermeneutical theologian whose reflection on God's action in the world was shaped in decisive ways by his reading of Israel's sacred texts.[11]

It would therefore be highly artificial to suppose that Scripture plays an important role in Paul's thought only in those cases where he quotes a text explicitly. There can be no serious doubt that Scripture shapes his symbolic world in a more pervasive manner.[12] That means that our efforts to interpret his writings must deal also with allusions to and echoes of Scripture in his writings.

8. I continue to believe (as I suggested in *Echoes*, 85) that the prepositional phrase περὶ τοῦ υἱοῦ αὐτοῦ is most naturally to be read as modifying γραφαῖς ἁγίαις, rather than εὐαγγέλιον θεοῦ, so that the sentence should be read "which he promised beforehand in holy writings concerning his Son, who came from the seed of David according to the flesh." My present point does not depend on this construal of the sentence, though this reading is not unrelated to the problem of the role of Isa 53 in Paul's Christology. It should also be recalled, as noted above, that the conclusion of Romans associates τὸ κήρυγμα Ἰησοῦ Χριστοῦ with the revelation of a hidden mystery that is now disclosed through "prophetic Scriptures" (διὰ γραφῶν προφητικῶν) to all the Gentiles (Rom 16:25-26).

9. According to the count of Koch (*Schrift als Zeuge*, 88), there are sixty-five OT quotations in Romans, fifty-six of them explicitly marked as such.

10. Several years ago, while on sabbatical in Jerusalem, I met an American doctoral student who informed me that her NT professor at an American graduate school had told his class that there are actually no OT quotations in Paul's letters. All the apparent quotations, he said, are actually better explained on the basis of Greco-Roman parallels! This absurd claim — even if the student's account was somewhat exaggerated — demonstrates the lengths to which some scholars will go to sever Paul from his Jewish roots.

11. I explored some aspects of this problem in *Echoes of Scripture in the Letters of Paul*. For a brief discussion of the state of the question prior to my work, see *Echoes*, 5-14.

12. That is by no means to say that his symbolic world is shaped *only* by Scripture. Many other factors are part of the mix: the social and political realities of his day, popular Greco-Roman philosophical traditions, the distinctive experiences and traditions of the emergent Christian movement, and so forth.

Some of these allusions and echoes may have been deliberately crafted by the apostle, presupposing recognition from Christian readers in the Pauline communities whom Paul himself had explicitly trained to understand certain scriptural motifs. Others may be less deliberate, simply bubbling up out of Paul's mind in the same way allusions to Shakespeare or Milton might arise unbidden for any English writer educated in the English literary tradition — or, let us say, allusions to Luther or Goethe for the German writer. From this distance in time, however, it is difficult to distinguish between intentional and unintentional intertextual references in Paul. Because the question of authorial intentionality is a slippery one, we should not place too much weight upon it; for the present let us simply say that to interpret Paul discerningly, we must recognize the embeddedness of his discourse in scriptural language (or the embeddedness of scriptural language in his discourse) and explore the rhetorical and theological effects created by the intertextual relationships between his letters and their scriptural precursors.

Identifying allusions and echoes of an earlier text in a later one, however, poses a daunting challenge, especially when we encounter texts that come to us from the ancient world. Thomas Greene, a literary scholar who has studied the use of classical sources in Renaissance literature, describes the difficulty of this sort of intertextual reading: "[It] makes even larger claims on the historical imagination than most reading, and underscores even more cruelly our cultural solitude. It asks us not only to intuit an alien sensibility from a remote *mundus significans,* but also that sensibility's intuitions of a third. Nothing perhaps is more calculated to impress upon us our temporal estrangement."[13] Thus, this sort of interpretative task calls for close attention and discernment by the reader, or more precisely, by the reading community. The danger of rampant subjectivity and misinterpretation is very great.

Consequently, we must consider how we as a community of trained and presumably competent readers shall discipline our intuitions about the role of Scripture in Paul's *mundus significans.* If the identification of allusions and echoes in Paul is not to be a purely private romp through infinite fields of intertextual possibility, what are the *criteria* that might be applied to test our hunches about Paul's indirect literary gestures toward the OT, particularly toward Isaiah?

13. Thomas M. Greene, *The Light in Troy: Imitation and Discovery in Renaissance Poetry* (New Haven: Yale University Press, 1982), 53.

29

I have some proposals to make about the criteria we might use, but before stating my positive criteria, I want to voice three preliminary cautions and clarifications about this enterprise, in hopes of heading off certain confusions.

1. Paul had no conception of "the Servant Songs" as a distinct collection or genre within the Isaianic prophetic material. The idea of a cycle of Servant Songs is a construct of modern critical scholarship. Our tendency to focus especially on the Servant material, a tendency which arises partly from the way the texts were later used in the construction of Christology and partly from the development of form-critical methods for studying the OT, may create a distortion of perspective. Paul seems to have used the Isaiah material in an undifferentiated manner, without paying any special attention to the passages about the Servant, though, as we have noted, he does cite and allude to Isa 40–55 with particular frequency. Thus, rather than asking, at least in the first instance, "How did Paul interpret the figure of the Servant in Isaiah 53?" we should begin by asking inductively, "How does Paul employ the Isaiah material that he cites?"

2. The identification of allusions and especially of echoes is not a strictly scientific matter lending itself to conclusive proof, like testing for the presence or absence of a chemical in the bloodstream. The identification of allusions, rather, is an art practiced by skilled interpreters within a reading community that has agreed on the value of situating individual texts within a historical and literary continuum of other texts (i.e., a canon). The "yes" or "no" judgment about any particular alleged allusion is primarily an *aesthetic* judgment pronounced upon the fittingness of a proposed reading. This does *not* mean, I hasten to add, that such judgments are purely arbitrary, any more than judgments about the quality of a particular performance of a Mozart piano concerto are arbitrary; there are norms and standards internal to the practice, and those who have studied the practice closely should be able to develop significantly convergent judgments. The ability to recognize — or to exclude — possible allusions is a skill, a reader competence, inculcated by reading communities.

3. Finally, we must consider the aims of the interpretative task we are undertaking. Are we trying to prove a historical hypothesis about Isaiah's direct influence on the early church's development of the idea that Jesus' death had atoning significance? Or, alternatively, are we trying to understand the way in which an author (Paul) creates meaning effects in a text through artful reminiscences of another text well-known to the commu-

nity? These are very different tasks: the former is primarily historical, the latter literary and theological. Both are perfectly legitimate pursuits — indeed, they are methodologically intertwined — but it is important to be clear about where the focus of our attention lies.

Much of the debate about the use of Isaiah in the NT has dealt with the historical issues. Consider, by way of illustration, the following quotation from Hooker, in which I have underlined the phrases that indicate her concentration on proving historical claims about Isa 53 as the unique source of christological ideas:

> [N]o attempt to <u>resolve the dilemma</u> on linguistic grounds alone can be successful if the <u>evidence</u> is only <u>probable</u>. To claim that there is a verbal similarity between a New Testament passage and an Old Testament one cannot be taken as <u>conclusive evidence</u> of <u>direct influence</u> unless it can be shown that the language and ideas found in the New Testament reference have come from, *and could only have come from,* that particular Old Testament passage. Unless the New Testament passage is an actual quotation from the Old Testament, or contains an idea found <u>uniquely</u> in that Old Testament reference, then the claim remains only as subsidiary <u>evidence</u>, and cannot be accepted as <u>proof</u> of any identification.[14]

In the nature of the case, of course, it is difficult to *prove* things about sources and direct influences, given the paucity of evidence at our disposal. That is one reason why Hooker's book had such an impact on the discussion in the English-speaking world: given her stringent criteria for proof, her arguments seemed nearly irrefutable. Indeed, the book served the important purpose of clearing away a lot of wild and undisciplined claims about the Servant image; particularly valuable was her demonstration that Jews in the first century C.E. were not looking for a Messiah to fulfill the Suffering Servant role.

More recent scholarship, however, has begun to articulate a different paradigm for thinking about intertextual relations. My own work on Paul's use of Scripture has sought to explore in the epistles what John Ciardi

---

14. Hooker, *Jesus and the Servant*, 62, italics in original. This quotation comes from her chapter "The Servant in the Synoptic Gospels" rather than from her discussion of Paul, but her aims are constant throughout. She is seeking definitive proof that the NT's language has come exclusively from a particular source.

called the "rippling pools" of metaphor and allusion, and other interpreters have become more attuned to the rhetorical effects within the Pauline texts. In point of fact, such approaches may also contribute to the formation of judgments about historical questions: for example, if we develop a reading of Romans that discovers an extensive network of allusions to Deutero-Isaiah, that will enhance the likelihood (but not "prove") that Isa 53 is one of the significant sources for Paul's interpretation of Jesus. But the primary interest of such readings lies elsewhere, in the literary and theological implications of observable intertextual linkages.

To clarify what I mean by speaking of a different paradigm, let us consider one nonscriptural example, an example not freighted with the theological baggage of past debates in our guild.[15] Near the end of the "Fire Sermon" section of *The Waste Land,* a section of the poem that vividly depicts the decaying, lustful, and meaningless condition of life in twentieth-century London, T. S. Eliot abruptly writes:

To Carthage then I came

Burning burning burning burning
O Lord Thou pluckest me out
O Lord Thou pluckest

burning

This looks like a random and puzzling series of lines: Why Carthage? What has this to do with London or the decay of modern life? The lines are puzzling, that is, unless we recognize the allusion to the opening of book 3 of Saint Augustine's *Confessions:* "To Carthage then I came, where a cauldron of unholy loves sang all about mine ears." With this connection made, Eliot's deft allusion conjures up Augustine's image of the corrupt city and his own immersion in it. Augustine's Carthage becomes a metaphor for Eliot's London, and the "burning" language — initially borrowed by Eliot from the Buddhist Fire Sermon's aversion to the world of the senses — becomes identified, on at least one level, with the burning of the youthful lusts that Augustine retrospectively deplores. (On another level, "burning"

---

15. For bringing this example to my attention and for much fascinating conversation about it I am indebted to Christopher B. Hays.

is also probably a figure for judgment and destruction, the reduction of the city to rubble; the two levels are intimately connected.) The line "O Lord Thou pluckest me out" should also then be recognized as an allusion to *Confessions* 3.11: "Et misisti manum tuam ex alto, et de hac profunda caligine eruisti animam meam."[16] The fact, however, that Eliot's affirmation trails off and collapses back into "burning" at the end of the unit marks the distance between the bishop of Hippo and the desolate modern poet: Augustine's confident cry of gratitude to God has become for the speaking persona of *The Waste Land* only a forlorn hope.

Beyond all this, we may note one more nearly subliminal but intriguing echo created by Eliot's allusion to Augustine. The final sentence of *Confessions* 2.10, the line just *preceding* "To Carthage then I came," reads as follows: "I sank away from Thee, and I wandered, O my God, too much astray from Thee my stay, in these days of my youth, and I became to myself *a barren land.*" This is an elegant and tantalizing example of metalepsis, the suggested but unspoken evocation of an image from the precursor text, echoing in the Waste Land of the latter.

The purpose of this excursus into the world of twentieth-century English poetry has been to illustrate something about the way allusion and echo work as *tropes,* figurative modes of speech whose efficacy depends partly upon their initial obscurity. We do not make much progress in reading such figures if we confine our inquiry to asking questions like, "Is Eliot's line an allusion to Augustine, yes or no?" and "Can we prove that the *Confessions* was a source for *The Waste Land*?" (I'm afraid that many readers trained in the usual methods of biblical studies might insist that Eliot intended no reference to the "cauldron of unholy loves," because he did not actually quote that part of the line!) We attain an illuminating reading of Eliot's text only when we follow the play of allusion and see where it leads. In the previous paragraphs I have sketched briefly one such reading of the intertextual figuration.

That is the sort of reading that also yields, I believe, considerable fruit when employed in relation to Paul's letters. Let us turn, then, to consider some criteria for evaluating alleged allusions and echoes.

---

16. "And Thou sentest Thine hand from above and drewest (*eruisti*) my soul out of that profound darkness." English translations here are taken from *The Confessions of Saint Augustine*, trans. E. B. Pusey (New York: Modern Library, 1949). I have not been able to determine what translation (if any) Eliot was using. "Pluckest" is actually a very good — and far more vivid — translation of *eruisti*.

The Seven Criteria of *Echoes* Applied to Paul's Use of Isaiah

In *Echoes* I proposed seven tests for discerning the presence of intertextual echoes in Paul.[17] As I have already indicated, precision in such matters is not attainable, but these are — it still seems to me — modestly useful rules of thumb. For our present purposes I will restate them and elaborate on them, with particular application to the question about Paul's reading of Isaiah. It should be kept in mind that no one of these criteria is decisive: they must be employed in conjunction with one another. We should also bear in mind that the use of such criteria will often yield only greater or lesser degrees of probability about any particular reading, especially where echoes are concerned.

Availability

Was the proposed source of the echo available to Paul and/or his original readers? In the case of Isaiah, there can be no doubt about this. Isaiah was broadly recognized as Scripture in the Judaism of Paul's time, and Paul quotes it as such repeatedly, using explicit citation formulas, such as λέγει γὰρ ἡ γραφή (Rom 10:11), γέγραπται γάρ (Rom 14:11), καθὼς γέγραπται (Rom 2:24; 9:33; 10:15; 11:26; 15:21), ἐν τῷ νόμῳ ['] γέγραπται ὅτι (1 Cor 14:21), and a series of formulas that mention Isaiah by name: Ἡσαΐας δὲ κράζει ὑπὲρ τοῦ Ἰσραήλ (Rom 9:27), καθὼς προείρηκεν Ἡσαΐας (Rom 9:29), Ἡσαΐας γὰρ λέγει (Rom 10:16), Ἡσαΐας δὲ ἀποτολμᾷ καὶ λέγει (Rom 10:20), and καὶ πάλιν Ἡσαΐας λέγει (Rom 15:12). Paul certainly knew Isaiah and cited it frequently. His interpretations of the text may have been controversial, but he expected his readers to recognize the source of his quotations and acknowledge it as Scripture.

Volume

How "loud" is the echo; that is, how explicit and overt is it? Of the seven tests suggested in *Echoes,* this one has been perhaps the most subject to misunderstanding, because I did not explain it very fully there. The general

17. Hays, *Echoes,* 29-33.

notion of the variable "volume" of echoes is derived from the richly suggestive work of John Hollander, whose book *The Figure of Echo* was a major stimulus to my work on echoes in Paul.[18] The basic question here is how insistently the echo presses itself upon the reader. Let me try to unpack the elements involved in assessing this issue.

a. The primary factor is *the degree of verbatim repetition of words and syntactical patterns.* For example, in Rom 8:32 (ὅς γε τοῦ ἰδίου υἱοῦ οὐκ ἐφείσατο), the words "did not spare his own son" can be heard as an echo of Gen 22:16 because the words "son" and "did not spare" reproduce the language of the LXX closely. The whole expression, however, has been transferred from the second person to the third, and the subject of the verb in Romans is God rather than, as in Genesis, Abraham. Thus, the volume of this echo is only moderate, and interpreters have long been divided on how to assess its significance or even whether to hear it as an echo at all. To take another example, a much louder echo is to be found in Rom 8:33-34, where we have not only the language of judgment (Isa 50:8: τίς ὁ κρινόμενός μοι; Rom 8:34: τίς ὁ κατακρινῶν) and God's vindication of the elect (Isa 50:8: ἐγγίζει ὁ δικαιώσας με; Rom 8:33: θεὸς ὁ δικαιῶν), but even the same syntactical pattern of brief diatribal rhetorical questions in both texts. Here the echo is very loud indeed; only the most stubborn or tone-deaf reader would deny its presence in Paul's text. To give an example at the other end of the decibel spectrum however, consider this: Should Paul's use of the term καινὴ κτίσις (2 Cor 5:17; Gal 6:15) be understood as an echo of Isa 43:18-19 and/or 65:17? I would argue that it should be so understood, because the echo meets several other important criteria, particularly the criterion of thematic coherence (see below), but the *volume* of the echo — in terms of verbatim repetition of Isaiah's language — is low: it is only the word pair ἀρχαῖα/καινή (hardly an unusual juxtaposition) that suggests a connection.[19]

Of course, to speak of "verbatim repetition" presumes that we know what text form of the scriptural passages was available to Paul and his readers. This is, unfortunately, a complex technical problem that admits few certain answers.[20] It has been established that Paul's quotations of the

---

18. J. Hollander, *The Figure of Echo: A Mode of Allusion in Milton and After* (Berkeley: University of California Press, 1981).

19. Actually, even ἀρχαῖα is lacking in Isa 65:17, which refers only to τῶν προτέρων. On the other hand, the "new heaven and new earth" of Isa 65:17 certainly suggests — even more clearly than Isa 43:18-19 — the Pauline idea of a "new creation."

20. For the most comprehensive study of this problem, see Christopher D. Stanley, *Paul*

OT generally follow the LXX against the MT where the two are divergent. Thus, our normal procedure should be to compare alleged scriptural allusions in Paul first of all to the LXX, as I have done in the examples cited in the previous paragraph. If in some instances evidence from later Greek versions agrees with Paul's wording against the LXX, this opens the possibility that Paul may be echoing a Greek text — presumably known to his readers — that differs from extant LXX manuscripts, or that he is modifying the LXX in accord with common linguistic usage of his own day.[21] Sometimes scholars claim to hear in Paul's letters echoes or allusions of an underlying Hebrew or Aramaic text that differs from any of the Greek versions; such proposals are not impossible (my own view is that Paul surely must have known Hebrew), but they will always remain speculative,[22] enjoying a lower degree of probability than alleged echoes of a Greek textual source. Most of Paul's readers surely did not know Hebrew or Aramaic; therefore, any echoes of such linguistic origin would have fallen on deaf ears.

b. "Volume" also depends, however, on *the distinctiveness, prominence, or popular familiarity of the precursor text.* For example, in 1 Cor 8:6 Paul's confessional formula echoes Deut 6:4: "For us there is one God, the Father, . . . and one Lord, Jesus Christ." Even though the number of words repeated from Deuteronomy is small, the Shema is such a familiar and foundational text within Judaism that only a slight verbal cue is needed to trigger the full-volume echo. For an analogy we might consider how the simple words "Our Father" serve to conjure up the entire text of the Lord's Prayer for any Christian reader.[23] American readers might compare the way any passing reference to "self-evident truths" is likely to be heard as an echo of the Declaration of Independence, or the way the simple phrase "I

---

and the Language of Scripture: Citation Technique in the Pauline Epistles and Contemporary Literature, SNTSMS 69 (Cambridge: Cambridge University Press, 1992).

21. Of course, it is equally possible that later Christian scribes copying the Greek OT might have altered the text to conform to Paul's citations; such problems must be assessed on a case-by-case basis.

22. For an illustration of how I think such problems should be handled, see my treatment of the possible echo of the MT's image of God as Rock (Deut 32:4, 15, 18, 30, 31) in 1 Cor 10:4 (*Echoes,* 94).

23. In 1 Cor 8 context also plays a role: the fact that Paul is contrasting Christian confession to polytheistic idolatry helps to confirm the resonance of the Shema behind 1 Cor 8; this again shows how the criterion of thematic coherence (see below) comes into play to complement other criteria.

have a dream" can no longer be uttered without echoes of Martin Luther King, Jr., being heard in the background.

c. Finally, the volume of an echo is affected subtly by the rhetorical stress placed upon the phrase(s) in question, both within the precursor text and in Paul's discourse. This is more difficult to illustrate concisely, but I have in mind the recurrence of language that comes from keynote or summary passages in the source text, or language that is placed at a climactic (clinching) point in Paul's own discourse. The echo of Gen 1:3-5 in 2 Cor 4:6 is an example of this sort of thing.[24]

In short, when we speak of the *volume* of an echo, we must consider not only the degree of exact verbal correspondence but also the relative weightiness of the material cited.

Recurrence or Clustering

How often does Paul elsewhere cite or allude to the same scriptural passage? We might also call this "multiple attestation." This criterion is a very important one indeed, and it will play a crucial role in our consideration of echoes of Isaiah in Paul. Authors tend to work with a de facto canon within the canon, certain texts that are more important, more frequently read and adduced. Paul is no exception: there are several instances of passages that he seems to have mulled over at some length. *When we find repeated Pauline quotations of a particular OT passage, additional possible allusions to the same passage become more compelling.* I use the term "passage" broadly to indicate not just a particular verse quoted explicitly on more than one occasion (such as Hab 2:4 or Gen 15:6) but also larger units of Scripture to which Paul repeatedly refers. One example of this would be Deut 32, which turns up repeatedly in Paul's letters (e.g., explicit quotations in Rom 10:19; 12:19; 15:10 and clear allusions in 1 Cor 10:20, 22 and Rom 11:11).[25] The parade example of this phenomenon in the Pauline letters, however, is his use of Isa 40–55.[26] Paul returns again and again to this text, especially in Romans.

---

24. Hays, *Echoes*, 30, 152-53. See my further suggestion there (153) that 2 Cor 4:6 also echoes Isa 9:2.

25. For a full discussion see R. H. Bell, *Provoked to Jealousy: The Origin and Purpose of the Jealousy Motif in Romans 9–11*, WUNT 2, ser. 63 (Tübingen: J. C. B. Mohr [Paul Siebeck], 1994).

26. I noted this phenomenon in *Echoes* (30), but did not develop its significance sufficiently.

Here we find clear evidence of the *clustering* of citations from one special scriptural context. Figure 1 on page 39 graphically displays the data concerning Paul's direct quotations of Isaiah in Romans.[27] The evidence is even more impressive if we include allusions in our purview: according to the table of "Loci citati vel allegati" in the 27th edition of Nestle-Aland, there are, by my count, fourteen quotations from Isa 40–55 in the Pauline letters[28] (seven of them in Romans) and twenty-six more allusions, for a total of forty references in all. I suspect that this tabulation only scratches the surface of the intertextual networking between Paul and Deutero-Isaiah. In any case, no matter how we might tabulate the precise extent or number of allusions, it is difficult to avoid the impression that Paul was deeply engaged in reflection about this particular passage of Scripture.

Of course, it is in principle possible that Paul merely treated Isa 40–55 as a loose anthology of favorite religious quotations, without considering its overall meaning; readers will have to form their own judgment on this point. Even if so, however, the criterion of recurrence would still be useful for identifying the *presence* of allusions to Isaiah. The question of the *meaning* of such allusions, however, leads us to the next criterion.

Thematic Coherence

How well does the alleged echo fit into the line of argument that Paul is developing? Does the proposed precursor text fit together with the point Paul is making? Can one see in Paul's use of the material a coherent "reading" of the source text? Is his use of the Isaiah texts consonant with his overall argument and/or use made of other texts? Of course, it is perfectly possible for random isolated echoes to occur that do not contribute coherently to the argument, but it would be difficult to test intuitions about such echoes with much confidence. When, however, an echo does fit into a larger thematic pattern, we may more securely identify it.

In fact, when we assemble the evidence, it is possible to mount a strong argument that Paul is not just randomly proof-texting in his allu-

27. This figure was devised by Diana Swancutt, now assistant professor of New Testament at Yale Divinity School. I use this material here with her permission and with gratitude to her.

28. One of these, however, the quotation of Isa 49:18 in Rom 14:11, should probably be described as an echo rather than a quotation.

Figure 1. Explicit Citations of Isaiah in Romans

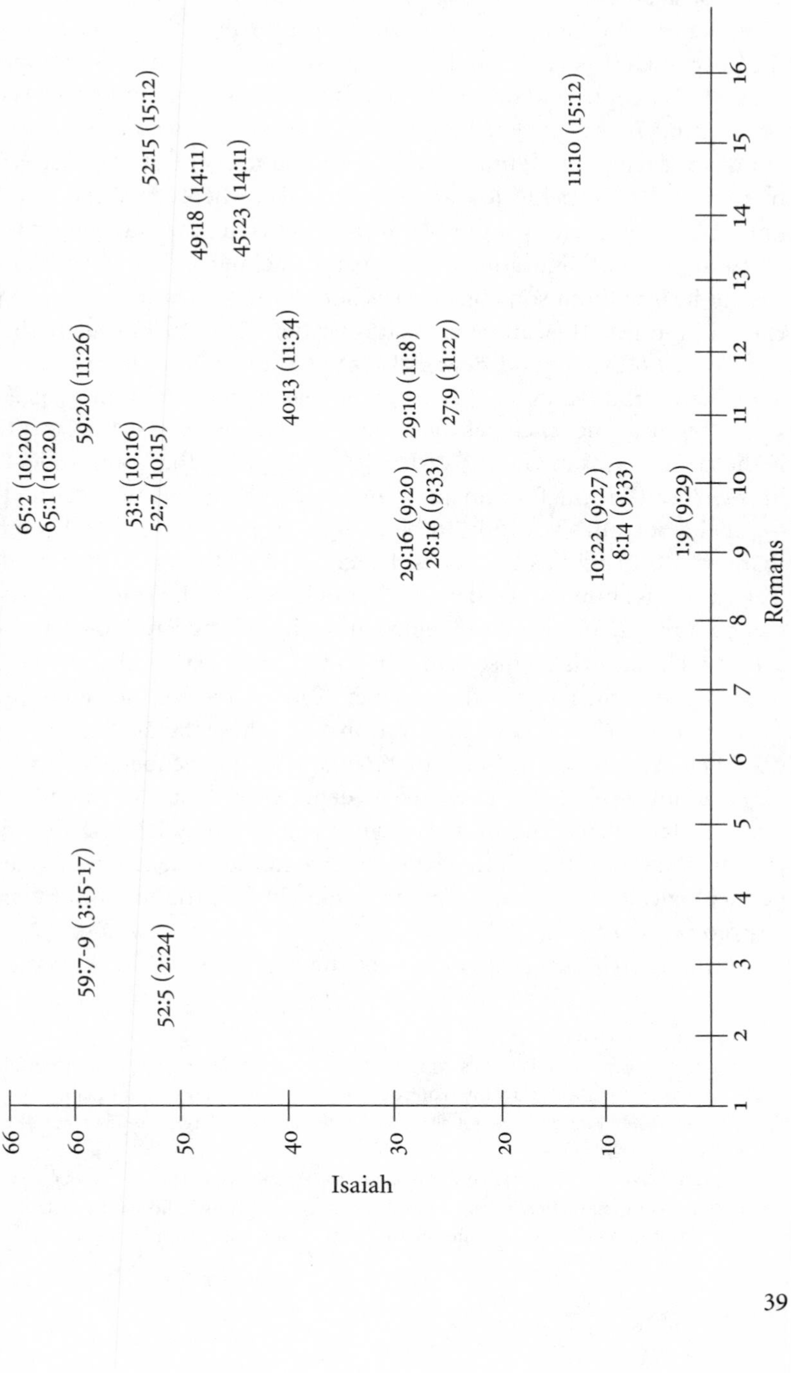

Isaiah

66

60   59:7-9 (3:15-17)

50   52:5 (2:24)

65:2 (10:20)
65:1 (10:20)
59:20 (11:26)

53:1 (10:16)
52:7 (10:15)

52:15 (15:12)

49:18 (14:11)
45:23 (14:11)

40   40:13 (11:34)

30   29:16 (9:20)
28:16 (9:33)

29:10 (11:8)
27:9 (11:27)

20   10:22 (9:27)
8:14 (9:33)

11:10 (15:12)

10   1:9 (9:29)

Romans

1   2   3   4   5   6   7   8   9   10   11   12   13   14   15   16

sions to Isaiah but that Isa 40–55 is fundamentally formative for his understanding of what God is doing in the world through the proclamation of the gospel: God is revealing his eschatological righteousness, ending the exile of his people, and bringing the Gentiles to see and understand (Rom 15:21, citing Isa 52:15). Furthermore, as J. Ross Wagner has shown, Paul "finds in Isaiah a prefiguration or pre-announcement of his own proclamation of the Gospel to Jew and Gentile alike, wherever Christ is not yet known."[29] Consider, for example, in Rom 10:15-16, the way Paul cites Isa 52:7 and 53:1 as prefigurations of his own preaching activity: "And how are they to hear without someone to proclaim him? And how are they to proclaim him unless they are sent? As it is written, 'How beautiful are the feet of those who bring good news!' [Isa 52:7].[30] But not all have obeyed the good news; for Isaiah says, 'Lord, who has believed our message?' [Isa 53:1]."[31] Many other such passages could be adduced. Of particular interest is the strong echo in Gal 1:15 of Isa 49:1, suggesting that Paul understood his own "call" as the fulfillment — or at least the typological counterpart — of the Servant's vocation to be a "light to the nations," and (perhaps thereby?) to bring Jacob (that is, Israel) back to the Lord; cf. Isa 49:5-6. Thus, there is abundant evidence in Paul's letters that he read Isa 40–55 as a coherent prophetic vision foretelling and authorizing Paul's own apostolic activity. The surprising disclosure of God's righteousness, the proclaiming of the word to the nations, the unbelief of Israel, the apostle's commission to announce the good news of salvation — all these themes are richly suggested by the passages in Isaiah that Paul quotes and echoes. (See the summary on pp. 44-46.) Where we see evidence of such sustained and reflectively patterned reading of a particular text, we may assume that other possible echoes of that same text elsewhere in the same letter are likely to be theologically significant rather than merely the product of our own interpretive fantasy.

Although Hooker's early study of the Servant denies a thematic link

29. Wagner, "Heralds," 194.

30. As Wagner notes, Paul has converted Isaiah's singular messenger to a plural (τῶν εὐαγγελιζομένων), without warrant in any extant Greek or Hebrew text of Isaiah. This shows that Paul interpreted the passage not christologically but as a reference to the (plural) Christian preachers of the gospel.

31. Here again we note that Paul's lone citation of a passage from Isa 53 focuses not on the mysterious figure of the Servant but on the activity of those who have proclaimed the message about him — a message met by the hearers with considerable skepticism.

between Isa 52–53 and Pauline Christology, her actual interpretation of the material is convergent with the point I am making here: "[T]here is a consistent interpretation of the 'Servant' which stretches from Deutero-Isaiah, through Judaism, to Jesus himself [and, I would add, to Paul as well]: an interpretation which arises, not from the concept of the 'Servant,' but from the thought of the mission of people of God to the world."[32] If indeed that is how Isa 52–53 was understood in the Judaism of Paul's day, then is it not credible to find allusions to this text in Paul's theological reflection upon his own mission?

Historical Plausibility

Could Paul in fact have intended the alleged meaning effect of any proposed allusion, and could his first-century readers have understood it? The criterion of historical plausibility requires that the historical situatedness of Paul's letters, as acts of communication, be taken seriously. Paul was a Pharisaic Jew and also a member of the early Christian movement; consequently, he was the heir of certain interpretative traditions within both of these communities. At the same time, he was seeking to mediate to predominantly Gentile readers the meaning of Israel's Scripture in the new eschatological situation. In such a situation, and against such a background, what sorts of allusions and echoes would make sense? Here there is much room — indeed, great need — for further research and reflection. How did other Jews in Paul's time read Isaiah? How are his readings like and unlike theirs? What use was made of Isaiah's prophecies in other early Christian interpretations? Can we find parallels to Paul's readings?

This criterion should not necessarily function as a negative constraint, because Paul was no doubt a reasonably original thinker who was capable of formulating fresh echoes and unprecedented readings. Furthermore, many of his more subtle allusions might have eluded his Gentile readers. If, however, it can be shown that Paul's allusions to Scripture do have analogies and parallels in other contemporary writings, then we are on firmer ground in placing interpretive weight upon them. For example, should Paul's strange gloss (ὅς ἐστιν Χριστός) in Gal 3:16 on the promise to Abra-

---

32. Hooker, *Jesus and the Servant*, xi-xii. She describes this as one of the two main points that emerge from her study of the problem.

ham and to his "seed" (σπέρματι) be understood as a covert allusion to 2 Sam 7:12-14, in which God promises to "raise up" a "seed" (σπέρμα) of David and "establish the throne of his kingdom forever"? This suggestion is made more convincing by the discovery that 4Q Florilegium 1:10-11 includes 2 Sam 7:12-14 in an anthology of messianic texts.[33] Or again, Paul's strange christological interpretation of Deut 30:12-14 in Rom 10:6-8 is rendered more comprehensible in light of Bar 3:29-30, which had already transferred Deuteronomy's language about the Torah onto the personified figure of Wisdom:

> Who has gone up into heaven and taken her,
> and brought her down from the clouds?
> Who has gone over the sea and found her,
> and will buy her for pure gold?[34]

The use of this criterion requires of us a broad historical construction of the hermeneutical horizon and reader-competence of Paul and his first-century readers. I am not aware of a scholarly monograph thoroughly surveying interpretations of Deutero-Isaiah in the Second Temple period,[35] but some such study would be of great help in our efforts to identify and interpret Pauline allusions to Isaiah.

---

33. For discussion see G. J. Brooke, *Exegesis at Qumran: 4Q Florilegium in Its Jewish Context*, JSOTSup 29 (Sheffield: JSOT, 1985), 197-205; D. Juel, *Messianic Exegesis: Christological Interpretation of the Old Testament in Early Christianity* (Philadelphia: Fortress, 1988), 59-77; Hays, *Echoes*, 85.

34. For discussion of this example see Hays, *Echoes*, 77-82. In a response to my work, Craig A. Evans has also pointed out that *Targum Neofiti* on Deut 30:12-13 fills in even more possible background for Paul's interpretation of Deut 30. See Craig A. Evans, "Listening for Echoes of Interpreted Scripture," in *Paul and the Scriptures of Israel*, ed. C. A. Evans and J. A. Sanders, JSNTSup 83 (Sheffield: JSOT, 1993), 47-51.

35. The recent collection of essays *Der leidende Gottesknecht: Jesaja 53 und seine Wirkungsgeschichte*, ed. B. Janowski and P. Stuhlmacher, Forschungen zum Alten Testament 14 (Tübingen: Mohr Siebeck, 1996) is a step in the right direction, but by focusing only on Isa 53 it runs the risk of drawing the circle of attention too narrowly and thus prejudging the questions I am seeking to raise here. Florian Wilk's study, *Die Bedeutung des Jesajabuches für Paulus*, FRLANT 179 (Göttingen: Vandenhoeck & Ruprecht, 1998), without seeking to survey Jewish interpretations of Isaiah comprehensively, does call attention to a number of parallels in Jewish sources.

History of Interpretation

If the previous criterion attends to readings of Scripture *contemporary with* Paul, this one attends to *the subsequent history of the reading of Paul's epistles*. Have other readers in the tradition heard the same echoes that we now think we hear? Or can the history of interpretation alert us to echoes that we might otherwise have missed?

Again, this criterion may serve more to expand than to veto our intuitions about particular echoes. The Christian tradition early on lost its vital connection with the Jewish interpretive matrix in which Paul had lived and moved; consequently, later Christian interpreters missed some of Paul's basic concerns. For example, the Christian fixation on christological proof texts may have caused readers to zero in on texts like Isa 53 and to overlook Paul's concern for explaining the mission to the Gentiles and the fate of Israel in relation to Scripture. This tendency, in turn, may have caused most readers to lose sight of the ecclesiocentric hermeneutic operative in Paul's larger pattern of allusions to Isaiah.[36] Thus, the tradition of interpretation has its blind (or deaf) spots. Traditional readings will need to be supplemented by new readings that benefit from a scholarly recovery of the "cave of resonant signification" within which Paul's voice originally sounded.[37]

Still, we stand only to gain from a careful examination of the history of readings of Paul's use of Isaiah. The fact that the subsequent tradition has made so much of Isa 53, despite the lack of explicit citations of the passage in Paul's letters, might suggest that there is a metaleptic suppression of Isa 53 in Paul that has worked effectively as a trope to highlight the uncited material.[38] In *Echoes* I described the situation as follows:

> The letter to the Romans is salted with numerous quotations of and allusions to Isaiah 40–55, including several passages that seem to echo the Suffering Servant motif of Isaiah 53 (e.g., Rom 4:24-25, 5:15-19, 10:16,

36. Wagner prefers to speak of a "missiological hermeneutic."

37. Cf. Hollander, *The Figure of Echo*, 65-66.

38. In brief, "metalepsis" is a rhetorical figure that creates a correspondence between two texts such that text B should be understood in light of a broad interplay with the precursor text A, encompassing aspects of A beyond those explicitly cited. See Hays, *Echoes*, 18-21. For an informative discussion tracing the history of this terminology back at least to Quintilian, see Hollander, *The Figure of Echo*, 133-49.

15:21). Why, then, does Paul not draw this prophecy into the open and use the servant figure as an explicit basis for his interpretation of Israel, or of the church, or of Jesus? Paul's motive for this evasion or reticence, whichever it is, remains forever lost to us, but the effect of his rhetorical strategy can be readily described. He hints and whispers all around Isaiah 53 but never mentions the prophetic typology that would supremely integrate his interpretation of Christ and Israel. The result is a compelling example of metalepsis: Paul's transumptive silence cries out for the reader to complete the trope.[39]

Perhaps that is exactly what the history of interpretation in the church has done.

Satisfaction

Does the proposed intertextual reading illuminate the surrounding discourse and make some larger sense of Paul's argument as a whole? This final criterion is elusive but important to the task of critical interpretation in the community. It is related to the criterion of thematic coherence, but it differs in the following way: whereas the criterion of thematic coherence asks whether the content of an individual precursor text is materially related to the sense of Paul's argument at the place where the putative echo occurs (see examples above), the criterion of satisfaction asks more broadly whether the resultant reading of Paul's discussion is clarified and enhanced by an awareness of the proposed intertexts. This criterion calls for an integrative act of discernment about the meaning of the epistle as a whole, or at least the meaning of the local context within the epistle, in light of the proposed intertextual links. A proposed intertextual reading fulfills the test of satisfaction when we find ourselves saying, "Oh, so *that* is what Paul means here in passage *x;* and furthermore, if that's right, then we can begin to understand what he means in passage *y* and why he uses *these* certain words in that place." For example, if Isa 40–55 really does play the role in Romans that I have been proposing here, then our understanding of Rom 1:16-17, the keynote of the letter, will be illuminated by reading it in counterpoint with Isa 51:4-5:

39. Hays, *Echoes*, 63.

Hear me, hear, my people,
And kings, give ear to me.
For the Law will go forth from me,
And my judgment will go forth as a light to the Gentiles [ἐθνῶν],
My righteousness [ἡ δικαιοσύνη μου] draws near quickly,
And my salvation [τὸ σωτήριόν μου] will go forth as a light,
And in my arm [cf. δύναμις in Rom 1:16] will Gentiles [ἔθνη] hope.

Or again, Isa 52:10:

And the Lord will reveal [ἀποκαλύψει] his holy arm
    before all the Gentiles [ἐθνῶν],
And all the corners of the earth will see the salvation [σωτηρίαν]
    that is with God.

I leave it to the reader to decide whether some such account of the good news is the message (εὐαγγέλιον in Rom 1:16, echoing Isa 52:7; ἀκοή in Rom 10:16, quoting Isa 53:1) that Paul believed himself commissioned to proclaim.

Paul's Reading of Isaiah's Story: The Explicit Quotations

A full study of Paul's reading of Isaiah should begin with an inductive examination of all the passages in the letters where Paul quotes Isaiah explicitly. Such an examination should ask what motifs Paul spotlights in the text of Isaiah and how these motifs are related to the argument of the letters in which the quotations appear. Further, an attempt should be made to see whether these motifs can be plotted as part of a coherent narrative structure. In a paper of this length, such an inductive survey is impossible, but I will nonetheless venture a synthetic statement of the findings that I believe would issue from such a survey.

Paul reads Isaiah as having narrated beforehand the events that have at last been set in motion in Paul's generation through the death and resurrection of Jesus. These events may be summarized in the following way.

1. Israel has fallen into hard-hearted disobedience; their iniquities have separated them from God. Their disloyalty to the covenant brings discredit

to God's name among the nations. Despite God's long-suffering fidelity to the covenant, Israel is "a disobedient and contrary people."

Isa 59:7-8	Rom 3:15-17
Isa 52:5	Rom 2:24
Isa 65:2	Rom 10:21

2. Even so, God has not abandoned Israel. He has preserved a remnant of those who remain faithful.

Isa 1:9	Rom 9:29
Isa 10:22	Rom 9:27

3. God has now acted to bring the promise of eschatological salvation into fulfillment in the present time. But he has done so in a way that calls for trust (in Christ), causing the majority of Israel to stumble. Those who trust him will not be put to shame.

Isa 49:8	2 Cor 6:2 (cf. Isa 43:18-19/2 Cor 5:17)
Isa 8:14	Rom 9:32-33
Isa 28:16	Rom 9:33; 10:11

4. This is the message that Paul, apostle to the Gentiles, has been called to announce to the nations. Contrary to all expectation, the Gentiles are receiving this good news gladly. The Gentile mission is bearing fruit.

Isa 52:7	Rom 10:15 (cf. Isa 49:1/Gal 1:15)
Isa 11:10	Rom 15:12
Isa 45:14	1 Cor 14:25
Isa 52:15	Rom 15:21
Isa 54:1	Gal 4:27 (a revisionary interpretation of Isa 54:1, reading Sarah as mother of the "children of promise" [= Gentile believers])[40]
Isa 65:1	Rom 10:20

5. But not all believe, because the message is an affront to human wisdom. In the present time both Israel and the Gentile world are full of people who consider themselves wise, though actually they are blind and foolish. God will bring judgment upon them. In a mysterious way God's judgment on

---

40. See Hays, *Echoes*, 105-21.

disobedient Israel has taken the form of closing their eyes and hardening their hearts.

Isa 53:1	Rom 10:16
Isa 22:13	1 Cor 15:32
Isa 28:11	1 Cor 14:21
Isa 29:14	1 Cor 1:19
Isa 29:16; 45:9	Rom 9:20
Isa 29:10	Rom 11:8 (cf. also Isa 6:9-10)
Isa 65:2	Rom 10:21

6. Nonetheless, in the end God will redeem Israel, forgive their sin, and establish sovereignty over the whole world, so that every knee will bow and every tongue give praise to God. This divine eschatological triumph will include God's overcoming the power of death.

Isa 27:9	Rom 11:27
Isa 59:20	Rom 11:26
Isa 45:23	Rom 14:11 (cf. Phil 2:10-11)
Isa 25:8	1 Cor 15:54

7. God's mercy is finally overwhelming and incomprehensible.

Isa 40:13	Rom 11:34; 1 Cor 2:16
Isa 64:4?	1 Cor 2:9

All of this Paul finds foretold in Isaiah. It should be noted that, with the possible (and contested) exception of the "stone of stumbling" (Isa 8:14 + 28:16/Rom 9:32-33), Paul does not resort to christological typology in his interpretation of Isaiah. The story he reads in the Isaiah scroll is closely constrained by Isaiah's original plotline of Israel's exile and restoration, accompanied by God's radical eschatological renewal that embraces the whole Gentile world.

Conclusion: Theses for Disputation

The limited goals of this paper have been to set forth some criteria for identifying allusions and echoes of the OT in Paul, to make some observations about the application of these criteria to some illustrative passages where Paul seems to be echoing Isaiah, and to sketch the story line implied by Paul's explicit citations of this prophetic book. To carry the investigation to its conclusion, we would have to comb thoroughly through the letters seeking possible allusions to Isaiah and evaluating them one by one. That is far too large an undertaking for the present essay.[41] I have not, for example, taken up the familiar debates about whether we should hear allusions to Isa 53 in Rom 4:24-25, Rom 5:15-19, 1 Cor 15:3, and Phil 2:6-11. Readers who find my proposed criteria useful can take up the task of applying them to these texts. I offer, however, in conclusion, a number of summary remarks and provocations.

1. Paul reads in Isaiah the story of God's eschatological redemption of the world. His extensive allusions to Isa 40–55 suggest that he has pondered this text repeatedly and found in it a prefiguration of his own apostolic mission to announce God's good news to the Gentile world. Or, to put the same point the other way around, Paul's reading of Isaiah is shaped by his own experience of the Gentile mission. The claim that Paul does see there a coherent *story,* not merely a grab bag of isolated oracles, is very important for understanding his interpretation of the texts he cites and echoes.

2. Paul's primary interest in his actual *use* of Isaiah does not seem to be christological. Here, as elsewhere, his hermeneutic is ecclesiocentric, focusing on the manifestation and operation of God's grace in the church, the eschatological people of God. This is related to the concrete purpose of Paul's letters: Romans, for example, is not a treatise on Christology but a theological reflection on the outworking of God's mysterious purposes for Jews and Gentiles in the drama of salvation. Thus, Christology remains at an implicit, presuppositional level in the argument. That is why we find in Romans only allusions and echoes of early christological readings of the OT. Paul was not so much interested in proving that Jesus "was" the Servant. Rather, Paul was seeking to show that Isaiah revealed the prophetic promise of God's redemption of the world, embracing Gentiles as well as Jews. Consequently, we must keep reminding ourselves that Paul might have alluded to Isaiah for purposes other than those that have propelled much modern scholarly investigation.

---

41. Note: this essay was written in the spring of 1998, just prior to the publication of Florian Wilk's comprehensive study of Paul's citations of passages from Isaiah (see n. 35 above). Wilk's findings are entirely independent of mine, but they converge with and confirm many of the suggestions made here.

3. Where we find citations and allusions in Paul's letters, we must always ask what they are doing in the argument, how they serve Paul's rhetorical and theological agenda. That is, we should come back again and again to the question of how the proposed intertextual collocations shape our reading of the epistles. There is an inescapable hermeneutical circle here: if our hypotheses about intertextual links yield illuminating readings of the letters, this result will increase our confidence about the validity of the hypotheses.

4. Paul was formed deeply by his reading of Scripture. One consequence of this is that he may from time to time echo texts unconsciously or in passing, without thinking through all the possible implications of the intertextual links created by his own discourse. Later readers may recognize Paul's echoes of Isaiah and legitimately develop some theological implications of the intertextual links that had not occurred to Paul himself. It is possible (though in my view not likely) that the christological reading of Isa 53 could fall into this category.

5. We should give Paul and his readers credit for being at least as sophisticated and nuanced in their reading of Scripture as we are. Everything about Paul's use of OT texts suggests that his "implied reader" not only knows Scripture but also appreciates allusive subtlety. Whether the reader accepts the compliment or not, the apostle still delights in intertextual play.

6. Finally, there is the matter of what sort of readers we must be to read Paul's texts rightly. He calls upon his readers to present their bodies as a living sacrifice and to be transformed by the renewing of their minds. That is not exactly a *criterion* for rightly identifying allusions; it is something more like a *prerequisite*. As I have argued at length in *Echoes*, Paul believes that the veil over Scripture is lifted only for those who turn to the Lord and that the meaning of Scripture becomes clear only as the Spirit works to embody the sense of the text in concretely transformed communities.[42] If that is right, Paul's allusive texts will not yield up their treasures to the merely curious (sobering word for us scholars): they will speak only to those actively engaged in carrying out the ministry of reconciliation by embodying the righteousness of God, as a light to the nations.

---

42. Hays, *Echoes*, 122-53. See now also the sixth of the "Nine Theses on the Interpretation of Scripture," in *The Art of Reading Scripture*, ed. E. F. Davis and R. B. Hays (Grand Rapids: Eerdmans, 2003), 3: "Faithful interpretation of Scripture invites and presupposes participation in the community brought into being by God's redemptive action — the church."

Psalm 143 as Testimony
to the Righteousness of God

Much of the scholarly battle about the meaning of "the righteousness of God" in Paul has been fought over the wrong ground. Ernst Käsemann, reviving an interpretation first suggested by Adolf Schlatter,[1] touched off a storm of controversy in 1961 with his essay "Gottesgerechtigkeit bei Paulus,"[2] in which he challenged the traditional Protestant interpretation of the expression δικαιοσύνη θεοῦ ("the righteousness of God") in certain passages in Paul's letter to the Romans. Protestant exegesis from Luther onward had taken the expression to refer to an imputed, "alien" righteousness that individuals receive as a gift by believing in Jesus Christ. Käsemann contended, however, that δικαιοσύνη θεοῦ, in passages such as Rom 3:21 and 10:3, means God's *own* righteousness, which encounters humanity as a "salvation-creating power" which "reaches out for the world" and establishes God's rightful claim to sovereignty over his creation.[3] One of the key moves in Käsemann's argument was his claim that the meaning of δικαιοσύνη θεοῦ could best be understood within the context of apocalyptic thought, as illustrated by the Thanksgiving Hymns of the Qumran community, in which Käsemann finds δικαιοσύνη θεοῦ to be a "ready-made formulation" with apocalyptic overtones.[4]

His claim that δικαιοσύνη θεοῦ was a technical term in apocalyptic be-

---

1. A. Schlatter, *Gottes Gerechtigkeit: Ein Kommentar zum Römerbrief* (Stuttgart: Calwer, 1935), 35-38, 135-39.

2. Käsemann, "Gottesgerechtigkeit bei Paulus," *ZTK* 58 (1961): 367-78. This essay is available in English translation in *NT Questions of Today* (Philadelphia: Fortress, 1969), 168-82. Subsequent references will be to this translation.

3. Käsemann, *NT Questions of Today*, 181-82.

4. Käsemann, *NT Questions of Today*, 172, 178-82.

came a major point of controversy which unfortunately diverted attention from the more substantive theological issue he had intended to raise. Rudolf Bultmann, for instance, in his attempt to refute Käsemann, flatly denied any apocalyptic context for the expression and insisted, remarkably enough, that it was "ein Neuschöpfung des Paulus."[5] On the other side of the debate, Christian Müller and Peter Stuhlmacher, both Käsemann's students, produced monographs that sought to establish apocalyptic foundations for Paul's use of δικαιοσύνη θεοῦ.[6] Various responses, pro and con, ensued.[7]

Subsequently E. P. Sanders undertook a detailed exegetical analysis of the Qumran passages adduced by Käsemann and his supporters.[8] Sanders concluded that צדקה (= δικαιοσύνη) in these texts is simply equivalent to "mercy," and that it has neither the status of a technical term nor the connotation of active salvation-creating power.[9] Sanders's case was considerably strengthened by the observation that the צדקה terminology occurs not in apocalyptic narrative contexts but primarily in hymns and prayers, whose vocabulary is heavily influenced by the OT Psalms.[10] This observation sug-

---

5. R. Bultmann, "Δικαιοσύνη θεοῦ," *JBL* 83 (1964): 16.

6. C. Müller, *Gottes Gerechtigkeit und Gottes Volk: Eine Untersuchung zu Römer 9–11*, FRLANT 86 (Göttingen: Vandenhoeck & Ruprecht, 1964); P. Stuhlmacher, *Gerechtigkeit Gottes bei Paulus*, FRLANT 87 (Göttingen: Vandenhoeck & Ruprecht, 1965).

7. In particular, see the following: K. Kertelge, *"Rechtfertigung" bei Paulus* (Münster: Aschendorf, 1967); H. Conzelmann, "Die Rechtfertigungslehre des Paulus: Theologie oder Anthropologie?" *EvT* 28 (1968): 389-404, ET, "Paul's Doctrine of Justification: Theology or Anthropology?" in *Theology of the Liberating Word*, ed. F. Herzog (Nashville: Abingdon, 1971), 108-23; G. Klein, "Gottes Gerechtigkeit als Thema der neuesten Paulus-Forschung," in *Rekonstruktion und Interpretation* (Munich: Chr. Kaiser, 1969), 225-36; Klein, "Righteousness in the NT," in *IDBSup*, 750-52; M. Barth, "Rechtfertigung: Versuch einer Auslegung paulinischer Texte im Rahmen des Alten und Neuen Testaments," in AnBib 42 (1970), 137-207, ET, *Justification* (Grand Rapids: Eerdmans, 1971); N. A. Dahl, "The Doctrine of Justification: Its Social Function and Implications," in *Studies in Paul* (Minneapolis: Augsburg, 1977); J. Reumann, "The Gospel of the Righteousness of God: Pauline Reinterpretation in Romans 3:21-31," *Int* 20 (1966): 432-52. For a summary of the basic positions in the debate, see M. T. Brauch, "Perspectives on 'God's Righteousness' in Recent German Discussion," appendix to E. P. Sanders, *Paul and Palestinian Judaism* (Philadelphia: Fortress, 1977), 523-42.

8. Sanders, *Paul and Palestinian Judaism*, 305-12. Sanders does not explicitly present his exegesis of these texts as a refutation of Käsemann, but if his interpretation is correct, it deals a damaging blow to Käsemann's position.

9. Sanders, *Paul and Palestinian Judaism*, 307.

10. Cf. the judgment of Dahl, "The Doctrine of Justification," 99: "What the Qumran

gests the possibility that the OT Psalms themselves may prove to be the most illuminating backdrop for Paul's usage of the expression δικαιοσύνη θεοῦ, though this suggestion may lead us beyond Sanders's findings.

In this essay I propose that the interpretation of δικαιοσύνη θεοῦ as God's own salvation-creating power can be shown to be correct without any appeal to Qumran materials. The weight of the argument rests on two other types of evidence: a consideration of the internal logic of Paul's argument in Rom 3 and an examination of Ps 143 as the background for that argument.

The debate over the meaning of δικαιοσύνη θεοῦ comes to its decisive point in the interpretation of Rom 3 because it is here that this theme, so prominently announced in Rom 1:17, finally appears on center stage in Paul's exposition. Interpretations of this chapter often subdivide it into discrete pericopes which are then discussed separately, as if they had no relation to one another — as if, for example, the meaning of δικαιοσύνη θεοῦ in 3:22 could be determined without reference to its meaning in 3:5.[11] A proper understanding of the expression, however, can be attained only through taking the context and flow of the argument into serious consideration.

At the beginning of chapter 3 Paul is wrestling with the problem of the

---

texts really prove is that the OT idea of God's righteousness was alive in Judaism at the time of the NT. . . . It is not necessary to suppose that the Pauline terminology is directly taken over from circles in Qumran or related groups."

11. Commentaries often refer back to Rom 1:17, but most treat 3:21-26 entirely without reference to the foregoing discussion in vv. 3-7. See, for example, C. K. Barrett, *A Commentary on the Epistle to the Romans*, HNTC (New York: Harper and Row, 1957), 72-82; E. Käsemann, *An die Römer*, HNT 8a (Tübingen: Mohr, 1973), 84-94; K. H. Schelkle, *The Epistle to the Romans* (New York: Herder and Herder, 1964), 66-68; E. Brunner, *Der Römerbrief* (Berlin: Evangelische Verlagsanstalt, 1951), 21-25; K. Barth, *The Epistle to the Romans* (London: Oxford University Press, 1933), 91-107; A. Nygren, *Der Römerbrief* (Göttingen: Vandenhoeck & Ruprecht, 1951), 109-18; C. E. B. Cranfield, *A Critical and Exegetical Commentary on the Epistle to the Romans*, vol. 1, ICC (Edinburgh: T. & T. Clark, 1975), 202-3; C. H. Dodd, *The Epistle of Paul to the Romans*, MNTC (New York: Harper and Bros., 1932), 48-61; J. Murray, *The Epistle to the Romans*, vol. 1, NICNT (Grand Rapids: Eerdmans, 1959), 108-12. An exception is H. Schlier (*Der Römerbrief*, HTKNT [Freiburg, Basel, and Vienna: Herder, 1977], 104), who at least notes the connection between 3:5 and 3:21-22, without, however, allowing this observation to shape his interpretation. O. Michel (*Der Brief an die Römer*, MeyerK [Göttingen: Vandenhoeck & Ruprecht, 1963], 105) also recognizes the connection but argues that δικαιοσύνη θεοῦ is used differently in vv. 21-22: "Das Subjekt δικαιοσύνη θεοῦ wird wieder aufgenommen, aber nun auf den Menschen bezogen: Die Gerechtigkeit Gottes wird durch den Glauben an Jesus Christus geschenkt." Here Michel makes explicit the view that other exegetes seem to assume without comment.

allegedly special status of the Jew before God. He has argued in the foregoing paragraph that the Jew has no reason to boast of his possession of the
law, because "real circumcision is a matter of the heart, spiritual and not
literal" (2:29 RSV). That argument leads him into difficulty, however, because it seems to imply that the specificity of Jewishness is meaningless,
that its particularity is subsumed and negated by a nebulous universal
spirituality.[12] Paul is unwilling to accept that conclusion for very definite
theological reasons, since the particularity of Jewish identity is rooted in
claims about God's dealings with his people in history. If Paul's gospel now
somehow invalidates the special relationship established through these
past events, it means that God's past dealing with his people was false dealing, that he made promises on which he is now backing out. Paul, however,
is committed to the affirmation that the God who raised Jesus from the
dead is the same God who gave the promises to Israel; consequently, the
trustworthiness of the God who made these promises must be affirmed.
This issue is, at bottom, the question of God's integrity.[13] This is the concern that undergirds and animates the discussion in Rom 3.

In view of these considerations, Paul affirms that "the advantage of the
Jew" is "much in every way," and he also anticipates and rejects the suggestion that God could somehow be relieved of the obligation to keep his promises because Israel failed to hold up its end of the bargain. At this point (3:5)
the term δικαιοσύνη enters the discussion.[14] How are we to interpret it?

12. This is precisely the conclusion drawn by Daniel Boyarin, *A Radical Jew: Paul and
the Politics of Cultural Identity* (Berkeley: University of California Press, 1994). Paul has certainly left himself open to such a critique. Boyarin's trenchant reading, however, gives insufficient attention to Paul's persistent efforts, in Romans, to rebut precisely this interpretation
of his message.

13. See the lucid discussion in "The Moral Integrity of God and the Human Situation,"
by L. E. Keck (*Paul and His Letters,* Proclamation Commentaries [Philadelphia: Fortress,
1979], 117-30). Keck proposes to "restate the point" of Paul's phrase "the righteousness of
God" by using the phrase "the moral integrity of God."

14. Δικαιοσύνη echoes the word δικαιωθῇς in the immediately preceding citation of Ps
51:4 (= Ps. 50:6 LXX). Müller (*Gottes Gerechtigkeit und Gottes Volk,* 65-68) believes that the
language of this passage, as shown especially by the psalm quotation, is informed by the idea
of the cosmic trial *(Rechtsstreitgedanke)* in which God is metaphorically depicted as going to
court to establish his rightful claim over the world. Müller is certainly correct to observe that
terms such as δικαιοῦν and κρίνειν have their origin in the language of legal process, but one
should be cautious about interpreting the present text in light of the clusters of images associated with the root meanings of such words. Ps 51, in fact, is a good example of a text in

This expression does not occur independently, but it stands as one of a series of apparently synonymous expressions, all affirming God's integrity as contrasted to humanity's lack of integrity. The antitheses can be seen in schematic fashion as follows:

ἄνθρωπος	θεός
3:3 ἡ ἀπιστία αὐτῶν	τὴν πίστιν τοῦ θεοῦ
3:4 πᾶς ἄνθρωπος ψεύστης	ὁ θεὸς ἀληθής
3:5 ἡ ἀδικία ἡμῶν	θεοῦ δικαιοσύνη
3:7 ἐν τῷ ἐμῷ ψεύσματι	ἡ ἀλήθεια τοῦ θεοῦ

Clearly, the expressions in each column function interchangeably in this passage and therefore interpret one another.[15] Ἡ πίστις τοῦ θεοῦ, being contrasted to the unfaithfulness of (some) Jews, must be translated as "the faithfulness of God," an unambiguous subjective genitive. Likewise, ἡ ἀλήθεια τοῦ θεοῦ, in contrast to "my falsehood," must mean "the truthfulness of God," again unambiguously a subjective genitive.[16] These observa-

---

which the juridical connotations of the terms have already been absorbed into the language of confessional piety. (Müller's assertion [65 n. 51] that "Sündenbekenntnis und Busse rechtliche Vorgänge sind" begs the question.) Paul introduces the psalm quotation into his argument as a proof text (καθὼς γέγραπται) for his foregoing affirmation (Rom 3:4) that God is "true" (ἀληθής), which means in this context that God is faithful to his word. Since Paul is using the psalm citation merely to reinforce his point about God's faithfulness, it seems methodologically dubious to interpret the surrounding text in Rom 3 within the conceptual framework of a *"Rechtsstreitgedanke"* which is not even explicit in Ps 51.

15. James Barr (*The Semantics of Biblical Language* [Oxford: Oxford University Press, 1961], 187-94) delivers a withering critique of Thomas Torrance's claim that "where we have the words πίστις and δικαιοσύνη in the New Testament we must see behind them the Hebrew words 'emet and 'ĕmunāh, and where in the New Testament we have ἀλήθεια we must understand that not simply as a Greek word but in the light of the Biblical inclusion of πίστις and δικαιοσύνη in the concept of truth" (T. Torrance, "One Aspect of the Biblical Conception of Faith," *ExpTim* 68 [1956-57]: 111-14, here 112). Barr's cogent criticisms of Torrance and of A. G. Hebert (" 'Faithfulness' and 'Faith,' " *Theology* 58 [1955]: 373-79) do not, however, apply to the present exegetical observations about Rom 3. Barr's basic objection is directed against the linguistically naive assumption that there is a distinctive (Hebraic) "fundamental meaning" that governs the semantic range of ἀλήθεια, πίστις, and δικαιοσύνη in the NT without regard to context and usage. My observations here, rather than resting upon an alleged fundamental linguistic equivalence, proceed from the evidence of Paul's *usage* of these words as functionally equivalent terms within this particular discourse.

16. It is interesting to note the progression in Paul's way of identifying the human side

tions suggest strongly that θεοῦ δικαιοσύνη, in antithesis to "our unrighteousness," should be understood, on the analogy of the parallel expressions, as another subjective genitive construction, designating God's *attribute* of righteousness. Thus, "the righteousness of God" in Rom 3:5 appears as a functional equivalent of "the faithfulness of God" (3:3) and "the truthfulness of God" (3:7).[17] To say this, however, is not to interpret these phrases as designations for a static attribute of God; rather, all three serve to affirm that God makes his integrity known through his active faith keeping.[18]

The idea of the covenant is not explicitly mentioned here, but it is unmistakably present: the righteousness of God consists in his persistence in keeping his covenant intact in spite of human unfaithfulness.[19] While this

---

of these antitheses: "*Their* unfaithfulness . . . *every man* false . . . *our* unrighteousness . . . *my* falsehood." The indictment spirals inward.

17. A similar conclusion is reached by Stuhlmacher (*Gerechtigkeit Gottes bei Paulus,* 86) and by Kertelge (*"Rechtfertigung" bei Paulus,* 67). Even Klein ("Righteousness in the NT," 751) recognizes that θεοῦ δικαιοσύνη is a subjective genitive in Rom 3:5; thus, he is forced to argue that this usage is exceptional and that it has no bearing on the meaning of the expression δικαιοσύνη θεοῦ just a few verses later. The arbitrariness of this exegesis bears eloquent testimony to the stubborn power of the usual exegesis of Rom 3:21, which regards this verse as the beginning of an entirely new phase of Paul's argument ("man under faith" as opposed to "man prior to the revelation of faith," to use Bultmann's labels).

18. Cf. Schlatter, *Gottes Gerechtigkeit,* 36: "Es ist offenkundig, dass sich die Aussage des Paulus über die Gerechtigkeit Gottes nicht auf die Eigenschaft einer ruhenden Substanz beziehen liess. Paulus denkt in jeder Aussage über Gott an den Schöpfer, an den der will und wirkt, sich offenbart und den Menschen in das von ihm gewollte Verhältnis zu sich bringt."

19. Stuhlmacher (*Gerechtigkeit Gottes bei Paulus,* 86) sees this point clearly, but he goes on to argue (90), as do Müller (*Gottes Gerechtigkeit und Gottes Volk,* 108-13) and Käsemann (*An die Römer,* 73-74, 93-94), that there is a critique of "covenant" theology in Rom 3, that Paul seeks to replace the particularistic idea of God's covenant faithfulness (*"Bundestreue"*) with a more universalistic idea of "creation faithfulness" (*"Schöpfungstreue"*). This claim rests upon a very complex exegesis of Rom 3:24-26. (See P. Stuhlmacher, "Zur Neueren Exegese von Rom 3:24-26," in *Jesus und Paulus: Festschrift für Werner Georg Kümmel zum 70. Geburtstag,* ed. E. E. Ellis and E. Grässer [Göttingen: Vandenhoeck & Ruprecht, 1975], 315-34.) According to this interpretation, Paul both quotes and "corrects" an early Christian tradition which understands God's "righteousness" as his covenant faithfulness. It is not possible here to respond in detail to this reading of vv. 24-26, but the following objections may be stated briefly: (1) The idea of creation faithfulness is not explicitly present in the text; instead, it has to be imported by the exegete as an explanatory device. (2) To give a theological account for the gospel's universality of scope, Paul characteristically appeals not to a doctrine of creation but to the universal implications of the covenantal promise to Abraham (cf.

understanding of "righteousness" as persistent faithfulness is not exactly identical to Käsemann's conception of δικαιοσύνη θεοῦ as "salvation-creating power," that idea lies very close at hand, especially when we realize that God's faithfulness/righteousness is manifested in his saving *activity*, not as a property of God *in se*.[20]

Verses 7-8 touch on the problem of the relation between δικαιοσύνη θεοῦ and ethics, a problem that arises irrepressibly out of the claim that human unfaithfulness cannot nullify the faithfulness of God. Paul digresses briefly into a complaint about some adversaries who misrepresent his gospel as a license for libertinism (3:8),[21] but then he suddenly recalls the discussion (τί οὖν, 3:9) to the question with which he began the chapter, to which he now, surprisingly, gives the diametrically opposite answer: Jews are *not* better off, because everybody, Jew and Greek alike, is ὑφ' ἁμαρτίαν. This assertion is supported by a lengthy catena of OT passages (3:10-18) that establish the thorough depravity of humanity. We cannot pause here to consider the composition of this catena.[22] Let us simply take it as a unitary block and make some brief observations about its relation to the flow of the argument.

It seems apparent that Paul is attracted to this catena by the catchword δίκαιος in its opening line. Indeed, this line sums up the point of the whole quotation, which here serves to reinforce Paul's claim that everyone is "under sin." This point, in case the reader has forgotten it, is reiterated in 3:19 at the end of the catena, with the additional claim that the function of the law is to "stop every mouth" by ensuring that the whole world will be accountable (ὑπόδικος) to God. The connection here between the expres-

---

Rom 3:29–4:25; Gal 3:1-29). (3) The exegesis advocated in this essay suggests that God's faithfulness to the covenant with Israel is precisely what Paul wants to affirm.

20. Cf. K. Barth, *Church Dogmatics* II/1 (Edinburgh: T. & T. Clark, 1957), 257-72 ("The Being of God in Act"). Barth surely offers a faithful reflection of Pauline thought when he declares that "When we ask questions about God's being, we cannot in fact leave the sphere of his action and working as it is revealed to us in His Word" (260).

21. This verse is the most difficult one to fit into the flow of the argument. It seems that Paul has gotten ahead of himself here, and v. 9 returns the discussion to the matter at hand. The question in v. 8, unanswered in chap. 3, is picked up once again in chap. 6 and given more thorough consideration.

22. For a discussion of the catena, see L. E. Keck, "The Function of Romans 3:10-18 — Observations and Suggestions," in *God's Christ and His People: Studies in Honour of Nils Alstrup Dahl*, ed. J. Jervell and W. A. Meeks (Oslo, Bergen, and Tromsö: Universitetsforlaget, 1977), 141-57.

sions ὑφ' ἁμαρτίαν . . . οὐκ ἔστιν δίκαιος . . . ὑπόδικος is hardly accidental; this sequence of phrases provides the framework for the movement of Paul's thought in 3:9-19:

3:9   πάντας ὑφ' ἁμαρτίαν
3:10-18   οὐκ ἔστιν δίκαιος
3:19   ὑπόδικος πᾶς ὁ κόσμος

The traditional way of reading Rom 3 regards verses 3-8 as a parenthetical digression after which Paul returns (v. 9) to a primary concern with the δικαιοσύνη of human beings. However, if we put aside the presupposition that Romans is a treatise answering the question "How can I be saved?"[23] it at once becomes clear that Paul's underlying purpose in 3:9-20 is to establish beyond all possible doubt the affirmation that God is *just* in his judgment of the world. In other words, 3:9-20 forms an extended rebuttal to the rhetorical suggestion in verses 5-7 that God might be considered unfair (ἄδικος). Verses 9-18 establish the proposition that all deserve God's condemnation, and verse 19 makes it clear that the silencing of protests against God's justice is indeed the main point of this section of the discourse.[24] Thus, we can see in broad outline the movement of the argument:

3:1-8   Has God abandoned his promises to Israel? Is he inconsistent or unjust?

3:9-20   All such objections are invalid: humanity, not God, is guilty of injustice.

3:21-26   God has not abandoned his people.[25] He has now revealed his justice/righteousness in a new way, overcoming human unfaithfulness by his own power and proving himself faithful/just.

---

23. Cf. the remarks of K. Stendahl in *Paul among Jews and Gentiles* (Philadelphia: Fortress, 1976), especially 1-4, 78-96.

24. The development of Paul's thought here runs closely parallel to Rom 9:14-24: "Is there injustice on God's part? By no means! . . . You will say to me then, 'Why then does he still find fault? For who can resist his will?' But who indeed are you, a human being, to argue with God?" (9:14, 19-20 NRSV).

25. Cf. Rom 11:1. The interpretation advocated here reveals the striking interrelationship between the concerns of Rom 3 and of Rom 9–11, an interrelationship pointed out also by Müller (*Gottes Gerechtigkeit und Gottes Volk*, 51).

This way of reading the passage shows the continuity of the discussion and makes sense out of the otherwise-baffling emphasis in verses 25-26 on the "demonstration" (ἔνδειξις) of God's righteousness and the insistence that God himself is δίκαιος: Paul closes the circle in verses 21-26 by answering the objections raised in verses 1-7.[26]

If this proposed reconstruction of the internal logic of Rom 3 is correct, how are we to understand the transition from verse 20 to verse 21? In verse 20 Paul wraps up the argument of verses 9-19 by citing yet another OT passage, this time from Ps 143:2: οὐ δικαιωθήσεται πᾶσα σάρξ ἐνώπιον αὐτοῦ.[27] It is almost universally held by commentators that this citation summarizes and brings to a close a major section of the discussion.[28] Virtually no one, however, has noticed that Ps 143 also provides the point of departure for what *follows*.[29] In addition to the dictum that "no living being will be justified in his sight," Ps 143 contains several references to God's *righteousness*. The verse immediately preceding the one from which Paul quotes reads as follows:

> Κύριε εἰσάκουσον τῆς προσευχῆς μου,
> ἐνώτισαι τὴν δέησίν μου ἐν τῇ ἀληθείᾳ σου,
> ἐπάκουσόν μου ἐν τῇ δικαιοσύνῃ σου.
>
> (Ps 142:1 LXX)

26. When this connection between vv. 1-7 and vv. 21-26 is not recognized, additional complication is created for the interpretation of the latter verses. Käsemann (*An die Römer*, 85) cites with approval J. Weiss's opinion that this paragraph (vv. 21-26) is "einer der schwerfälligsten und undurchsichtigsten des ganzen Briefes."

27. LXX (Ps 142:2) actually reads οὐ δικαιωθήσεται ἐνώπιόν σου πᾶς ζῶν. Paul appears to be citing loosely from memory. This is a fact of some importance for our assessment of the way in which Ps 143 informs the larger movement of the argument of Rom 3. See n. 33, below.

28. All the commentators cited in n. 11 above treat Rom 3:20 as the end of a major section of the letter. Typical is Nygren's comment (*Der Römerbrief*, 107): "Wir stehen nun am Schluss des Gedankenganges, der seinen Anfang mit Kap. 1,18 nahm." W. Sanday and A. C. Headlam (*A Critical and Exegetical Commentary on the Epistle to the Romans*, 2nd ed., ICC [New York: Scribner's, 1920], 76) actually include in their translation of 3:20 the words "This is the conclusion of the whole argument." Apparently this is intended as a free rendering of διότι.

29. One exception is F. J. Leenhardt (*The Epistle to the Romans* [London: Lutterworth, 1961], 97), who calls attention in a somewhat tentative way to the presence of the word δικαιοσύνη in Ps 143(142):1. He does not, however, develop the implications of this observation for the unity of Rom 3.

The LXX phrases ἐν τῇ ἀληθείᾳ σου and ἐν τῇ δικαιοσύνῃ σου translate the Hebrew באמנתך and בצדקתך. What is the proper translation of these phrases? Does the prayer ask God (depicted as clothed or dwelling or sub-sisting in faithfulness and righteousness) merely to hear the psalmist's cry, or does the expression "hear my prayer" already imply the idea "hear and answer"?[30] In the latter case the prepositions (ἐν, ב) might best be trans-lated in the instrumental sense, yielding the meaning "answer me by your righteousness." Decisive evidence for this instrumental translation is pro-vided by the anticipated answer to this prayer later in the same psalm: ἐν τῇ δικαιοσύνῃ σου ἐξάξεις ἐκ θλίψεως τὴν ψυχήν μου (Ps 142:11 LXX). Here the ἐν is clearly instrumental, and God's righteousness is conceived as a power that will reach out to save the psalmist.

Now let us take stock of what we have observed here. Paul cites Ps 143 to sum up his argument that no one is righteous (= no one will be justified before God). This same psalm prays for and anticipates a salvation that will be effected by *God's* faithfulness (ἀλήθεια) and righteousness (δικαιο-σύνη). These terms are strikingly reminiscent of the discussion in Rom 3:3-7.[31] Even more significant, however, is the fact that the language of the psalm provides an illuminating background for the key transition that Paul makes in Rom 3:21: "But now apart from law δικαιοσύνη θεοῦ has ap-peared." God's saving righteousness for which the psalmist had hoped (μαρτυρουμένη ὑπὸ τοῦ νόμου καὶ τῶν προφητῶν)[32] has at last appeared! This righteousness, according to Paul's proclamation, has now been made

---

30. RSV, for example, adopts the latter interpretation.

31. Is it possible that the language of Ps 143 was already in Paul's mind in vv. 3-7? This is possible, but not necessary. See n. 33 below.

32. Müller (*Gottes Gerechtigkeit und Gottes Volk*, 67-68) takes this phrase as evidence that the metaphor of the cosmic litigation *(Rechtsstreit)* between God and the world still controls the development of Paul's thought in 3:21: "'Gesetz und Propheten' 'zeugen' für die 'Gerechtigkeit' Gottes, indem sie die Schuldverfallenheit des Kosmos richtig feststellen. Die so 'bezeugte' δικαιοσύνη θεοῦ ist demnach wie 3,5 der Sieg des Anspruches Gottes über den schuldverfallenen Kosmos." This interpretation at least has the merit of attempting to take seriously the continuity of chap. 3 and to interpret δικαιοσύνη θεοῦ in 3:21 in a way consis-tent with 3:5. Müller's view rests upon the observation that the only explicit citations from "the law and the prophets" in the immediate context are testimonies of condemnation (vv. 10-18, 20). It is doubtful, however, whether Müller's interpretation adequately accounts for the positive salvific function of δικαιοσύνη θεοῦ in vv. 21-26. The evidence of Ps 143 proves that the law and the prophets do not only witness *against* the world; they also bear witness to δικαιοσύνη θεοῦ as a power of deliverance.

manifest in Jesus Christ (3:22).[33] Thus, Ps 143 illuminates the structure of the logic that underlies Rom 3 because the psalm already contains both an affirmation of the unconditional inadequacy of human beings to stand before God (cf. Rom 3:9-20) and an appeal to God to exercise his own righteousness to rescue the psalmist (cf. 3:21-26). There is no possibility of construing the δικαιοσύνη of the psalm to mean some kind of imputed righteousness; it unambiguously means God's own righteousness, and this righteousness appears in Ps 143 as a power of deliverance. Thus, because Paul actually quotes from it at precisely this point in his argument, Ps 143 actually provides much stronger support for Käsemann's interpretation of δικαιοσύνη θεοῦ as "the power that brings salvation" than do any possible Qumran parallels.[34]

Our evidence converges on a single conclusion. The major structural break that commentators usually posit between Rom 3:20 and 3:21 has no "justification" in the text, and Paul's continuing use of terminology from Ps 143 (δικαιοσύνη) shows clearly the intended continuity. Rom 3:21 carries on the discussion from the earlier part of chapter 3. Thus, the problem in view here is not, as Hans Conzelmann thinks, "the subjective quest for salvation,"[35] but still, as in Rom 3:5, the issue of God's integrity,[36] God's justice that persistently overcomes human unfaithfulness.

---

33. In what sense can God's own saving righteousness be said to manifest itself διὰ πίστεως Ἰησοῦ Χριστοῦ? Certainly the traditional "objective genitive" translation, "through faith in Jesus Christ," makes little sense here. The logic of the present interpretation suggests the necessity of a reconsideration of the meaning of the phrase διὰ πίστεως Ἰησοῦ Χριστοῦ; but that is a project beyond the scope of this essay. See Richard B. Hays, *The Faith of Jesus Christ: The Narrative Substructure of Galatians 3:1–4:11*, 2nd ed. (Grand Rapids: Eerdmans, 2002).

34. Did Paul have vv. 1 and 11 of the psalm in mind? This suggestion is, of course, not susceptible of proof. But the pattern of thought is the same in the psalm and in Rom 3. Even if Paul was not consciously constructing a midrash on Ps 143, he *was* operating out of a background of theological categories and assumptions into which Ps 143 provides a very helpful insight.

35. Conzelmann, "Paul's Doctrine of Justification," 118.

36. This interpretation is corroborated by Paul's closing recapitulation of his argument in Rom 15:8: "For I am saying that Christ became a servant of circumcision for the sake of the truthfulness of God (ὑπὲρ ἀληθείας θεοῦ), in order to confirm the promises given to the fathers."

Abraham as Father
of Jews and Gentiles

How does the figure of Abraham in Rom 4 function in Paul's exposition of the gospel? While this question has drawn the insistent attention of NT exegetes,[1] many studies in the past tended to treat Rom 4 as an isolated unit of material. Two significant dissertations by S. K. Stowers and C. T. Rhyne have moved the discussion forward by demonstrating that formal considerations require this chapter to be read in a larger context;[2] however, even in these treatments, major obscurities remain concerning the meaning and function of Rom 4:1. This essay seeks to clarify the discussion of Rom 4 by reexamining this verse, which introduces Abraham into Paul's argument, and offering a new proposal for translating the Greek text. This proposal, if viable, will cast new light on the way in which Paul employs the figure of Abraham in his discussion, and it will consequently make the continuity of the argument in Rom 3 and 4 more readily discernible.

---

1. In addition to the commentaries, the following studies may be mentioned: G. Klein, *Rekonstruktion und Interpretation* (Munich: Kaiser, 1969), 145-224; U. Wilckens, "Zu Römer 3,21–4,25," in *Rechtfertigung als Freiheit* (Neukirchen: Neukirchener Verlag, 1974), 50-76; K. Berger, "Abraham in den paulinischen Hauptbriefen," *MTZ* 17 (1966): 47-89; L. Goppelt, "Paulus und die Heilsgeschichte," *NTS* 13 (1966-67): 31-42; H. Boers, *Theology out of the Ghetto* (Leiden: Brill, 1971), 74-104; E. Käsemann, "The Faith of Abraham in Romans 4," in *Perspectives on Paul* (Philadelphia: Fortress, 1971), 79-104; L. Gaston, "Abraham and the Righteousness of God," *HBT* 2 (1980): 39-68; C. K. Barrett, *From First Adam to Last: A Study in Pauline Theology* (New York: Charles Scribner's Sons, 1962), 22-45; H. J. van der Minde, *Schrift und Tradition bei Paulus* (Paderborn: Schöningh, 1976), 68-106; U. Luz, *Das Geschichtsverständnis des Paulus*, BevT 49 (Munich: Kaiser, 1968), 168-86.

2. S. K. Stowers, *The Diatribe and Paul's Letter to the Romans*, SBLDS 57 (Chico, Calif.: Scholars, 1981), 155-74; C. T. Rhyne, *Faith Establishes the Law*, SBLDS 55 (Chico, Calif.: Scholars, 1981), 25-61.

Romans 4:1: "Our Forefather according to the Flesh"?

Much of the difficulty of determining the relation of Rom 4 to the larger context of Paul's argument arises from the notorious unclarity of the sentence (Rom 4:1) that introduces Abraham into Paul's discussion. The textual problems in this verse are no doubt a reflection as well as a cause of the interpretive problem.[3] Against the RSV, which chooses to follow Codex Vaticanus in dropping the infinitive εὑρηκέναι out of the text,[4] there is a solid consensus among recent commentators that the manuscript evidence clearly favors the following reading:

Τί οὖν ἐροῦμεν εὑρηκέναι Ἀβραὰμ τὸν προπάτορα ἡμῶν κατὰ σάρκα.[5]

The rather peculiar εὑρηκέναι is then usually explained, following the suggestion of Otto Michel,[6] as an echo of the LXX expression εὑρίσκειν χάριν (e.g., Gen 18:3), and the sentence is interpreted to mean, "What then shall we say that Abraham, our forefather according to the flesh, found?"[7] The difficulties with this rendering are at least fourfold: (a) the allusion to Gen 18:3 is opaque and awkward, because nothing in the foregoing discussion prepares the reader for it; (b) in fact, the expression εὑρίσκειν χάριν occurs

3. For discussions of the textual problem, see C. E. B. Cranfield, *A Critical and Exegetical Commentary on the Epistle to the Romans,* ICC (Edinburgh: T. & T. Clark, 1975), 1:226-27; M. Black, *Romans,* NCB (London: Oliphants, 1973), 74-75; B. M. Metzger, *A Textual Commentary on the Greek New Testament* (London and New York: United Bible Societies, 1971), 509-10.

4. Thus yielding the meaning "What shall we say (about) Abraham our forefather according to the flesh?" This reading was accepted by W. Sanday and A. C. Headlam, *A Critical and Exegetical Commentary on the Epistle to the Romans,* ICC (New York: Charles Scribner's Sons, 1895), 98-99; K. Barth, *The Epistle to the Romans* (London: Oxford University Press, 1933), 117; C. H. Dodd, *The Epistle of Paul to the Romans,* MNTC (New York: Harper and Bros., 1932), 65. However, as Cranfield (*Romans,* 1:226) remarks, this is "certainly very odd Greek."

5. In addition to Metzger (*Textual Commentary,* 509), see also C. K. Barrett, *The Epistle to the Romans,* HNTC (New York: Harper and Row, 1957), 85 n. 1; E. Käsemann, *Commentary on Romans* (Grand Rapids: Eerdmans, 1980), 106; Cranfield, *Romans,* 1:226-27; U. Wilckens, *Der Brief an die Römer,* EKKNT VI/I (Zürich: Benziger Verlag; Neukirchen-Vluyn: Neukirchener Verlag, 1978), 1:260-61.

6. Michel, *Paulus und seine Bibel,* BFCT 2/18 (Gütersloh: Bertelsmann, 1929), 57.

7. The NRSV translates as follows: "What then are we to say was gained by Abraham, our ancestor according to the flesh?"

nowhere in the Pauline corpus;[8] (c) it seems unlikely that Paul would choose to designate Abraham as "our forefather according to the flesh" (cf. Rom 9:6-8);[9] (d) it is by no means clear that the ensuing discussion answers the question thus posed. If we suppose that Romans is a treatise on the problem of how a person may "find" justification,[10] it is possible to make some sense out of the sentence, but the construction in Rom 4:1 remains, at best, a very odd way for Paul to express himself.

The matter is made worse rather than better if κατὰ σάρκα is taken to modify εὑρηκέναι, so that the question is understood to mean, "What then shall we say that Abraham our forefather found according to the flesh?" Even if we grant that the discussion in the following verses is concerned with Abraham's "finding" of something, the point at issue, as Ulrich Luz points out, is not *what* Abraham found but *how* he found it.[11] In view of these considerations, we may concur with Matthew Black's observation: "No solution hitherto proposed is without serious difficulties."[12]

A fresh approach to the problem is possible, however, through an investigation of Paul's use of the rhetorical formulation τί οὖν ἐροῦμεν, which occurs repeatedly in Romans.[13] Aside from Rom 4:1, Paul uses this expression six times in Romans (counting Rom 3:5, which lacks οὖν). These occurrences may be set forth as follows:

---

8. The only NT occurrences of the expression are found in Luke 1:30, Acts 7:46, and Heb 4:16. Εὑρίσκειν ἔλεος does occur in 2 Tim 1:18.

9. The oddity of the expression was already noted by J. A. Bengel (*Gnomon Novi Testamenti* [Berlin: Schlawitz, 1855; based on the 3rd ed. of 1773], 354), who concluded that κατὰ σάρκα should therefore be taken as a modifier of εὑρηκέναι.

10. This supposition is one which recent study of Paul has rendered increasingly doubtful. See K. Stendahl, *Paul among Jews and Gentiles* (Philadelphia: Fortress, 1976); E. P. Sanders, *Paul and Palestinian Judaism* (Philadelphia: Fortress, 1977); R. B. Hays, "Psalm 143 and the Logic of Romans 3," *JBL* 99 (1980): 107-15; S. K. Williams, "The Righteousness of God in Romans," *JBL* 99 (1980): 241-90.

11. Luz, *Geschichtsverständnis*, 174 n. 148. The same observation was made, e.g., by Sanday and Headlam, *Romans*, 99.

12. Black, *Romans*, 75. Black is so pessimistic about making sense out of the text that he is willing to entertain conjectural emendations. Bultmann (*TDNT* 3:649) also regarded the text as "hopelessly corrupt."

13. Interestingly, this formulation is found in none of the other Pauline letters. For more extensive surveys of Paul's use of such formal dialogical expressions, see Stowers, *Diatribe*, 133-37; Rhyne, *Faith Establishes the Law*, 41-59; A. J. Malherbe, "ΜΗ ΓΕΝΟΙΤΟ in the Diatribe and Paul," *HTR* (1980): 231-40.

Table 1.
Paul's usage of τί οὖν ἐροῦμεν in Romans
(apart from Rom 4:1)

3:5	τί ἐροῦμεν;	εἰ δὲ ἡ ἀδικία ἡμῶν θεοῦ δικαιοσύνην συνίστησιν, . . . μὴ ἄδικος ὁ θεὸς ὁ ἐπιφέρων τὴν ὀργήν; κατὰ ἄνθρωπον λέγω. μὴ γένοιτο.
6:1	τί οὖν ἐροῦμεν;	ἐπιμένωμεν τῇ ἁμαρτίᾳ, ἵνα ἡ χάρις πλεονάσῃ; μὴ γένοιτο.
7:7	τί οὖν ἐροῦμεν;	ὁ νόμος ἁμαρτία; μὴ γένοιτο.
8:31	τί οὖν ἐροῦμεν	πρὸς ταῦτα; εἰ ὁ θεὸς ὑπὲρ ἡμῶν, τίς καθ᾽ ἡμῶν;
9:30	τί οὖν ἐροῦμεν;	ὅτι ἔθνη τὰ μὴ διώκοντα δικαιοσύνην κατέλαβεν δικαιοσύνην, δικαιοσύνην δὲ τὴν ἐκ πίστεως, Ἰσραὴλ δὲ διώκων νόμον δικαιοσύνης εἰς νόμον οὐκ ἔφθασεν;

A survey of these texts yields the following observations:

1. In every case except Rom 8:31, τί οὖν ἐροῦμεν constitutes a complete sentence, punctuated with a question mark immediately following ἐροῦμεν.
2. In all six instances this formulation introduces another rhetorical question.
3. In all six instances the second rhetorical question articulates an inference that might be drawn from the foregoing discussion.
4. In four of the six cases this inference is a false one. (Rom 8:31 clearly does not conform to this pattern. In Rom 9:30-31 the issue is more complicated, but it appears that here the inference is correct, though scandalous.)

These observations may be reinforced by a consideration of three other passages in Romans (3:9; 6:15; 11:7) in which Paul employs a briefer form of the same rhetorical device (τί οὖν), and one analogous passage in 1 Cor 10:19 (τί οὖν φήμι). Rom 11:7 closely resembles Rom 9:30-31, but the other three texts conform to the pattern described above: τί οὖν introduces a rhetorical question that poses a false inference.[14]

14. Both Stowers and Malherbe refer to these false inferences as "objections." This is an

In view of the prevalence of this rhetorical pattern, we may explore the possibility that Rom 4:1 ought to be punctuated and understood analogously. The text would then read: τί οὖν ἐροῦμεν; εὑρηκέναι Ἀβραὰμ τὸν προπάτορα ἡμῶν κατὰ σάρκα. If so, however, how would the question about Abraham be translated and interpreted?

Luz, who recognizes the importance of Paul's patterned rhetorical usage of τί οὖν ἐροῦμεν, punctuates the text as I have suggested here and translates the question as follows: "Hat es unser Vorvater Abraham nach dem Fleische gefunden?"[15] Although Luz does not actually employ the word "grace" in his translation, he thinks it unavoidable to acknowledge that "χάριν offenbar selbstverständlich vorschwebt," and he points again to the idiom εὑρίσκειν χάριν. This general approach to interpreting Rom 4:1 is of course not a novel one. John Wesley, for example, punctuated the text in the same way: "What shall we say then? That our father Abraham hath found according to the flesh?" His explanatory note on the text states that the unexpressed object of εὑρηκέναι should be understood to be "acceptance with God."[16]

The merit of these suggestions is twofold: they take seriously Paul's characteristic rhetorical constructions with τί οὖν ἐροῦμεν, and, just as importantly, they interpret 4:1 in a way that makes the transition to 4:2 smooth and intelligible. The γάρ of 4:2, according to this reading, would serve to introduce an explanation of the way Abraham might hypothetically have

appropriate term if one thinks of the text as a dialogue between Paul and an imaginary interlocutor. In the absence of specific indicators in the text (as in a Platonic dialogue), however, it would seem preferable not to posit an actual change of speakers. Even though Paul states in the form of a rhetorical question a view which is opposed to his own, *Paul* remains the speaker; even though there are two points of view, there is only one *voice*. Stowers's otherwise excellent study fails to make this distinction. See now also S. K. Stowers, *A Rereading of Romans: Justice, Jews, and Gentiles* (New Haven: Yale University Press, 1994), along with my review essay: R. B. Hays, "'The Gospel Is the Power of God for Gentiles Only'? A Critique of Stanley Stowers' *A Rereading of Romans*," *Critical Review of Books in Religion* 9 (1996): 27-44. Wilckens, on the other hand, while recognizing the dialogical character of Paul's argumentation in Romans, notes correctly that in Rom 3:27-31 "Paulus sowohl die Fragen stellt als auch selbst die Antworten gibt. Der Partner kommt seinerseits gar nicht zu Wort" (*Römer*, 1:244). For this reason I prefer to call the counterquestions which follow Paul's use of τί οὖν ἐροῦμεν false inferences rather than objections.

15. Luz, *Geschichtsverständnis*, 174.

16. J. Wesley, *Explanatory Notes upon the New Testament* (1755; reprint, London: Epworth, 1966), 531. In taking κατὰ σάρκα as a modifier of εὑρηκέναι, Wesley was following Bengel against the KJV.

found grace/justification "according to the flesh." Why then has some such solution not found grace in the eyes of the commentators? There are at least three considerations that seem to tell against it. First is the matter of word order. The reading τί οὖν ἐροῦμεν Ἀβραὰμ τὸν πατέρα ἡμῶν εὑρηκέναι κατὰ σάρκα appears in a number of later manuscripts, but it manifestly represents a secondary attempt to clarify the sense of a difficult text. No modern critic accepts this reading. Given the text of the 27th edition of Nestle-Aland (based on ℵ, A, C, etc.), the wide separation between εὑρηκέναι and κατὰ σάρκα is very peculiar if the latter is intended to modify the former; κατὰ σάρκα is more naturally taken with Ἀβραὰμ τὸν προπάτορα ἡμῶν. This is the consideration most frequently mentioned in the commentaries. Second, the use of εὑρίσκειν in the sense of "gain, acquire" with no expressed object is unparalleled in Paul's usage or, indeed, in the NT.[17] Finally, in terms of this interpretation it is difficult to see why Paul should employ a perfect, rather than an aorist, infinitive. There are so many other perplexities surrounding this verse that few exegetes have worried over this last point, but for reasons that will become apparent, the question is well worth asking.

In any case, the interpretation illustrated here through Luz and Wesley shares with the more popular interpretation recounted above the Western exegetical tradition's characteristic preoccupation with the problem of how Abraham found (and how we might find) justification. I would suggest that this preoccupation has prevented commentators on Romans from recognizing a more satisfactory way of reading Rom 4:1. If we under-

---

17. The verb is used absolutely, with no explicit object, in expressions such as ζητεῖτε καὶ εὑρήσετε (Matt 7:7 = Luke 11:9) or in elliptical constructions where the object is explicitly named in the previous clause (Matt 2:8; 12:43; Acts 11:25-26; etc.). In every case of the latter kind in the NT, εὑρίσκειν is juxtaposed to a verb of seeking in the preceding clause. Clearly none of these conditions pertains in Rom 4:1. The LXX does provide a few instances of the absolute use of εὑρίσκειν with the meaning "acquire possessions, become rich." See, for example, Lev 25:47: ἐὰν δὲ εὕρῃ ἡ χεὶρ τοῦ προσηλύτου ἢ τοῦ παροίκου τοῦ παρὰ σοὶ ("If a proselyte or sojourner with you becomes rich . . ."). This seems to be an idiom which occurs only with ἡ χείρ (τινος); however, if Rom 4:1 were understood on the analogy of this idiom, the meaning would be "What then shall we say? Did our father Abraham become rich according to the flesh?" This translation (which I have found neither advocated nor even considered by any commentator) is certainly a more defensible reading of the Greek than the RSV's reading, and it would be consistent with the economic imagery of Rom 4:4. The position of κατὰ σάρκα in the sentence's word order remains problematical for this interpretation, but it is not impossible. The reader will have to judge whether this translation suits the wider context of Paul's argument as well as the proposal put forward in this essay.

stand Ἀβραὰμ not as the subject but as the *direct object* of the infinitive εὑρηκέναι, whose subject would then be understood as the "we" of the immediately preceding ἐροῦμεν,[18] we could translate the verse in the following way: *"What then shall we say? Have we found Abraham (to be) our forefather according to the flesh?"*[19]

Unlike other proposed solutions to the exegetical riddle of Rom 4:1, this interpretation requires no textual emendation, no strained syntax, no awkward ellipsis.[20] The verb εὑρίσκειν here would be understood not as a cryptic allusion to the theological idiom of Gen 18:3 but as a straightforward exegetical-dialogical term, referring to the "findings" (results) of a discussion or inquiry.[21] Paul uses the word in precisely this way elsewhere in Romans (7:10, 21).[22] Indeed, the construction featuring εὑρίσκειν complemented by an unexpressed εἶναι and a predicate nominative or adjective is a common one in Paul: "to find (someone) to be (something)." For instances of this construction see, for example, 1 Cor 4:2, 15:15, 2 Cor 5:3, 9:4, 12:20, Gal 2:17.[23]

Furthermore, it is not difficult to hear in this reading of Rom 4:1 echoes of the specialized usage of the verb "to find" in rabbinic exegetical idiom, where the common question מה מצינו ב׳ means "What do we find (in Scripture) concerning . . . ?"[24] This usage of the verb מצא is illustrated (though not in its interrogative form) by a text from the *Mekilta* which may be quoted here at some length.

18. This is an impeccable construction, common in classical Greek: "The complement of verbs of (perceiving), believing, (showing), and saying which indicate the content of the conception or communication, is formed to a great extent by the infinitive. If the subject of the infinitive is the same as that of the governing verb, it is not expressed" (BDF §396).

19. Precisely this reading of the text was proposed by T. Zahn, *Der Brief des Paulus an die Römer* (Leipzig: Deichert, 1910), 215. Zahn's extremely thorough discussion of this verse (212-19) has been almost completely overlooked by recent commentators.

20. Zahn (*Römer*, 215) describes this interpretation as "grammatisch unanfechtbar."

21. This is a very common meaning of the word; see, e.g., Plato, *Meno* 74 a8. BAGD (325) cites an extensive list of passages where εὑρίσκειν is used "of intellectual discovery based upon reflection, observation, examination, or investigation."

22. The only other appearance of this verb in Romans is at 10:20, in an OT quotation.

23. The same construction is illustrated by Acts 13:22b: εὗρον Δαυὶδ τὸν τοῦ Ἰεσσαὶ ἄνδρα κατὰ τὴν καρδίαν μου ("I have found David the [son] of Jesse [to be] a man after my heart").

24. This idiom is noted by M. Jastrow, *A Dictionary of the Targumim, the Talmud Babli and Yerushalmi, and the Midrashic Literature* (Brooklyn: Traditional Press, [1903]), 825.

> Great indeed is faith before Him who spoke and the world came into be-
> ing. . . . R. Nehemiah says: Whence can you prove that whosoever ac-
> cepts even one single commandment with true faith is deserving of hav-
> ing the Holy Spirit rest upon him? We *find* (מצינו) this to have been the
> case with our *fathers*. For as a reward for the faith (בשכר האמנה) with
> which they believed, they were considered worthy of having the Holy
> Spirit rest upon them, so that they could utter the song, as it is said:
> "And they believed in the Lord. . . . Then sang Moses and the children of
> Israel." And so also you *find* that *our father Abraham* inherited both this
> world and the world beyond (העולם הזה יהעולם הבא) *only* as a reward
> for the faith (אמנה בשכר) with which he believed, as it is said: "And he
> believed in the Lord," etc. (Gen 15:6). . . . He keeps in remembrance the
> faith of the *fathers*.[25]

In this text the verb "to find" (מצא) means "to draw a conclusion on the
basis of exegetical evidence." Similarly, Rom 4:1 could very well mean
"Have we found (on the basis of Scripture) that Abraham is our forefather
according to the flesh?"

Thus, my proposed interpretation of Rom 4:1 has much to be said for
it on syntactical grounds. It allows the text to be read as lucid and unforced
Greek, and it construes the syntax of the passage in accordance with the
rhetorical pattern which obtains in Paul's other uses of the expression τί
οὖν ἐροῦμεν.[26] Furthermore, this rendering of the passage accords to the
perfect infinitive a readily intelligible function. If Paul's question were
about what Abraham found, we should expect the aorist infinitive; however, if Paul's question is about what we have found Abraham to be, the
perfect infinitive is precisely the appropriate form of the verb. Thus, on the
basis of grammatical and syntactical considerations, this interpretation is
clearly preferable to any other that has been proposed.

We must still ask, however, whether this reading makes sense in the
context of Paul's argument. We may pursue this matter under two headings.

---

25. *Mekilta* Beshallaḥ 7 (Lauterbach I, 252-53). The translation is Lauterbach's, the emphasis mine.

26. It might be objected that in none of the other cases does Paul follow this rhetorical
question with an infinitive dependent on ἐροῦμεν. This observation is correct, but inconse-
quential; the variety of the formulations collected in table 1 is sufficient to illustrate that Paul
is certainly capable of syntactical variation. We are dealing here with a thought pattern, not a
fixed formula.

1. Is the proposition that "Abraham is our forefather according to the flesh" an intelligible inference — whether true or false — from Paul's foregoing discussion in Rom 3?

2. Is the question of Rom 4:1, as I have translated it, a suitable starting place for the discussion to follow in Rom 4? Each of these questions will be addressed in turn.

God of the Jews Only? Romans 4:1 in Relation to the Foregoing Discussion

To see how Rom 4:1 fits into Paul's line of thought, we must look carefully at the preceding paragraph (Rom 3:27-31).[27] In verses 27-28 Paul articulates one implication of his discussion of δικαιοσύνη θεοῦ in chapter 3: boasting is excluded because justification is by faith apart from works of Law. This affirmation is not, however, the goal toward which Paul's argument is driving; instead, it functions as a necessary step toward the assertion that God justifies Gentiles and Jews in the *same* way (i.e., apart from Law). The fundamental problem with which Paul is wrestling in Romans is *not* how a person may find acceptance with God; the problem is to work out an understanding of the relationship in Christ between Jews and Gentiles. This is the concern that surfaces clearly in verses 29-30. Is God the God of the Jews only (as he would be if justification were contingent upon keeping the Law)? Is he not the God of the Gentiles also?

To understand Paul's answer to these rhetorical questions we must reconsider the punctuation of verses 29-30. These verses are usually punctuated and translated as follows:

ἢ Ἰουδαίων ὁ θεὸς μόνον; οὐχὶ καὶ ἐθνῶν; ναὶ καὶ ἐθνῶν, εἴπερ εἷς ὁ θεὸς ὃς δικαιώσει περιτομὴν ἐκ πίστεως καὶ ἀκροβυστίαν διὰ τῆς πίστεως.

Or is God the God of Jews only? Is he not the God of Gentiles also? Yes, of Gentiles also, since God is one; and he will justify the circum-

---

27. In treating Rom 3:27–4:25 as a unit, I am in agreement with Stowers, *Diatribe,* 155-74. Rhyne (*Faith Establishes the Law,* 63-93) argues for 3:21–4:25 as the requisite boundaries of the pericope. As I have argued elsewhere, however ("Psalm 143 and the Logic of Romans 3"), the division between 3:20 and 3:21 is not appropriate.

cised on the ground of their faith and the uncircumcised through their faith.[28]

A different punctuation of these words, however, produces an interpretation that carries the development of Paul's thought through with greater clarity. I propose to read a full stop after ἐθνῶν at the end of verse 29 and a comma after πίστεως in verse 30, so that the words καὶ ἀκροβυστίαν διὰ τῆς πίστεως become the elliptical apodosis of a conditional sentence whose protasis is introduced by εἴπερ.[29] The unexpressed verb of this elliptical clause would be δικαιώσει, implicit after its explicit occurrence in the protasis of the sentence. The result would be as follows:

ἢ Ἰουδαίων ὁ θεὸς μόνον; οὐχὶ καὶ ἐθνῶν; ναὶ καὶ ἐθνῶν· εἴπερ εἷς ὁ θεὸς ὃς δικαιώσει περιτομὴν ἐκ πίστεως, καὶ ἀκροβυστίαν διὰ τῆς πίστεως.

Or is God the God of Jews only? Is he not the God of Gentiles also? Yes, of Gentiles also. If indeed God, who will justify the circumcised on the basis of faith, is one, he will also justify the uncircumcised through faith.

According to the RSV interpretation, Paul concludes that because God is one, he must be the God of the Gentiles also; on this reading Paul is simply stating a commonplace maxim.[30] According to my proposed interpretation, Paul concludes that because God is one, he must *justify* Gentiles in the same way he justifies Jews.

---

28. This is the RSV translation. I leave aside for the moment whether it is appropriate to supply the possessive pronoun "their" before the word "faith" in this sentence. The NRSV reads "he will justify the circumcised on the ground of faith and the uncircumcised through that same faith." This represents a clear improvement.

29. See the apt remarks of Stowers (*Diatribe*, 166) on the RSV's rendering of εἴπερ as though it were ἐπείπερ. While Stowers recognizes the conditional meaning of εἴπερ, he treats it as an elliptical clause in its own right, equivalent to "if he really is God of the Gentiles also." This is certainly a possible way of reading the text. But why make εἴπερ into a separate elliptical clause when it can be read quite naturally as the first word of a conditional clause which is explicit in the text?

30. See the comments of N. A. Dahl ("The One God of Jews and Gentiles," in *Studies in Paul* [Minneapolis: Augsburg, 1977], 189): "No Jew or Jewish Christian would deny that God, being one, is not only the God of the Jews but also the God of the Gentiles. The discussion partners agree in upholding a universal monotheism."

The difference between these interpretations is not great. In either case the text affirms that Jews and Gentiles alike are justified through faith. To read the text as I have proposed, however, is to call attention more pointedly to a fact too little recognized: Paul assumes without defense or fanfare that "God will justify the circumcised ἐκ πίστεως." Paul did not invent the doctrine of justification by faith. He could assume it as the common conviction of Jewish Christianity, as Gal 2:15-16 unmistakably shows. "We ourselves who are Jews by birth and not Gentile sinners, knowing that a person is not justified on the basis of works of Law but through the faith of Jesus Christ, have believed in Christ Jesus in order that we might be justified on the basis of Christ's faith and not on the basis of works of Law, because on the basis of works of Law no flesh shall be justified." There, as here, the thrust of Paul's argument is directed against Christians who confess themselves to be justified ἐκ πίστεως Χριστοῦ ("on the basis of Christ's faith")[31] but who fail to draw what Paul sees as the logical corollary of this confession: that Gentiles need not come under the Law to be justified. There lies the disputed issue.[32]

In view of these considerations, Paul poses another question in verse 31: If Gentiles need not come under the Law to be justified, then through faith do we abrogate the Law? This inference Paul decisively rejects (μὴ γένοιτο), and he claims instead that through faith "we confirm the Law." Interpreters of Romans have long recognized that the discussion of Abraham in chapter 4 is Paul's attempt to give some exegetical grounding to his provocative claim that the gospel confirms rather than overturns the Law. He is arguing that the *Law* already teaches that Abraham was justified by

31. Those who find this a peculiar translation may consult M. Barth, "The Faith of the Messiah," *HeyJ* 10 (1969): 363-70; L. T. Johnson, "Romans 3:21-26 and the Faith of Jesus," *CBQ* 44 (1982): 77-90; R. B. Hays, *The Faith of Jesus Christ: The Narrative Substructure of Gal 3:1–4:11*, 2nd ed. (Grand Rapids: Eerdmans, 2002).

32. Precisely because the doctrine of justification by faith is known to us in its Pauline form, which, in a very polemical manner, formulates it in sharp antithesis to "works of Law," it requires an act of the imagination to project ourselves back into Paul's time and to realize that there might well have been Jewish Christians who believed themselves to be justified ἐκ πίστεως Χριστοῦ and who, without sensing any contradiction, at the same time would have insisted that Gentile believers ought to adhere to the Law. Only when we are able to fix this picture clearly in our minds do the letters to the Galatians and Romans really begin to make sense; in both letters Paul treats the doctrine of justification by faith as an agreed-upon premise *from* which he can construct his position about the relation between Jews and Gentiles and the role of the Law in the life of the Christian community.

faith.[33] What then shall we say about Rom 4:1? How does it fit into or advance the argument?

It must be granted that Abraham is introduced into the discussion rather abruptly at this point.[34] The relevance of the figure of Abraham to the problem of how God justifies Gentiles will become apparent only in the course of Paul's exegesis of Gen 15. On the face of the matter, it is difficult to see how the proposition that "Abraham is our forefather according to the flesh" could be drawn as an inference — whether true or false — from Paul's argument up to this point.[35] This observation poses an apparent obstacle to our proposed interpretation of Rom 4:1.

The obstacle is hardly an insuperable one, however. To follow Paul's argument we need only recognize that the inference ("Abraham is our forefather κατὰ σάρκα") is not developed directly from Paul's immediately preceding statement ("We confirm the Law") but from the previous hypothetical (and false) suggestion that "God is the God of the Jews only" (3:29). Such a belief would represent a type of Judaism that Paul regards as inappropriately ethnocentric. In 4:1 Paul takes up this line of thought again with the intent of demonstrating its falsity. Thus, the phrase τί οὖν ἐροῦμεν in 4:1 introduces an inference that continues to draw out the implications of the position *against which* Paul is arguing.[36] The clearest evi-

---

33. It is rarely noticed, however, that this evaluation of the Law conflicts with the strongly negative interpretation traditionally given to Law in chap. 3. See my article "Psalm 143 and the Logic of Romans 3" for an attempt to accord to Law its more proper Pauline function as a testimony to δικαιοσύνη θεοῦ. See now also Rhyne, *Faith Establishes the Law,* passim.

34. This fact leads E. E. Ellis (*Prophecy and Hermeneutic in Early Christianity,* WUNT 18 [Tübingen: J. C. B. Mohr (Paul Siebeck), 1978], 217) to hypothesize that Rom 4 might be a preformed block of midrashic exegesis, here incorporated by Paul into a new argumentative setting.

35. The major difficulty with Zahn's treatment of the passage (*Römer,* 212-19) lay in his inability to give a credible explanation of the logic of Paul's argument here. Zahn assumed that the "we" of 4:1 must mean "we Christians" (as opposed to Jews); consequently, he supposed that the rhetorical accusation that Christians are Abraham's children only κατὰ σάρκα must reflect a charge flung by Jews against *Jewish* Christians, since such a charge would make no sense against Gentile Christians. This understanding of 4:1-2, however, disregards the larger argumentative context: Paul is concerned here about relations not between Jews and Jewish Christians but between Jews and Gentiles in Christ (cf. 3:29-30; 4:11-12).

36. This observation explains the absence of an explicit negation (μὴ γένοιτο) of the inference, a point that Käsemann (*Romans,* 106) regards as decisive evidence against the interpretations of both Zahn and Luz.

dence that this is so can be found in the characterization of Abraham as τὸν προπάτορα ἡμῶν κατὰ σάρκα. Does Paul intend, as the usual interpretation of this passage would require, to affirm that Abraham is the forefather of Christians "according to the flesh"?[37] Surely this is an inadmissible interpretation. In Rom 9:7-8 Paul insists that it is not the "children of the flesh" who are reckoned as Abraham's "seed," but the "children of the promise." (Cf. also Gal 4:21-31.) Thus the description of Abraham as "our forefather according to the flesh" can hardly be a casual introductory epithet; it must represent an understanding of Abraham (and of the relation of God's people to him) that Paul is seeking to refute.

The logic of Paul's argument may be clarified by a paraphrase: "Is God the God of Jews only and not also of Gentiles? Of course not! He is surely the God of Gentiles also. But that means that if God, who justifies Jews on the basis of faith, is consistent and whole, he must justify Gentiles also through faith. Then through this faith are we invalidating the Law? No! Instead, we are confirming the Law. What then shall we say? Have we found (in this chain of argument) that Abraham is our forefather according to the flesh — i.e., that we belong to the physical family of Abraham?"

Paul is going to argue that those who are in Christ — including not only Gentiles but also Jewish believers — claim their relation to Abraham not by virtue of physical descent from him (κατὰ σάρκα)[38] but by virtue of

37. Stowers's treatment of the passage as a dialogue circumvents this difficulty: the words are attributed not to Paul but to the interlocutor (*Diatribe*, 164-67). Although Stowers has a fundamentally correct insight (the point of view expressed here is not Paul's own), he does not recognize the extent to which Paul's response is designed precisely as a rebuttal to this characterization of Abraham as "forefather according to the flesh."

38. This represents a slight modification of my argument in the originally published version of this essay, in which I wrote: "Paul is going to argue that Judaism itself, rightly understood, claims its relation to Abraham not by virtue of physical descent from him." I have been persuaded to change my interpretation by N. T. Wright, "Romans and the Theology of Paul," in *Pauline Theology*, volume 3: *Romans*, ed. D. M. Hay and E. E. Johnson (Minneapolis: Fortress, 1995), 30-67. Wright accepts my proposed translation, but interprets the question as follows: "Does this mean that we Christians, Jews and Gentiles alike, now discover that we are to be members of the fleshly family of Abraham?" (40). This reading clarifies the overall coherence of Rom 4, particularly the logical connection between v. 1 and vv. 2-8 (see R. B. Hays, "Adam, Israel, Christ," in *Pauline Theology*, volume 3, 81). Of course, the expression κατὰ σάρκα is a theologically loaded one for Paul. At the superficial level it refers simply to the process of natural physical descent, but there are at least two other levels of meaning in Paul's usage of the term: it alludes to circumcision and, at the same time, to the mode of human existence apart from God. The meaning of the expression in Rom 4:1 is to be de-

sharing his trust in the God who made the promises.[39] In that sense the gospel, which invites all people, including Gentiles, into right relation with God through faith, confirms the Law; it is consistent with the real substance of the Law's teaching. This is the proposition Paul now sets out to demonstrate, beginning in Rom 4:3, through his exposition of Genesis.

This reading of the text will appear odd only if we are committed to the presupposition that Paul is expounding a message that stands in an antithetical relation to Judaism. If we do not hold this view a priori, it will be clear enough that Paul means precisely what he says: the gospel confirms the Torah. Only a narrowly ethnocentric form of Judaism would claim that God is the God of the Jews only,[40] or that Abraham is the progenitor of God's people only "according to the flesh," i.e., by virtue of natural physical descent. For the purpose of his argument Paul associates these (evidently false) claims with the (disputed) claim that Gentile Christians must come under the Law. Paul, speaking from *within* the Jewish tradition,[41] contends that the Torah itself provides the warrant for a more universally inclusive theology which affirms that the one God is God of Gentiles as well as Jews and that Abraham is the forefather of more than those who happen to be his physical descendants. This is the case to be made in chapter 4.

Thus, our proposed reading of Rom 4:1 does link this verse to the foregoing discussion in a thoroughly coherent way. The major theme of Rom 3:27-31 is the affirmation that the one God deals with Jews and Gentiles alike.[42] This claim is played off against a rhetorical "straw man" position that would claim special status for the circumcised and/or demand that Gentiles adopt the physical sign of Jewish ethnic identity. In Rom 4:1 Paul formulates, with some incredulity, the consequence of such a position: Abraham is "our forefather according to the flesh." Paul's ensuing exegesis will seek to rip this straw man apart.

---

termined not by choosing among these possibilities but by discerning their complex interweaving in the present context.

39. This line of thought parallels the position already articulated by Paul in Rom 2:26-29, where he asserts that "circumcision of the heart," not physical circumcision (ἐν σαρκί), characterizes the person who is truly a Jew.

40. Cf. Dahl, "The One God," 182-88.

41. This approach to the texts stands in agreement with the hermeneutical principles elucidated by Gaston ("Abraham," 39-41, 59).

42. Cf. J. M. Bassler, *Divine Impartiality, Paul and a Theological Axiom*, SBLDS 59 (Chico, Calif.: Scholars, 1982), 156-58.

Abraham as Forefather: Romans 4:1
in Relation to the Following Discussion

In what way does the rhetorical question posed in 4:1 orient the reader toward the content of the discussion that follows? What is the subject matter that the question introduces?

The customary interpretation of Rom 4:1 would suggest that the issue concerns what Abraham "found": justification apart from works.[43] Indeed, this explanation appears to account very nicely for verses 2-8. In these verses Paul demonstrates, through close exegesis of Gen 15:6 and Ps 32:1-2, that the doctrine of justification by faith is to be found in Scripture; thus he supports his assertion (3:31) that the gospel confirms the Law.

However, we must consider Rom 4 as a whole, not just verses 2-8, and we must explore the question of its continuity with the preceding argument. My interpretation of Rom 3:27–4:1 has suggested that Paul's concern focuses not on the mechanics of justification but on the relation of Jews and Gentiles in light of the message of justification. Now it must be demonstrated that my proposed reading of Rom 4:1 provides a lens through which we may perceive the extension of this same theme through Rom 4 as the unifying concern.

In 4:1 Paul asks whether his insistence that his message confirms the Law (3:31) leads to the conclusion that Gentile believers must become part of Abraham's fleshly family (i.e., through the fleshly act of circumcision, which functions as a synecdoche for Torah observance). This inference is emphatically denied. Then, in verses 2-8, he demonstrates that Abraham himself was reckoned righteous (i.e., received into covenant relation with God) apart from "works" of Torah observance. In support of this claim Paul also adduces the words of David (Ps 31:1-2 LXX), understood as a future-looking prophetic blessing upon "the uncircumcision" (v. 9). This theme governs the discussion in verses 9-22. In verse 9 Paul asks, in relation to the quotation of Ps 32:1-2, "Is this blessing pronounced upon the circumcision (Jews) or upon the uncircumcision (Gentiles)?" This question is then smoothly transposed from the psalm context back into the discussion of Gen 15:6. At this point in the argument (vv. 9-12) Paul is concerned no longer with the problem of *how* Abraham was justified but instead with the question of *when* he was "reckoned righteous." Was it be-

---

43. See, e.g., Käsemann, *Romans*, 105-11; Cranfield, *Romans*, 1:224-32.

fore or after he received circumcision? It is very important to see *why* this question arises as a crucial one for Paul's argument. It does *not* arise (this can hardly be said too strongly) because Paul wants to refute the view that Abraham was justified by virtue of a "work" (circumcision). It arises because Paul regards Abraham as a *representative* figure whose destiny "contains" the destiny of others; the blessing pronounced upon him applies not only to him but to his "seed" as well.[44] Therefore, the fact that Abraham was "reckoned righteous" while still uncircumcised has *symbolic* significance: he can thereby be the "father" of Gentiles as well as Jews. Paul spells this out explicitly in verses 11-12:

> And he received a sign of circumcision, a seal of the righteousness of the faith which is in the uncircumcision, *in order that* he might be:
>
> a. the father of all who believe while uncircumcised, in order that righteousness might be reckoned to them;
> b. the father of circumcision to those who are not only circumcised but also walk in the footsteps of the faith that our father Abraham had while he was uncircumcised.

The story of Abraham is told as it is told (or, as Paul would say, these things happened to Abraham in the *order* in which they happened) *in order that* Abraham might fitly serve as the archetype for Gentile believers as well as Jewish believers. He is said to be the "father" of both groups *not* because they are descended from him κατὰ σάρκα but because their faith mirrors his (they walk "in his footsteps") and because their destiny is prefigured in him.

This same theme undergirds the discussion in the following section as well (vv. 13-18).[45] In verses 13-14, where his reasoning very closely resembles

44. This is especially clear in Rom 4:13, which speaks of ἡ ἐπαγγελία τῷ Ἀβραὰμ ἢ τῷ σπέρματι αὐτοῦ ("the promise to Abraham — or his seed"). Cf. Gal 3:8-9, where Paul first cites the promise that all the nations will be blessed ἐν σοὶ and then offers the exegetical comment that thus οἱ ἐκ πίστεως are blessed *along with* the faithful Abraham. For a full discussion of the latter passage, see Hays, *Faith of Jesus Christ,* chap. 5.

45. Remarkably, commentators often draw a line of division in the middle of v. 17, treating vv. 13-17a as one pericope and vv. 17b-22 as another. This tendency is illustrated by Cranfield (*Romans,* 1:225), who, while acknowledging that "v. 17b is grammatically part of the sentence which began with v. 16," still contends that "it belongs by reason of its content to what follows." Neither Cranfield nor any other commentator that I have consulted gives

the argument of Gal 3:15-18, Paul draws attention to the fact that the promise (ἐπαγγελία: a new term in the discussion) applies not only to Abraham but also to his "seed," and asserts that the promised inheritance is given[46] not διὰ νόμου but διὰ δικαιοσύνης πίστεως. Why? The argument again, as in verses 11-12, presses on to explain the purpose (God's purpose, we may infer) of this arrangement. The inheritance is given ἐκ πίστεως, Paul tells us, in order that everything might hinge upon grace, in order that the promise might be confirmed for "the whole seed," not only for the Jew (τῷ ἐκ νόμου) but also for the Gentile (τῷ ἐκ πίστεως Ἀβραὰμ). Here the theme of verses 11-12 is reiterated, and once again Abraham is designated by Paul as "father of us all . . . before God" (4:16, 17b), even if he is not the father of us all κατὰ σάρκα.

Paul buttresses his claim that Abraham is the father of Gentiles with another Scripture quotation: καθὼς γέγραπται ὅτι πατέρα πολλῶν ἐθνῶν τέθεικά σε (Rom 4:17a, quoting Gen 17:5 LXX). Then, as though the point had not been sufficiently made already, Paul drives it home one more time in verse 18: Abraham believed in hope against hope *in order that* he might thereby become the father of many nations (ἔθνη). Once again scriptural support is adduced, this time through a citation from Gen 15:5, which, in rabbinic fashion, employs a catchphrase to represent the fuller quotation (Rom 4:18b).

Verses 19-22 do not require detailed discussion here, but two things

---

due weight to the fact that v. 18 constitutes the second of two parallel relative clauses both of which modify Ἀβραὰμ (v. 16). The parallelism may be illustrated as follows:

Ἀβραὰμ

-ὅς ἐστιν πατὴρ πάντων ἡμῶν	affirmation
καθὼς γέγραπται ὅτι	citation formula
πατέρα πολλῶν ἐθνῶν τέθεικά σε . . .	proof text
-ὅς παρ' ἐλπίδα ἐπ' ἐλπίδι ἐπίστευσεν	affirmation
εἰς τὸ γενέσθαι αὐτὸν	
πατέρα πολλῶν ἐθνῶν	
κατὰ τὸ εἰρημένον	citation formula
οὕτως ἔσται τὸ σπέρμα σου	proof text

This structure is obscured by the punctuation of the Nestle-Aland[27] text, which indicates that a new period begins with v. 18. If a division must be made somewhere, it should be made at the beginning of v. 19, not v. 18.

46. Or received? Some verb must be supplied.

stand out as worthy of comment. First, it is here and only here that Paul calls attention to the strength or quality of Abraham's faith; thus, these verses mark Paul's closest approach in this chapter to a hortatory mode of discourse. Even here, however, it should be noted that there is no explicit appeal to the reader to imitate Abraham's example. The description of Abraham might still be regarded an implicit exemplum,[47] but some caution is appropriate in stating such a view. Paul was, as we know, not reticent about employing direct exhortations; it is perhaps significant that he does not do so here.

Second, another function of these verses is to emphasize that the fulfillment of the promise was contingent upon the promise and power of God, not upon the natural capacities of Abraham and Sarah. In other words, the promise was fulfilled κατὰ χάριν (cf. v. 16), not κατὰ σάρκα (cf. v. 1). Once again, Rom 9:8 provides an apt commentary: οὐ τὰ τέκνα τῆς σαρκὸς ταῦτα τέκνα τοῦ θεοῦ ἀλλὰ τὰ τέκνα τῆς ἐπαγγελίας λογίζεται εἰς σπέρμα. Even more important than Abraham's faith is God's faithfulness.

Before we move on to examine the concluding verses of the chapter, let us draw together the results of our observations up to this point. Paul conducts his argumentation in verses 3-22 on *exegetical* grounds, treating the story of Abraham as a divinely plotted drama whose purpose is to portray Abraham as the "father" of Jewish and Gentile believers. He is a representative figure in whom the destiny of all believers is included and figured forth; the promise given to him is ipso facto given to them as well. In that sense he is their father; physical descent from him is a matter of no consequence.

In view of this analysis, several significant conclusions may be drawn.

1. Paul has developed this interpretation of Abraham in Rom 4:1-22 directly through exegesis of Scripture, without any appeal to the language of Christian confession; this rendering of Abraham intends to be and is a *Jewish* theological interpretation of the significance of Abraham. Insofar as Paul has mounted a persuasive argument within the acknowledged rules of the Jewish exegetical game, he has sustained his claim (3:31) that his gospel of justification for Gentiles outside the Law is consistent with the Law.[48]

2. Throughout Paul's discussion from 3:27 to 4:22 there is an inter-

---

47. As it is by Stowers (*Diatribe,* 168-74).

48. This argument requires, of course, that "Law" be understood to mean in effect "Scripture." In no way does Paul's discussion at this point deal with the problem of the relation between the gospel and the Law of Sinai. Cf. Gal 3:15-29.

weaving — indeed a virtual equation — of three theoretically distinguishable motifs: justification by works of the Law, circumcision, and physical descent from Abraham. The connection of these motifs is not a systematic one; they are bound together, in a way characteristic of Paul, by an *associative* logic. All three are components of a particular "profile" of Jewish ethnic/religious self-understanding that Paul is seeking to correct. His tendency to employ them almost interchangeably makes the argument of Rom 4 difficult to follow.

3. Only in verses 2-8 does Paul's discussion center on the issue of justification by faith versus justification by works. In the development of the argument, these verses serve as a preliminary step toward the major thesis of the chapter, which is worked out painstakingly in verses 9-18: Abraham is the father of all, both Jews and Gentiles, who place their trust in the promise of God. This is the unifying concern of Rom 4.

When Rom 4 is understood in this way, it becomes clear that our proposed reading of Rom 4:1 offers an entirely appropriate introduction to Paul's interpretation of Abraham. The chapter as a whole revolves around the issue of Abraham's status as "father": Whose father is he really, and in what way is he related to his "seed"? With these concerns in view, it makes perfectly good sense for Paul to open the discussion by asking, "Have we found Abraham to be our forefather according to the flesh?" His exposition then works toward refuting such a position by showing that Abraham is the forefather, even for Jewish believers, not κατὰ σάρκα but in a more important way.

Romans 4:23-25: "It Was Not Written Only for His Sake . . ."

Paul finally turns, in the last sentence of chapter 4, to apply his "findings" about Abraham directly to the situation of Christian believers. In doing so, he is of course making explicit the application that has tacitly shaped the rest of the chapter. It is important, therefore, to pay close attention to exactly what he does and does *not* say here.

The christological formulation of Rom 4:25, which appears to be a confessional fragment, has attracted the extensive labors of exegetes,[49] but verses 23-24, in spite of their importance in the logical structure of the argu-

---

49. Cf. van der Minde, *Schrift und Tradition*, 89-102, and the literature cited there.

ment, have been little attended to, presumably because their meaning has been regarded as self-evident: just as Abraham believed and was reckoned righteous, so too will we be reckoned righteous if we believe. The case of Abraham, according to this interpretation, is an illustration of the general principle of justification by faith; if it worked for him, it will work for us, too. This interpretation is exemplified by Calvin's comment on the passage: "Paul expressly affirms that in the person of Abraham there had been exhibited an example of a common righteousness which applies equally to all."[50] This text does *not*, however, say explicitly what this interpretation requires; another meaning lies closer to hand: the pronouncement of Scripture applies not only to Abraham as an individual but also to others ("us") who are included *vicariously* in God's reckoning of righteousness.

Calvin's reading of the text, although it contains an element of truth, treats Abraham too much as an exemplary individual and neglects Paul's strong emphasis on Abraham as an inclusive representative figure. We must recall that several of the "promise" texts in Genesis that are crucial for Paul's interpretation of Abraham (e.g., Gen 12:3; 18:18; 22:18) declare that all nations will be blessed "in" Abraham.[51] In Gal 3:8 Paul, taking the idea of participation in Abraham very seriously, quotes precisely this promise, apparently conflating Gen 12:3 with 18:18 and/or 22:18. In Rom 4 the same idea surfaces in verses 9-12 when Paul first applies the words of Ps 32:1-2 to Abraham and then asks whether this blessing (on Abraham) applies to Jews or Gentiles. The clear implication is that the blessing pronounced on Abraham applies vicariously to others who are his "seed." This is precisely the point of verse 13, which regards the promise as applicable to "Abraham, or to his seed."

In view of all this, we may begin to suspect that Rom 4:23-24 carries a similar meaning, which may be paraphrased as follows: "Scripture says, 'Abraham believed God and it was reckoned to him as righteousness.' However, it was not just reckoned to him as an individual: these words apply also to us (who believe in God who raised Jesus from the dead) to

---

50. J. Calvin, *The Epistles of Paul the Apostle to the Romans and to the Thessalonians*, Calvin's Commentaries (Grand Rapids: Eerdmans, 1961), 100. Cf. L. Goppelt, *Typos* (Grand Rapids: Eerdmans, 1982), 136-38.

51. J. Van Seters (*Abraham in History and Tradition* [New Haven: Yale University Press, 1975], 272-78) thinks the notion of participation in Abraham's destiny is a result of the transference of originally royal motifs (cf. Ps 72:17) onto the Abraham tradition during the exilic period.

whom righteousness is going to be reckoned (vicariously, because we are Abraham's seed)." This way of reading the text should not be understood as antithetical to the customary interpretation. Clearly there is an analogy between Abraham's faith and the faith of the Christian believer; Paul chooses to stress this analogy not only in the characterization of "us" as οἱ πιστεύοντες (v. 24) but also in his approval (v. 12) of "those who walk in the footsteps of the faith which our father Abraham had while he was uncircumcised." The dichotomy between receiving a blessing vicariously as a result of the archetype's faith/obedience ("in Abraham") and receiving a blessing through reenacting the faith/obedience of the archetype ("like Abraham") is our dichotomy, not Paul's. Paul sees the two as indissoluble.[52] Because we participate in the blessing pronounced upon him, we mirror his faith; because our faith parallels his, we may be said to be his seed. Paul would be content, I think, with either formulation.

If this interpretation of Rom 4:23-24 is correct, it means, among other things, that in Rom 4 Paul is explicating his doctrine of justification in terms analogous to the Jewish idea of "the merits of the fathers." That this idea is a congenial one to Paul is demonstrated clearly by his evaluation of Israel's status before God (Rom 11:28): κατὰ μὲν τὸ εὐαγγέλιον ἐχθροὶ δι᾽ ὑμᾶς, κατὰ δὲ τὴν ἐκλογὴν ἀγαπητοὶ διὰ τοὺς πατέρας ("Although with regard to the gospel they are enemies for your sake, they are, with regard to election, beloved for the sake of the fathers"). The statement that Israel, in spite of some contemporary unfaithfulness, remains beloved by God for the sake of the fathers expresses the essence of the rabbinic understanding of the merits of the patriarchs.

C. K. Barrett, in his comments on Rom 11:28, notes the parallelism to rabbinic thought, but asserts that "the resemblance is only superficial, for Paul is not speaking of human merit but of divine election."[53] This view, however, reflects a misunderstanding that arises when the Jewish sources are read anachronistically through the filter of Reformation-era debates about justification and the "treasury of merits." As E. P. Sanders has shown in a helpful summary treatment of this issue,[54] the motif of the merits of the fathers can often be closely associated with the idea of God's faithful-

---

52. Only if we hold firmly to this insight can we properly begin to rethink the relation between Paul's Christology and his ethics. See, e.g., R. B. Hays, "Christology and Ethics in Galatians: The Law of Christ," *CBQ* 49 (1987): 268-90.

53. Barrett, *Romans*, 225; cf. Käsemann, *Romans*, 315.

54. Sanders, *Paul and Palestinian Judaism*, 183-98.

ness to his promises and with the motif of covenant election. Consider, for example, the declaration of Rabbi Eleazar ben Azariah: "Because of the merit of (כזכות) our father Abraham did God bring Israel out of Egypt, as it is said: 'For he remembered His holy word unto Abraham His servant,' and 'And he brought forth His people with joy.'"[55] Here Sanders contends that כזכות should be rendered in a simple prepositional sense (= "for the sake of"). No meritorious work of Abraham is adduced here; only the promise of God is in view.[56] This is certainly the case with regard to Rabbi Eleazar's proof text, Ps 105, which strongly emphasizes God's covenant faithfulness.

> He is mindful of his covenant forever,
> Of the word that he commanded for a thousand generations,
> The covenant which he made with Abraham,
> His sworn promise to Isaac. . . .
>
> . . .
>
> He opened the rock, and water gushed forth;
> It flowed through the desert like a river.
> For he remembered his holy promise,
> And Abraham his servant.
>
> (vv. 8-9, 41-42)

The continuity between this mode of thought and Paul's is apparent. Just as the psalmist can affirm that God gave Israel water in the wilderness because of his faithfulness to the promise given to Abraham his servant long before, so also Paul can affirm that "Christ became a servant of the circumcision for the sake of the truthfulness of God, in order to confirm the promises made to the fathers" (Rom 15:8).

Paul's use of this theological conceptuality is marked, however, by two distinctive developments. First, Paul has introduced a crucial new emphasis into the idea of the merits of the fathers by claiming, on the basis of the scriptural text, that Abraham's faithfulness was reckoned by God to the benefit not only of Israel (as in the rabbinic exegetical tradition) but also of the Gentiles. In the passage just cited from Rom 15, Paul declares that Christ "be-

---

55. *Mekilta* Pisḥa 16 (Lauterbach I, 140).

56. See Sanders, *Paul and Palestinian Judaism*, 195; cf. Gaston, "Abraham," 58-59: "What Abraham 'merited' for later generations is pure grace."

came a servant of the circumcision" not only "in order to confirm the promises made to the fathers" but also "in order that the Gentiles might glorify God for (his) mercy." Second, while Sanders contends that the Tannaitic rabbis never related their discussion of *zekut* (merits) to soteriology,[57] Paul manifestly has escalated the meaning of the blessing reckoned to Abraham onto the level of eschatological salvation. Nonetheless, the distinctive features of Paul's presentation should not be allowed to obscure its very definite continuity with rabbinic traditions about the vicarious effects of Abraham's faithfulness. Paul, reading Gen 15:6 with rabbinic eyes, asserts that the dictum of Scripture (ἐλογίσθη αὐτῷ) applies, not just potentially but actually, to Christian believers, whose present faith in the risen Jesus is a sign of participation in the blessing pronounced upon Abraham.

Conclusion

Having embarked on an effort to reconsider the meaning of Paul's apparently obscure Greek in Rom 4:1, we have arrived at a reading of the whole of Rom 4 that differs slightly but significantly from traditional ways of understanding the figure of Abraham in Paul's argument. *The crucial issue in the chapter is not how Abraham got himself justified but rather whose father he is and in what way his children are related to him. The central thrust of Paul's argument is to affirm that Abraham is the father of Jews and Gentiles alike and that Jews and Gentiles alike are included vicariously in the blessing pronounced upon him by God, a blessing that is specifically said to apply to "all the nations"* (πάντα τὰ ἔθνη). This argument demonstrates to Paul's satisfaction that his gospel, which offers God's salvation to Gentiles apart from the Law, is in fact a consummation and confirmation of the Torah's promises. Jews (at least those with circumcised hearts; cf. Rom 2:28-29) have found Abraham to be their father not "according to the flesh," but according to promise.

The great theological difficulty with all of this is to know how *Christ* is related to the fulfillment of the promises to Abraham.[58] The exegesis put

57. Sanders, *Paul and Palestinian Judaism*, 198. Sanders's statement is perhaps slightly misleading; it is true only if one defines "soteriology" so as to exclude blessings received within a community's historical experience.

58. This problem is posed sharply by Boers's discussion "The Significance of Abraham

forward in this essay suggests that a solution to this problem might be sought along the lines of the following sketch. Abraham's faith/obedience (which has vicarious soteriological consequences for those who know him as father) ought to be understood not primarily as a paradigm for the faith of Christian believers but first of all as a prefiguration of the faith of Jesus Christ (cf. Rom 3:22), whose faith/obedience now has vicarious soteriological consequences for those who know him as Lord.[59] Broadly speaking, then, the relevance of Paul's appeal to the story of Abraham would lie in the fact that he finds there a precedent *within Scripture* for the idea that the faithfulness of a single divinely chosen protagonist can bring God's blessing upon "many" whose destiny is figured forth in that protagonist's action. In this respect Abraham serves for Paul not just as an exemplar of Christian believing but also as a typological foreshadowing of Christ, the "one man" (Rom 5:19) through whose obedience "the many were constituted righteous."

---

for the Christian Faith" (in *Ghetto*, 74-104): "In Rom. 4, with remarkable keenness, [Paul] tried to discover . . . what the essence of justification through faith was. In doing so he could not prevent the reference to Christ in the justification of the believer from becoming an accidental in the definition of the justification through faith" (102).

59. For an interpretation of Rom 3:21-26 in these terms, see Johnson, "Faith of Jesus," 87-90. Johnson suggests that "Rom 5:19 is the plain explication of Rom 3:21-26" (89).

Three Dramatic Roles:
The Law in Romans 3–4

Like the stone steps of an ancient university building, the topic "Paul and the Law" has been worn smooth by the passing of generations of scholars. I suspect that few of our remarks on this topic will be surprising or original. The aim of this essay, therefore, is to consolidate the results of recent study and to identify some areas of consensus as well as the major loci for continuing debate. We will attend particularly to Paul's statements about the Law in Rom 3–4 and then offer some judgments about the state of the question.

I propose three theses concerning the role of the Law within Paul's argument in Rom 3–4. Paul contends that: (a) the Law defines the identity of the Jewish people; (b) the Law pronounces condemnation on all humanity; and (c) the Law is an oracular witness that prefigures the righteousness of God disclosed in Jesus Christ. What I have to say about the first two theses is fairly straightforward and, I expect, relatively noncontroversial. The third thesis, however, may open up some issues that will require more detailed examination and debate.

The Law Defines the Identity of the Jewish People

In the first instance the term ὁ νόμος refers in Paul's usage to the Law given by Moses to Israel (Rom 9:4; 10:5). By prescribing distinctive standards of conduct, the Law simultaneously accomplishes two things: it positively discloses the will of God, and it marks off the elect people from other nations. Let us consider each of these points in turn.

First, the will of God is revealed in the Law, and the people of Israel are called to obey it unconditionally (cf. Deut 30:11-14) as an expression of their covenant relation to God. To be a member of God's people is to find oneself obligated to adhere to the norms articulated in the Mosaic Torah. That this covenant obligation was understood, within the context of Judaism, not as a burden but as a privilege[1] is clearly recognized in Paul's diatribal address to an imagined Jewish interlocutor who "boasts in the law" (Rom 2:23):

> But if you call yourself a Jew and rely on the Law and boast of your relation to God (καυχᾶσαι ἐν θεῷ) and know his will and determine what matters (τὰ διαφέροντα) because you are instructed in the Law, and if you are sure that you are a guide to the blind, a light to those who are in darkness, a corrector of the foolish, a teacher of children, having in the Law the embodiment of knowledge and truth, you, then, who teach others, will you not teach yourself? . . . You that boast in the law (ἐν νόμῳ καυχᾶσαι), do you dishonor God by breaking the Law? (Rom 2:17-21a, 23)

Knowing the will of God is, to be sure, not an unproblematic condition. Paul's argument challenges the Jewish reader to beware of a complacent sense of security that comes from having a special relation to God through the Law: it is only the *doers* of the Law who are to be justified (2:13).[2] The mere knowledge of the Law is of no value unless it is accompanied by obedience (cf. 2:25-29). Nonetheless, Paul never disputes the twin premises that the will of God is authentically revealed in the Law and that the Jew therefore possesses, through the Law, a privileged knowledge of what God requires (cf. 7:7-12; 9:1-5). This claim underlies Paul's apparently surprising assertion in 3:2 that "the advantage of the Jew" is "much in every way."

---

1. The work of E. P. Sanders (*Paul and Palestinian Judaism* [Philadelphia: Fortress, 1977]) has impressed this point upon Pauline scholarship. One hopes that the impression will prove indelible.

2. The well-known problems surrounding the relation of Rom 2 to the theology of justification expressed elsewhere in Paul cannot be pursued here. See, e.g., E. P. Sanders, *Paul, the Law, and the Jewish People* (Philadelphia: Fortress, 1983), 123-35; K. R. Snodgrass, "Justification by Grace — to the Doers: An Analysis of the Place of Romans 2 in the Theology of Paul," *NTS* 32 (1986): 72-93. N. T. Wright ("The Law in Romans 2," in *Paul and the Mosaic Law*, ed. J. D. G. Dunn, WUNT 89 [Tübingen: Mohr Siebeck, 1996], 131-50) offers an important proposal that may shed new light on these difficulties.

Even if "some were unfaithful," Israel — unlike pagans who are able to recognize God only through the created world (1:19-20) — has been given the benefit of knowing God's revealed will *expressis verbis*.

Second, the Law functions to set apart a particular people for God, a people who are to serve as "a light to those in darkness" (2:19, echoing Isa 49:6). Thus, one of the most salient features of the Law is its role as the creator of an *identity* for a particular people. That is why Paul can refer to the Jewish people with expressions such as οἱ ἐν τῷ νόμῳ (Rom 3:19) and οἱ ἐκ νόμου (4:14). Their identity is grounded in the Law; it provides the distinctive characteristics, the identity markers, that define the boundary between Israel and the Gentiles. The work of James D. G. Dunn has highlighted this identity-marking function;[3] he interprets "the works of the law" (3:20, 28; cf. 4:2-6) as a reference to "the social function of the law as marking out the people of the law in their distinctiveness."[4] Circumcision, dietary observance, and Sabbath keeping are the practices that most explicitly set the Jewish people apart from the rest of the world; thus, these practices symbolize the more comprehensive body of "works of the Law" that establish Jewish identity. This insight is critical to the interpretation of Rom 3–4, for it helps us understand that Paul's critique of "works of the Law" is not focused, as the Reformation supposed, on human efforts to achieve God's approval through "works righteousness." Instead, his critique of "boasting" targets the problem of ethnocentric exclusivism.

Michael Winger, in a recent study of the meaning of νόμος in Paul's letters, offers the following general definition of "Jewish νόμος": "Those words given to and possessed by the Jewish people, which guide and control those who accept them and according to which those who accept them are judged."[5] Or, as he rephrases his definition more succinctly, "Νόμος is what Jews do."[6] If indeed Νόμος is to be identified with the practices that constitute Jewish ethnic particularity — "what Jews do" — then it is not

---

3. See, e.g., Dunn, "Works of the Law and the Curse of the Law (Galatians 3:10-14)," *NTS* 31 (1985): 523-42; Dunn, *Romans 1–8*, WBC 38A (Dallas: Word, 1988), 153-55, 158-60; Dunn, "Yet Once More — 'The Works of the Law': A Response," *JSNT* 46 (1992): 100-104. Cf. also F. Watson, *Paul, Judaism, and the Gentiles*, SNTSMS 56 (Cambridge: Cambridge University Press, 1986).

4. Dunn, *Romans 1–8*, 159. For more extensive discussion see lxiii-lxxii.

5. Michael Winger, *By What Law? The Meaning of Νόμος in the Letters of Paul*, SBLDS 128 (Atlanta: Scholars, 1992), 104.

6. Winger, *By What Law?* 109.

difficult to understand why Paul resists the imposition of nomistic practices upon Gentiles who have come to trust in Jesus Christ.

Only when this understanding of νόμος is kept clearly in view does Paul's line of argument in Rom 3:27-31 come into focus. Boasting — i.e., Jewish ethnic pride in the Law (2:17, 23) — is excluded (3:27) by the gospel that declares that "there is no distinction" between Jew and Gentile, for all are justified by God's grace as a gift (3:22b-24). But such boasting can hardly be excluded by the Law "of works," which is itself the basis for Jewish distinctiveness. Paul therefore asserts, in a deft rhetorical play on words, that boasting is excluded διὰ νόμου πίστεως (3:27). The precise meaning of νόμος πίστεως is difficult to determine because the phrase, coined spontaneously by Paul here in counterpoint to νόμος τῶν ἔργων, does not appear elsewhere in his writings.[7] If, however, νόμος τῶν ἔργων means something like "Torah construed through the hermeneutical filter of distinctively Jewish practices," then its opposite, νόμος πίστεως, must mean "Torah construed through the hermeneutical filter of πίστις," the Law as read through the eyes of faith.[8] (A striking example of this sort of reading is given in 10:6-13.) To interpret the word νόμος in this formulation as having merely the generic meaning of "principle" or "rule" is to underinterpret Paul's theologically laden language and to disregard the fact that he has been consistently using νόμος to refer to Israel's Law.[9] The "Law" that excludes boasting is precisely the Law that Paul has already called as witness to humanity's universal implication in sin (3:10-20) and

---

7. Cf., however, analogous formulations such as ὁ νόμος τοῦ πνεύματος τῆς ζωῆς ἐν Χριστῷ Ἰησοῦ (Rom 8:2) and ὁ νόμος τοῦ Χριστοῦ (Gal 6:2).

8. See C. E. B. Cranfield (A Critical and Exegetical Commentary on the Epistle to the Romans, ICC [Edinburgh: T. & T. Clark, 1975], 1:219-20), H. Hübner (Law in Paul's Thought [Edinburgh: T. & T. Clark, 1984], 210), and Dunn (Romans 1–8, 185-87), all of whom hold that νόμος πίστεως refers to the Mosaic Law newly construed hermeneutically from the perspective of Christian faith. F. Thielman (Paul and the Law [Downers Grove, Ill.: IVP, 1994], 183) suggests that "the law of faith" is an expression equivalent to "the new covenant." This comes close to C. K. Barrett's suggestion that "here and elsewhere for Paul law (νόμος) means something like 'religious system'" (The Epistle to the Romans, HNTC [New York: Harper and Row, 1957]).

9. The position taken here represents a change of mind for me. The draft of this essay originally presented at the symposium was more receptive to interpreting νόμος πίστεως as "principle of faith," but I was persuaded by the group's subsequent discussion to adopt the view articulated in this paragraph. I would like to record my particular gratitude to Prof. Otfried Hofius for a helpful conversation on this issue.

as witness to God's saving righteousness (3:21-22). In other words, the Law *read as Paul has already claimed it should be read* is the νόμος πίστεως.

The rhetorical questions in 3:29 confirm that the phrase "works of the Law" must designate the distinctive markers of Jewish ethnic identity: "Or is God the God of Jews only? Is he not the God of Gentiles also?" If righteousness were attainable only through works of the Law (as embodied in circumcision and *kashrut*), then God would be — Paul suggests — the God of the Jews only, a tribal deity concerned only with a single people. But, Paul insists, it is not so. His argument against this view is based on a fundamental tenet of Israel's confession, articulated in the Shema: God is one. Paul concludes from this that God's way of dealing with Jews and Gentiles alike must finally be the same: "Since God is one, who will justify the circumcision on the ground of faith, he will also justify the uncircumcision through faith" (3:30).[10] Thus, the very fact that the Mosaic Law serves to identify Israel as a distinctive people disqualifies it from serving as the basis of God's more universal setting-right *(Rechtfertigung)* of all peoples.

This theological claim inevitably raises an objection that Paul anticipates in 3:31: "Do we then abolish the Law through this faith?" Almost everything Paul has said up to this point would lead us to expect him to say, "Yes, we do abolish the Law, and good riddance!" Instead, however, he introduces a dialectical reversal that has kept the heads of Christian thinkers spinning from his time to ours: "By no means! On the contrary we uphold the Law" (3:31). In what sense does the gospel uphold the Law? His discussion of Abraham in chapter 4 seeks to show that the νόμος πίστεως is consistent with the Law — now understood to mean, however, not the Mosaic covenant but Scripture taken as a *narrative* whole. This is the hermeneutical transmutation that allows Paul to claim continuity between Law and gospel. The story of Abraham, read through the lens of Gen 15:6, serves to reinforce the claims Paul has made about justification through faith; indeed, it clarifies that God justifies the ungodly (Rom 4:3-8). Furthermore, God reckoned Abraham righteous *prior to* his circumcision; therefore, he

10. My translation of the passage places a full stop at the end of v. 29, takes εἴπερ as the beginning of a new sentence, and reads καὶ ἀκροβυστίαν διὰ τῆς πίστεως as an elliptical clause requiring the verb δικαιώσει to be understood from the previous clause. This makes it clear that the justification of the uncircumcised through faith is a conclusion drawn from the premises that God is one and that God justifies the circumcised ἐκ πίστεως. For a fuller defense of this reading see R. B. Hays, "Have We Found Abraham to Be Our Forefather according to the Flesh?" *NovT* 27 (1985): 76-98; reprinted in the present volume (pp. 61-84).

stands symbolically as the "father" of uncircumcised believers as well as of circumcised believers who walk in the footsteps of his faith (4:9-12). All this demonstrates three points crucial to Paul's argument: (1) that the inheritance promised to Abraham is to be received not through adherence to the practices of the Law but solely through God's grace (4:13-17); (2) that the promise is for "the whole seed" of Abraham (παντὶ τῷ σπέρματι, 4:16), not just for the Jewish people; and (3) that the gospel is the narrative completion, rather than the nullification, of Law (= Scripture).[11] The implications of this hermeneutical shift must be left for consideration in the third part of this essay.

The Law Pronounces Condemnation

The second major function of the Law in Rom 3–4 is to pronounce judgment upon the unrighteousness of all human beings. Jews and Greeks alike are under the power of sin (ὑφ' ἁμαρτίαν, 3:9), and the Law discloses their true condition through its emphatic proclamation of judgment: "There is no one who is righteous, not even one." The catena of citations in 3:10-18 establishes that all humanity has turned away from God into disobedience and bloodshed.[12] (Interestingly, the emphasis in the catena lies upon deceptive speech and violence rather than the sexual offenses highlighted in 1:24-27.) Consequently, the whole world is "accountable to God," standing under God's righteous sentence of judgment (3:19-20; cf. 3:3-7).

Even here, however, Paul has introduced a distinctive hermeneutical "spin" on the texts he cites. As Dunn notes, the five Psalm citations in the catena (Pss 13:2-3; 5:10; 139:4; 9:28; 35:2, all LXX) are originally condemnations of Israel's enemies or of "the unrighteous" as distinguished from "the righteous." Paul has prefaced these with a universal indictment of human unrighteousness from Eccles 7:20 and interspersed a powerful passage from Isa 59:7-8 that prophetically decries Israel's unfaithfulness.[13] The re-

11. For further elaboration of my reading of the argument, see Hays, "Have We Found Abraham to Be Our Forefather according to the Flesh?"

12. For discussion of the composition of the catena, see L. E. Keck, "The Function of Romans 3:10-18 — Observations and Suggestions," in God's Christ and His People, ed. J. Jervell and W. A. Meeks, Festschrift for N. A. Dahl (Oslo, Bergen, and Tromsö: Universitetsforlaget, 1977), 141-57.

13. Dunn, Romans 1–8, 149-51.

sult of this composite citation is to convert the Psalm passages also into condemnations of Jews as well as Gentiles. Dunn sums up the effect: "[I]t is hard to doubt that Paul intended the Psalm citations as a turning of the tables on Jewish overconfidence in their nation's favored status before God. The very descriptions which the psalmist used for those outside God's favor and righteousness can be seen in the light of the Ecclesiastes and Isaiah passages as a self-description and self-condemnation."[14] Thus, the words of Scripture must be read in the spirit of humility demanded by Paul in Rom 2:1: "Therefore you have no excuse, whoever you are, when you judge others; for in passing judgment on another, you condemn yourself, because you, the judge, are doing the very same things."

Paul's hermeneutical warrant for reading these words of Scripture as addressed to Jews, not just to those outside the Law, is explained in 3:19: "Now we know that whatever the Law says, it speaks to those who are within the Law (τοῖς ἐν τῷ νόμῳ)." Although the citations are from Psalms, Ecclesiastes, and Isaiah, Paul treats these words as expressions of what "the Law says" (3:19), thereby demonstrating that he can sometimes treat the term νόμος as referring to Scripture as a whole, i.e., as a virtual synonym of γραφή.[15] (As we have already seen, this semantic linkage will be crucial for his argument in 3:31ff.) By reading these passages as the voice of "the Law," Paul establishes that the Law has the function of declaring condemnation on the whole world, "in order that every mouth might be stopped."[16] There can be no protest against God's justice, for the hypothetical protest (3:3-7) is answered decisively by appeal to the Law's indictment of human sin. Thus, θεοῦ δικαιοσύνη (3:5) is confirmed.

The case is rounded off by one more appeal to Scripture in 3:20: "For 'no human being will be justified in his sight' by works of the Law, for through the Law comes knowledge of sin." Here he is quoting Ps 143:2 (142:2 LXX), in its original context not a word of condemnation but of contrite appeal:

Do not enter into judgment with your servant,
for no one living is righteous before you.

---

14. Dunn, *Romans 1–8*, 151.
15. See also Gal 4:21; 1 Cor 14:21.
16. Cf. Gal 3:22a: "The Scripture locked all things up under sin. . . ."

To sharpen his point, Paul adds the words ἐξ ἔργων νόμου, not found in the psalm text. Theologically speaking, the addition is consonant with the emphasis of the psalm, which appeals to God's covenant faithfulness (ἀλήθεια) and righteousness (δικαιοσύνη) as the ground of the psalmist's hope (Ps 142:1 LXX). The prospect of vindication depends not upon human observance of the Law (or: not upon the practices of Jewish ethnic particularity) but upon God's gracious fidelity to his covenant promise. Thus, the use of Ps 143 anticipates the next turn in Paul's argument, his declaration that the answer to the human plight rests in "the righteousness of God."[17]

For the moment, however, Paul's point in Rom 3:20 is that "through the Law comes the knowledge of sin." This claim is explicated in 7:7-12, but it is perhaps a mistake to read the full psychological complexity of that discussion back into 3:20. In the immediate context, at the conclusion of the unit of thought in 3:9-20, "the knowledge of sin" seems to mean simply the awareness of standing under God's judgment — an awareness forced upon us by the Law's relentless condemnation.

That is perhaps also what Paul means by declaring enigmatically that "the Law brings wrath" (4:15): it announces "God's decree" (τὸ δικαίωμα τοῦ θεοῦ, 1:32), God's sentence of death upon a human race in rebellion against God (1:18-32). Alternatively, the Law may bring wrath in the sense of creating the conditions necessary for culpability, i.e., the knowledge of good and evil (cf. 5:13b: "sin is not reckoned when there is no law"). Either way, the Law, being associated with wrath and condemnation, is set in juxtaposition to faith and to the *promise* given to Abraham (4:13-17). The provocative rhetorical force of this move should not be overlooked. Against the common Jewish view that the Law is a secure foundation, a source of life and hope for the elect community,[18] Paul highlights its negative functions, its power to curse and condemn. Those who boast in the Law are confronted with the warning that the Law is not so easily domesticated, *nicht verfügbar.* Those who rely on the Law will find that it recoils upon them and calls them to account in unexpected ways. (One recalls Gal 4:21: "Tell me, you who are so eager to be under the Law, do you not hear the Law?")

Paul was not unacquainted with a positive view of the Law. Rom 2:17-

---

17. For elaboration of this argument, see R. B. Hays, "Psalm 143 and the Logic of Romans 3," *JBL* 99 (1980): 107-15; reprinted in the present volume (pp. 50-60).

18. See Hermann Lichtenberger, "Das Tora-Verständnis im Judentum zur Zeit des Paulus: Eine Skizze," in *Paul and the Mosaic Law,* 7-23.

24 and Phil 3:4-6 demonstrate that he knew perfectly well how the Law was typically seen in contemporary Judaism. He has chosen here in Romans, however, to focus on its awesome capacity to pronounce judgment and to bring condemnation by demanding a righteousness that it has no power to produce (cf. 8:3-4). It is important to see such statements about the Law both in the wider context of the letter and in relation to the letter's contingent argumentative purpose.[19] Paul is not stating a systematic doctrine of the Law; rather, in a deliberately provocative manner *he is seeking to destabilize an entrenched position that associates the Law with the privileged status of the elect Jewish people.* Consequently, he focuses with considerable rhetorical power on scriptural texts that demonstrate that the whole world is accountable to God and that "all have sinned and fall short of the glory of God" (3:23). At the same time, it must be emphasized that Paul is not merely employing cheap rhetorical tricks to discredit the Law; rather, his revisionary statements about its destructive power are a direct theological consequence of reading Scripture freshly through a new hermeneutical filter shaped by the cross and by the Gentile mission.

The Law Is an Oracular Witness

And yet, Paul's statements about the role of the Law are by no means entirely negative, even in Rom 3–4. Three passages in the text suggest a function of the Law distinguishable from the two functions we have already considered (defining a way of life for the Jewish people and pronouncing judgment on the world).

1. In 3:21 Paul affirms that although the righteousness of God has been disclosed apart from the Law (i.e., through Christ), it is nevertheless attested by the Law and the prophets (μαρτυρουμένη ὑπὸ τοῦ νόμου καὶ τῶν προφητῶν).

2. When Paul insists that through faith "we uphold the Law" (3:31) and then supports that claim by appealing to the story of Abraham, the "Law" being upheld seems to be not only the Shema (3:30a) but also the Pentateuchal narrative, construed as a prefiguration of the gospel.

---

19. Thielman *(Paul and the Law)* helpfully adopts the method of examining Paul's statements about the Law in each letter individually, seeking to demonstrate how Paul's handling of the issue is related to the contingent circumstances addressed.

3. In 3:2 Paul insists that the Jewish people do have an "advantage" (τὸ περισσὸν) because they were "entrusted with the oracles of God (τὰ λόγια τοῦ θεοῦ)." The term νόμος is not actually used here, but the context makes it clear that Scripture is meant.

These three passages share in common a view of the Law as proleptic, prefiguring the economy of salvation that is revealed in the gospel. This claim is explicit in the first and second of these texts, implicit in the third. Let us begin with the clearer instances before turning to Paul's unusual reference in 3:2 to "the oracles of God."

1. In what way is δικαιοσύνη θεοῦ attested by the Law and the prophets? Our earlier discussion has suggested one answer: Ps 142 LXX, quoted in Rom 3:20, contains two references to God's δικαιοσύνη as the focus of the psalmist's hope for deliverance. Especially noteworthy is Ps 142:11b LXX: ἐν τῇ δικαιοσύνῃ σου ἐξάξεις ἐκ θλίψεως τὴν ψυχήν μου ("By your righteousness you will rescue my life from affliction"). This subtext provides a metaleptic link between the plight evoked in 3:20 and the solution proclaimed in 3:21.[20] Paul quotes verse 2 of the psalm to declare that no one will be justified before God, but echoes recollecting God's righteousness ripple out from the citation and provide the new theme of the following sentence.

Of course, the idea of God's saving righteousness is hardly restricted to one OT psalm. Passages such as Ps 97:2-3 LXX and Isa 51:4-5 provide equally important background for Paul's thought. Let us consider the latter text as an example:

Hear me, hear, my people,
And kings, give ear to me.
For the Law (νόμος) will go forth from me,
And my judgment will go forth as a light to the Gentiles (ἐθνῶν).
My righteousness (ἡ δικαιοσύνη μου) draws near quickly,
And my salvation (τὸ σωτήριόν μου) will go forth as a light,
And in my arm will Gentiles (ἔθνη) hope.

It requires no great leap of the imagination to see how such a text stands behind Paul's declaration that the gospel is "the power of God for salvation

---

20. See R. B. Hays, *Echoes of Scripture in the Letters of Paul* (New Haven: Yale University Press, 1989), 51-53.

(εἰς σωτηρίαν) to everyone who trusts, to the Jew first and also to the Greek. For in it the righteousness of God (δικαιοσύνη θεοῦ) is revealed through faith for faith" (Rom 1:16-17). Consequently, to say that the Law and the prophets bear witness to δικαιοσύνη θεοῦ is simply to say that the promise of God's righteousness as a saving power for all nations is already explicitly announced in OT texts such as the ones just cited. (In passing, we should note that this simple observation of the announcement of God's saving righteousness in the Psalms and in Isaiah ought to put an end to the old Bultmann-Käsemann debate over δικαιοσύνη θεοῦ: Käsemann was right to say that God's righteousness is God's eschatological saving power but wrong to dissociate it from God's covenant faithfulness to Israel. It was also unnecessary to argue, as Käsemann did, that δικαιοσύνη θεοῦ was a *terminus technicus* in Jewish apocalyptic.[21] One need not ferret it out of Qumran texts; it is already explicitly present in OT texts from which Paul quotes extensively in this letter.)

Apart from such specific references to God's righteousness, the Law (= Scripture) also bears witness more generally, in Paul's understanding, to the gospel.[22] In the salutation of Romans, Paul declares that "the gospel of God" was "promised beforehand through his prophets in holy writings concerning his Son, who was descended from David according to the flesh" (1:1-3). English translations usually treat the prepositional phrase περὶ τοῦ υἱοῦ αὐτοῦ as a modifier of εὐαγγέλιον, but this is an artificial expedient designed to spare Paul the embarrassment of having claimed that the Scriptures are "about" Jesus Christ. In fact, however, anyone hearing Paul's sentence read aloud in Greek would naturally hear περὶ τοῦ υἱοῦ αὐτοῦ as modifying γραφαῖς ἁγίαις. Hence: "holy scriptures concerning his Son. . . ." The formula may of course be pre-Pauline, but there is no reason to suppose that Paul, along with other early Christians, did not believe that the OT pointed to Jesus. Indeed, elsewhere he asserts it as a matter of the first importance that the death and resurrection of Jesus occurred "according to the Scriptures" (1 Cor 15:3-4), and in a passage such as Rom 15:3 he assumes that Christ is the speaker in Ps 69, without feeling the need to supply any supporting argument for this extraordinary assertion.[23]

21. E. Käsemann, "Gottesgerechtigkeit bei Paulus," *ZTK* 58 (1961): 367-78.

22. Cf. D.-A. Koch, *Die Schrift als Zeuge des Evangeliums: Untersuchungen zur Verwendung und zum Verständnis der Schrift bei Paulus*, BHT 69 (Tübingen: J. C. B. Mohr [Paul Siebeck], 1986).

23. On Paul's reading of the Psalms as utterances of Christ, see R. B. Hays, "Christ Prays

The conclusion that follows from such observations is that the whole question of Paul's reading of Scripture as a witness to Jesus Christ demands careful attention.[24] The participial phrase μαρτυρουμένη ὑπὸ τοῦ νόμου καὶ τῶν προφητῶν is not explicated fully at Rom 3:22, but it may be a clue pointing to a hermeneutical substructure that is fundamental to Paul's interpretation of the Law. If so, the meaning of Rom 10:4 ("Christ is the τέλος of the law") would need to be considered afresh.

2. Paul's reading of the story of Abraham seeks to "uphold the Law" by showing that the gospel of righteousness through faith is prefigured in the Law, that is, in the Genesis narrative. Obviously, such a construal of the Law is possible only in light of a profound hermeneutical shift. This shift has at least two important dimensions.

First, Paul shifts from a reading of Law as *commandment* to a reading of Law as *narrative of promise*. As James A. Sanders has characterized this shift, Paul reads Torah not as halakah but as haggadah.[25] As I have stated the matter on an earlier occasion:

> Paul finds the continuity between Torah and Gospel through a hermeneutic that reads Scripture primarily as a *narrative* of divine election and promise. God is the protagonist in the story, the one who has formed and sustained Israel from Abraham onward . . . , and God's righteousness is the ground of the narrative unity between Law and gospel. . . . God's act in Jesus Christ illuminates, Paul contends, a previously uncomprehended narrative unity in Scripture. That is the burden of the argument in Romans 3 and 4: God has shown forth his righteousness in a new way in Christ, apart from Law, but the Law and the Prophets bear witness that this unforeseen act of grace is the supremely fitting climactic action of the same God whose character and purposes are disclosed in the narrative of his past dealings with Israel. . . . Moses and the Law of

---

the Psalms: Paul's Use of an Early Christian Exegetical Convention," in *The Future of Christology*, ed. A. J. Malherbe and W. A. Meeks (Minneapolis: Fortress, 1993), 122-36; reprinted in the present volume (pp. 101-18).

24. This *pace* my own earlier dictum that Paul's hermeneutic is "ecclesiocentric" rather than "christocentric" (*Echoes*, 84-121). For qualifying remarks to this position, see R. B. Hays, "On the Rebound: A Response to Critiques of *Echoes of Scripture in the Letters of Paul*," in *Paul and the Scriptures of Israel*, ed. C. A. Evans and J. A. Sanders, JSNTSup 83 (Sheffield: JSOT Press, 1992), 72-96, esp. 77-78; reprinted in the present volume (pp. 163-89).

25. J. A. Sanders, "Torah and Christ," *Int* 29 (1975): 372-90.

Sinai are assigned a temporary supporting role, not the lead, in the drama of God's redemptive purpose. Thus, the Torah is neither superseded nor nullified but transformed into a witness of the gospel.[26]

By moving the Abraham story into the hermeneutical center of attention, Paul argues that the Law is first of all the vehicle of God's covenant promise, a promise that extends to all nations, far beyond the more limited scope of the nation defined by the Sinai covenant.

Second, the promise expressed in Scripture's narrative is a word addressed immediately to the church of Paul's own time. Paul repeatedly assumes that the word of Scripture is addressed directly to himself and his readers, as he explains in a pair of important hermeneutical maxims:

These things happened to them τυπικῶς, and they were written down for our instruction, upon whom the ends of the ages have met. (1 Cor 10:11)

For whatever was pre-written was written for our instruction, so that by steadfastness and by the encouragement of the Scriptures we might have hope. (Rom 15:4)

Paul's point is not just that Scripture is profitable for doctrinal instruction, as in 2 Tim 3:16-17. Rather, he regards Scripture as a living voice speaking directly to the community.[27]

This is the sort of hermeneutic that is at work in Paul's reading of the Abraham story. The story is not merely an example of how God deals with human beings; instead, it is a word of promise addressed directly to Paul's readers, who are themselves Abraham's seed: "Now the words ἐλογίσθη αὐτῷ were not written for his sake alone, but also for our sake to whom it [righteousness] is going to be reckoned, to those who trust in the one who raised Jesus our Lord from the dead" (Rom 4:23-24). Thus the "Law" — the Abraham story — must be read as pointing forward to realities that can be discerned only retrospectively from within the community of faith — the

---

26. Hays, *Echoes,* 157.

27. For extended discussion see Hays, *Echoes,* 116-17, 165-68; H. Hübner, *Gottes Ich und Israel: Zum Schriftgebrauch des Paulus in Römer 9–11,* FRLANT 136 (Göttingen: Vandenhoeck & Ruprecht, 1984).

community that the Law always aimed to bring into being. From within the community of faith, the Law qua narrative is seen to *prefigure* the gospel and the church.

3. Finally, we must consider the meaning of Rom 3:2, in which Paul, using an expression unparalleled elsewhere in his letters, refers to τὰ λόγια τοῦ θεοῦ. The expression does occur in the OT, often in contexts where obedience to or defiance of God's word is emphasized: for example, Ps 107:10-11:

> Some sat in darkness and in gloom,
> prisoners in misery and in irons,
> for they had rebelled against the words of God
>   (LXX: τὰ λόγια τοῦ θεοῦ),
> and spurned the counsel of the Most High.

Thus, even though the expression τὰ λόγια τοῦ θεοῦ is unusual in Paul, it is consonant with his general fondness for OT diction, and it fits nicely into the immediate context of Rom 3:1-3, where Israel's unfaithfulness is being emphasized.[28]

However, the word λόγια in general Greek usage referred to the utterances of an oracle. (Philo frequently uses the term as a description of the content of Scripture, thereby stressing its divinely inspired character; he uses this language to refer not only to direct utterances of God but also to other passages in the narrative. See, for example, *De Abrahamo* 62; *De vita Mosis* 1.57 [used in synonymous parallelism with χρησμοί, as also in *De virtutibus* 63]; *De vita Mosis* 2.176; *De migratione Abrahami* 85, 166.)[29] This connotative nuance cannot have escaped Paul and his readers. Dunn's comment on the passage highlights the implications of Paul's particular word choice here:

---

28. Cf. also the use of τὸ λόγιον τοῦ ἁγίου Ἰσραηλ in Isa 5:24 LXX, in synonymous parallelism to τὸν νόμον κυρίου σαβαωθ.

29. For discussion of Philo's fondness for describing scriptural passages as "oracles," see H. Burkhardt, *Die Inspiration heiliger Schriften bei Philo von Alexandrien* (Giessen and Basel: Brunnen Verlag, 1988), 111-25, especially on λόγια, 119-22. See also Y. Amir, "Authority and Interpretation of Scripture in the Writings of Philo," in *Mikra: Text, Translation, Reading, and Interpretation of the Hebrew Bible in Ancient Judaism and Early Christianity*, ed. M. J. Mulder, CRINT (Assen and Maastricht: Van Gorcum; Minneapolis: Fortress, 1990), 421-53, especially 429-32.

[F]or a gentile readership the word "oracle" would evoke the thought of inspired utterances preserved from the past, often mysterious and puzzling in character, awaiting some key to unlock their meaning. Paul may well imply then that the Jews had been entrusted with the stewardship of safeguarding and preserving these oracles of God until the coming of the key, that is, the gospel of Christ Jesus, which unlocked the mystery of what had always been God's purpose but which had remained hidden hitherto until this time of the End (cf. 11:25-27; 16:25-26).[30]

In light of our foregoing observations about Law/Scripture as a proleptic prefiguration of the gospel, Dunn's reading is richly suggestive as an exegesis of Rom 3:2. I would add only one further point: the statement that the Jewish people had been "*entrusted* with the oracles of God (ἐπιστεύθησαν τὰ λόγια τοῦ θεοῦ)" also adumbrates Paul's later reflections in Rom 9–11 on the dialectical mystery of the relation between the Jewish people and Gentile believers. The Jews are entrusted with the oracular utterances of Scripture precisely *for the Gentiles,* who will ultimately receive these oracles as words spoken directly to and for them.[31]

One function of the Law, then — perhaps its most important function for Paul — is to point forward to the coming of Christ and to God's intent to call Jews and Gentiles together into a community that simultaneously confirms the fidelity of God and glorifies God for his mercy (cf. Rom 15:7-9). Readers of the Law who understand *that* meaning of the Law have truly understood the τέλος of the Law; readers who do not understand this prefigurative, oracular function of the Law remain ignorant of "the righteousness that comes from God" (10:3-4).

Conclusion

It remains to ask how the three functions of the Law that we have seen in Rom 3–4 fit together — if at all. The answer, I would suggest, is complex; the three functions are not complementary aspects of a single systematic doctrine. Rather, we see within Romans Paul's movement from one

---

30. Dunn, *Romans 1–8,* 138-39.

31. In our discussion of this passage at the symposium, this point was brought out with particular clarity by N. T. Wright.

hermeneutical perspective to another. The Law originally had the primary function of *defining the identity of God's elect people,* the Jews. Within that hermeneutical perspective, the Law was understood primarily as *commandment.* Because Paul became convinced, however, that the death and resurrection of Jesus was an apocalyptic event that had brought the old world order to an end, he moved to an entirely new hermeneutical perspective, within which the Law functioned primarily as *promise and narrative prefiguration of the gospel.* In between these two hermeneutical worlds stands the function of the Law as *pronouncing condemnation on the world.* Such a view (Law as word of condemnation) corresponds neither to Judaism's account of the purpose of the Law nor to Paul's distinctively Christian position that sees the Law as a positive foreshadowing of the righteousness of God. Perhaps then we should see Paul's account of the condemning function of the Law as *a transitional rhetorical move* in an argument designed to deconstruct Jewish "boasting" in the Law by showing how the Law itself undercuts confidence in anything other than God's radical grace.

If that is correct, then we should see Paul's account of the functions of the Law as narratively ordered in a three-act drama. In act 1 the Law defines the will of God and shapes the identity of a people who are summoned to live in accordance with God's revealed will. In act 2 it becomes clear that even the covenant people cannot stand before the radical demand of God's holiness. All fall short, and the Law pronounces sentence of condemnation upon them, as well as upon the rest of the world. In act 3, however, God acts for the salvation of the world through the death and resurrection of Jesus. In light of this event, everything is redefined and the Law assumes an entirely new role as witness and herald of God's saving righteousness. In each act the Law is God's servant, playing a different role — serving, as it were, as Ariel to God's Prospero. (And perhaps — like Ariel — finally being dismissed to join "the elements" when his service is completed.)[32] Ὁ νόμος is always the same collection of texts, but the import of those texts shifts dramatically in accordance with the hermeneutical perspective at each stage of the unfolding drama.

---

32. W. Shakespeare, *The Tempest,* act 5, scene 1; cf. Gal 4:9.

Christ Prays the Psalms:
Israel's Psalter as Matrix of Early Christology

In *Echoes of Scripture in the Letters of Paul,* I argued that Paul's use of the Old Testament is characterized by "ecclesiocentric hermeneutics": unlike Matthew, John, Justin Martyr, and other early Christian writers, he is not normally concerned to find christological proof texts in the Old Testament. What Paul finds in Scripture, above all else, is a prefiguration of the *church* as the people of God. We rarely find him using Scripture to define the identity of Jesus Christ or to reflect theologically about it.

But what about the exceptions to this generalization? Paul does, after all, insist that the death and resurrection of Jesus took place "in accordance with the Scriptures" (1 Cor 15:3-4). What about those texts in which Paul does interpret Israel's Scripture christologically? How is he using these texts, and why is he able to read them in this new, imaginative way? What sort of exegetical tradition is he presupposing, and what sort of hermeneutical transformation of that tradition has taken place in his hands? This essay will consider some of these passages — with a particular focus on Rom 15:3 — and consider their implications for the earliest formation of New Testament Christology.

Who Is Praying Here? The Problem in Romans 15

In Rom 15:3 Paul appeals to Scripture in a way that differs notably from his usual practice. Not only does he — uncharacteristically — read a passage from the Psalms as a reference to Christ,[1] but he also attributes the words

---

1. See my discussion of Paul's ecclesiocentric hermeneutics in R. B. Hays, *Echoes of Scripture in the Letters of Paul* (New Haven: Yale University Press, 1989), esp. 84-87.

THE CONVERSION OF THE IMAGINATION

of the psalm directly *to* Christ. In Paul's reading of Ps 69:9, it is the Christ,[2] speaking in the first person, who addresses God through the words of the biblical text. "We who are powerful ought to bear the weaknesses of the powerless and not to please ourselves. Let each of us please our neighbor for the good purpose of building up [the community].[3] For the Christ did not please himself; but, as it is written, 'The insults of those who insult you have fallen on me'" (Rom 15:1-3). Surprisingly, Paul does not seek to explain or justify his identification of the psalmist's first-person singular pronoun with the figure of the Christ. Thus, the christological interpretation of this psalm must have been an established tradition in early Christianity before Paul's writing of Romans.

Although the portrayal of Christ as the praying voice of the Psalms seems anomalous in Paul, we find the same hermeneutical device repeated just a few sentences later, when the "I" of Ps 18:49 is again taken as the voice of Christ:[4] "For I tell you that the Christ has become a servant of the circumcised for the sake of the truthfulness of God in order that he might confirm the promises given to the patriarchs, and in order that the Gentiles might glorify God for his mercy. As it is written, 'Therefore I will confess you among the Gentiles, and sing praises to your name'" (Rom 15:8-9). The notion of Christ as one who confesses and sings among the Gentiles appears so odd that some commentators have balked at it. Ernst Käsemann reads Rom 15:9b as Paul's reference to his own apostolic ministry among the Gentiles.[5] Dietrich-Alex Koch, after first tentatively agreeing with Käsemann, backs cautiously away from the suggestion: "Doch ist es überhaupt fraglich ob Pls, der ja primär an der Feststellung des Bereichs des Gotteslobs interessiert ist, das Zitat darüber hinaus mit einer derart

---

2. J. D. G. Dunn (*Romans 9–16*, WBC 38B [Dallas: Word, 1988], 840) rightly insists that the definite article in the expression ὁ Χριστός should be given weight here and in v. 7: the term is a title, not a proper name.

3. The NRSV seriously misconstrues Paul's πρὸς οἰκοδομὴν by reading it individualistically: "building up the neighbor." Paul's use of the term οἰκοδομή always has the community in view. Here and elsewhere in this chapter, the translation of the biblical text is my own.

4. So, e.g., C. E. B. Cranfield, *A Critical and Exegetical Commentary on the Epistle to the Romans*, ICC (Edinburgh: T. & T. Clark, 1979), 2:745-46; U. Wilckens, *Der Brief an die Römer*, 3 vols., EKKNT 6/3 (Zürich, Einsiedeln, and Cologne: Benziger; Neukirchen-Vluyn: Neukirchener Verlag, 1982), 3:108.

5. E. Käsemann, *Commentary on Romans* (Grand Rapids: Eerdmans, 1980), 386-87.

präzisen Interpretation verbunden hat."[6] James D. G. Dunn proposes that "these are the words of the devout Jew (David) foreshadowing the situation of the diaspora Jew, and now particularly of the Jewish Christian."[7]

These interpretations, however, weaken the connection of the four quotations in verses 9b-12 to their immediate context. In verses 7-9a, just as in verses 1-3, Christ has been held up as an example to be emulated: he has welcomed Jew and Gentile together. The function, then, of the citations in verses 9b-12 is to represent Christ as standing in the midst of an eschatological congregation composed of both Gentiles and Jews (see especially v. 10, quoting Deut 32:43), offering praise to God.[8] (This interpretation also explains why Paul's quotation in verse 9b, which otherwise follows Ps 17:50 LXX exactly, omits the vocative κύριε: it is the κύριος who speaks.) Thus, in some respects the passage closely resembles Heb 2:11-13.[9] The καθὼς γέγραπται (v. 9) links the string of Scripture citations not just to the preceding infinitive phrase (τὰ δὲ ἔθνη ὑπὲρ ἐλέους δοξάσαι) but also to the main assertion of the previous sentence (λέγω γὰρ Χριστὸν διάκονον γεγενῆσθαι περιτομῆς).

Leander Keck has suggested that the first three of the four citations in the catena of verses 9b-12 may originally have come from a separate source in which the "I" is to be understood as the preexistent Christ "declaring in advance the purpose of his incarnation."[10] It is difficult to see how this proposal accounts for the second and third quotations (vv. 10-11), and I shall challenge the suggestion that the psalm's words should be construed

---

6. D.-A. Koch, *Die Schrift als Zeuge des Evangeliums: Untersuchungen zur Verwendung und zum Verständnis der Schrift bei Paulus*, BHT 69 (Tübingen: Mohr-Siebeck, 1986), 282 n. 24.

7. Dunn, *Romans 9–16*, 849. Dunn's observation that the words of the psalm are specifically, in their Old Testament context, to be understood as the words of *David* is important; its significance will be developed further below.

8. The imitation theme, of course, began explicitly in 15:3. If Dunn is right that κατὰ Χριστὸν Ἰησοῦν in v. 5 also suggests "conduct modeled 'after Christ'" (*Romans 9–16*, 840), then the theme runs through this whole section of the text. And might we surmise that the exemplary character of Christ's sacrificial self-giving is already implicit in the σύγκρισις embedded in 14:15: "Do not let *your* food destroy that one for whom *Christ* died"?

9. The parallel is noted also by L. E. Keck, "Christology, Soteriology, and the Praise of God (Romans 15:7-13)," in *The Conversation Continues: Studies in Paul and John: In Honor of J. Louis Martyn*, ed. R. T. Fortna and B. R. Gaventa (Nashville: Abingdon, 1990), 93. For further discussion of the Hebrews passage, see below.

10. Keck, "Christology," 93.

as issuing from the *preexistent* Christ; nonetheless, Keck has rightly discerned a pre-Pauline exegetical tradition here and has called our attention to the need for a careful reconsideration of this peculiar but crucial portion of the Letter to the Romans.[11]

Why does Paul hear the voice of Jesus Christ in Pss 69 and 18? How can he assume that his readers will understand and accept this revisionary reading of Israel's psalter? What is the rhetorical effect created here by Paul's seeming departure from his more characteristic ecclesiocentric reading strategy? Finally, how will attention to these issues help us to understand the line of argument in Rom 15?

Keck sees the passage as so riddled with internal tensions that he must propose several layers of source material to account for it, including a gloss (15:4) by the hand of a later editor.[12] In this essay, however, I shall contend that delving into Paul's intertextual hermeneutics will enable us to trace some of the roots of Paul's Christology and, at the same time, clarify the logic of the passage as it stands.[13]

Christ as Speaker in the Psalms: Other Instances

Although Rom 15 appears to be an isolated case of christological ventriloquism in Paul's writings,[14] the technique is by no means unparalleled in the New Testament. There are several passages where analogous treatments of psalm texts as utterances of Christ appear. Since the Romans passage may well reflect pre-Pauline tradition, a preliminary survey of some of the most important non-Pauline examples may shed light on the convention that Paul presupposes.

After his account of Jesus' symbolic protest action against the merchants and money changers in the temple, the Fourth Evangelist reports

11. Despite the fact that Rom 15:7-13 functions as the *peroratio* for the letter as a whole, reprising its central themes, remarkably little attention is given to the passage by many of the standard commentaries; Käsemann and Dunn are notable exceptions to this generalization.

12. L. E. Keck, "Romans 15:4 — an Interpolation?" in *Faith and History: Essays in Honor of Paul W. Meyer,* ed. J. T. Carroll, C. H. Cosgrove, and E. E. Johnson (Atlanta: Scholars, 1991), 125-36.

13. Thus, this essay continues a long-running conversation with Lee Keck, who has been for me a teacher, a colleague, and an example to be imitated.

14. See, however, the discussion of 2 Cor 4:13 below.

that Jesus' disciples "remembered that it is written, 'Zeal for your house will eat me up'" (John 2:17, quoting Ps 69:9). Although Jesus is not represented in John's Gospel as having spoken these words at the time of his temple action, the quotation makes sense here only if the disciples understand the "me" of the psalm to be Jesus himself.[15] John does not, however, shape the narrative so as to put these words directly into Jesus' mouth; in all likelihood, he understood the psalm as a prophetic *prefiguration* of Jesus Christ. This would be consonant with his general tendency to see Old Testament figures such as Moses and Isaiah as having written "about" (περὶ) Jesus (John 5:46; 12:41).

It is of considerable interest that John 2:17 quotes the other half of the same psalm verse that Paul quotes in Rom 15:3. C. H. Dodd took this as an important piece of evidence for his hypothesis that the earliest church focused on certain key Old Testament passages, such as Ps 69, as seminal tracts for the development of Christology.[16] The detail of Jesus' thirst in the passion narrative (John 19:28) is apparently likewise seen by the Fourth Evangelist as a fulfillment of Ps 69.

The Markan passion narrative employs a more daring hermeneutical strategy: the dying Jesus actually utters the opening words of Ps 22, "My God, my God, why have you forsaken me?"[17] Earlier, in the Garden of Gethsemane, Mark's Jesus had voiced his anguish by using the words of Ps 42:6, 12: περίλυπός ἐστιν ἡ ψυχή μου. Here the narrative takes the Psalms utterances up into direct discourse. Unlike John, Mark does not call the reader's attention to this discourse as a species of performative utterance that forges

---

15. The evangelist's remark in v. 22 that it was only after the resurrection that the disciples remembered and "believed the Scripture and the word that Jesus had spoken" should probably be understood to apply to v. 17 as well as to v. 19. Otherwise, why the reference to believing the *Scripture?* On this point see R. B. Hays, "Reading Scripture in Light of the Resurrection," in E. F. Davis and R. B. Hays, *The Art of Reading Scripture* (Grand Rapids: Eerdmans, 2003), 221-24.

16. C. H. Dodd, *According to the Scriptures: The Sub-structure of New Testament Theology* (London: Nisbet, 1952), 57-60.

17. I do not necessarily mean to suggest that this is purely a matter of Mark's literary invention. It is not unreasonable to suppose that a faithful Jew in death's agony might find such words welling up; if so, and if Jesus' cry was heard and remembered, the allusion might have become a clue that sparked more extensive christological interpretation of the Psalms in the post-Easter community. It is beyond the scope of this chapter, however, to explore this question. See H. Gese, "Psalm 22 und das Neue Testament," in *Vom Sinai zu Zion*, BevT 64 (Munich: Chr. Kaiser, 1974), 180-201.

typological links with Scripture; still, despite the lack of overt authorial comment, the typological correlation is both evident and powerful. The linkage is reinforced by a series of narrated correspondences between Ps 22 and the details of Jesus' execution: Mark 15:24/Ps 22:18, Mark 15:30-32/Ps 22:7-8, and perhaps Mark 15:36/Ps 22:15. Jesus, in his death, enacts the destiny of the Righteous Sufferer whose voice is heard at prayer in the Psalms.[18]

The force of this hermeneutical convention within early Christianity is further demonstrated by Luke's redactional modification of the Markan death scene: finding Mark 15:34 incommensurable with his Christology, Luke replaces the cry of Ps 22:1 with the trusting declaration of Ps 31:5, another royal psalm of suffering: "Into your hands I commit my spirit." Thus, Luke achieves a reinterpretation of Jesus' death while abiding within the convention of reading the lament psalms as utterances of Christ.

The tradition that Jesus Christ was/is the speaker in Ps 22 generates a different use of this text in the Letter to the Hebrews. "For it was fitting for [God], on account of whom and through whom all things exist, in bringing many sons to glory, to perfect τὸν ἀρχηγόν ('the captain' or 'the pioneer') of their salvation through sufferings. For the one who sanctifies and those who are sanctified all come from One. That is why he is not ashamed to call them brothers, saying, 'I will proclaim your name to my brothers; in the midst of the congregation I will sing hymns to you'" (Heb 2:10-12, quoting Ps 22:22). The writer of Hebrews here cites the triumphant climax of Ps 22 as an utterance of the risen Christ standing in the midst of the congregation of God's people. Here surely the citation of Ps 22:22 presupposes the wider context of the psalm as a whole: the triumphant figure who prays and sings in the midst of the congregation (22:21b-31) is precisely the one who has endured mockery and sufferings (22:1-2a). The quotation serves to confirm the solidarity of Christ with his people, and this solidarity emerges not only from the fact that the Christ of Ps 22 (if we may put the matter thus) calls them brothers but also from the fact that he is united with them in suffering, as the rest of the psalm demonstrates.

Finally, Heb 10:5-7 reads Ps 40:7-9 as words spoken by Christ εἰσερχόμενος εἰς τὸν κόσμον: in place of burnt offerings and sin offerings,

18. This interpretation of Jesus' death is proposed by Lothar Ruppert, *Jesus als der leidende Gerechte?* SBS 59 (Stuttgart: KBW, 1972). The various Old Testament citations and allusions in the Markan passion narrative are scrutinized by J. Marcus, *The Way of the Lord: Christological Exegesis of the Old Testament in the Gospel of Mark* (Philadelphia: Westminster, 1992).

he offers himself in obedience as a sacrifice: "See, I have come (in the scroll of the book it is written about me) to do your will, O God."

This quick survey of familiar texts demonstrates how widespread was the hermeneutical convention of hearing Christ's voice in the Psalms: John, the Synoptics,[19] and Hebrews all bear witness, independently of Paul and of one another, to this interpretive tradition. Furthermore, all of them presuppose this remarkable convention without comment or justification, just as Paul does in Rom 15; evidently, this exegetical strategy was embedded in Christian reading of the Scriptures from the earliest identifiable time.[20] (The import of this observation for understanding the development of Christology in the early church is a matter that merits further investigation.) Rom 15:3 and 15:9, then, should be seen not as aberrations but as instances of a common early Christian tradition.

The passages surveyed here draw from a select group of the "psalms of David" (Pss 18; 22; 31; 40; 42; 69) that describe the unjust suffering of the righteous king and celebrate the hope, or experience, of God's deliverance of the sufferer. Furthermore, every one of these psalms is introduced in the LXX by the enigmatic superscription εἰς τὸ τέλος (rendering the Hebrew למנצח). Whatever this superscription may have meant originally, it is not hard to see how early Christian interpreters, reading the LXX, might have understood it as a hermeneutical instruction to construe these texts eschatologically.[21]

Traces of the Tradition in Paul

Once we see how pervasive the christological reading of the lament psalms is, we can identify other places in which Paul may be employing or presup-

---

19. To complete the roster of the evangelists, we could add to the list Matt 13:34-35, quoting Ps 78:2.

20. It would be speculation — but not implausible speculation — to suppose that the earliest extant formulation of the kerygma (1 Cor 15:3-5) has precisely the royal lament psalms in mind when it affirms that the death and resurrection of Jesus occurred κατὰ τὰς γραφάς.

21. On the problem of the psalm titles, see B. S. Childs, "Psalm Titles and Midrashic Exegesis," *JSS* 16 (1971): 137-50. On the messianic and eschatological trajectory of psalm interpretation, see Childs, *Introduction to the Old Testament as Scripture* (Philadelphia: Fortress, 1979), 515-18.

posing the same hermeneutical device. For instance, the citation of Ps 69:22-23 in Rom 11:9-10 assumes greater cogency when we consider the convention of reading this psalm as a portrayal of Christ's passion:[22] Israel's culpability is enhanced by its identification with enemies of the Righteous Sufferer. This link may lie behind the designation in Rom 11:28 of Israel as temporary ἐχθροί; compare the use of this term in Ps 69:4, 18 (= Ps 68:5, 19 LXX).

Another obscure Pauline passage, 2 Cor 4:13-14, is greatly clarified if we see in it another instance of Christ as the praying voice in the psalm quotation:[23] Ἔχοντες δὲ τὸ αὐτὸ πνεῦμα τῆς πίστεως — κατὰ τὸ γεγραμμένον· **ἐπίστευσα, διὸ ἐλάλησα** — καὶ ἡμεῖς πιστεύομεν, διὸ καὶ λαλοῦμεν, εἰδότες ὅτι ὁ ἐγείρας τὸν κύριον Ἰησοῦν καὶ ἡμᾶς σὺν Ἰησοῦ ἐγερεῖ. The whole passage (2 Cor 4:7-15) is a description of Paul's apostolic ministry and sufferings as an embodiment of the sufferings of Christ: ". . . always carrying around in the body the dying of Jesus, in order that the life of Jesus might be made manifest in your (ὑμῶν) body" (v. 10). Thus, Paul describes his own experience as a recapitulation of the christological paradigm. If we read Paul's citation of Ps 116:10 (= 115:1 LXX) as an utterance of Christ,[24] then the pattern plays itself through fully:

Jesus	*Paul*
died so that others might have life	suffers so that others have life
trusted and spoke	trusts and speaks
God raised him from the dead	will be raised with Jesus

Furthermore, at least two features of Ps 115 LXX might encourage Paul to interpret it christologically, even though it lacks the heading εἰς τὸ τέλος: (1) the "plot" of the psalm is the typical lament movement from abasement to praise; indeed, some of the vocabulary here is reminiscent of the Christ hymn of Phil 2 (ἐταπεινώθην, v. 1; δοῦλος, v. 7); and (2) the language of verses 4-6 could readily be construed as a prefiguration of the Lord's Sup-

22. As we have already seen, Rom 15:3 demonstrates Paul's assumption of exactly such a reading of this psalm. In Rom 11:9, however, the speaker is said to be David rather than Christ. For reasons that will be discussed below, the two voices seem to be virtually interchangeable.

23. This interpretation was first suggested, so far as I am aware, by A. T. Hanson, *Paul's Understanding of Jesus* (Hull: University of Hull Publications, 1963), 11-13.

24. Cf. the closely analogous quotation of the last clause of Isa 8:17 (LXX) in Heb 2:13a.

per as a means of proclaiming the Lord's death: "I will take the cup of salvation and call upon the name of the Lord. . . . Precious before the Lord is the death of his holy ones."

It seems probable, therefore, that 2 Cor 4:13 should be added to the list of passages in which the New Testament writer hears Christ praying in the psalm text. In this passage, as in the others we have noted, Paul makes no attempt to explain or defend his christological reading; it is treated as *selbstverständlich*. If it is less so for belated readers twenty centuries later, that is because we lack the necessary hermeneutical key: that ὁ Χριστός (Rom 15:3, 7) is the true and ultimate speaker of Israel's laments and praises.

Unless the rhetoric whereby Paul deploys these messianic psalms is misleading and manipulative (introducing novel claims under the tacit pretense that of course everyone already knows these things), we must assume that such readings were common in the earliest strata of tradition that we can identify. The typological messianic reading of the lament psalms may also underlie the pre-Pauline formula of Rom 1:2-4, which asserts that the gospel was "pre-promised through his prophets in holy writings concerning his Son, who came from the seed of David."[25] What writings? This notorious puzzle receives a satisfying answer if we suppose that these royal psalms are prominent among the writings in question: hence the reference to "seed of David." Whether that hunch is correct or not, it is indisputable that 1 Cor 15:25-27 presupposes a christological reading of Pss 8 and 110. Both are psalms of David, and the connection of Ps 110 to the Davidic kingship tradition is familiar as a topic of controversy in early Christianity (cf. Mark 12:35-37; Acts 2:33-36). Again, the most striking thing about Paul's use of these psalms is its allusive character; neither is introduced with a citation formula, and the messianic/eschatological interpretation is assumed rather than asserted. Of course, in neither case is Christ treated as the speaker. Nonetheless, we find here further evidence for an established pre-Pauline tradition of messianic psalm interpretation.[26]

---

25. For a defense of this translation, taking the phrase περὶ τοῦ υἱοῦ as a modifier of γραφαῖς ἁγίαις, cf. R. B. Hays, "ΠΙΣΤΙΣ and Pauline Christology," in *The Faith of Jesus Christ: The Narrative Substructure of Galatians 3:1–4:11* (Grand Rapids: Eerdmans, 2002), 280 n. 18.

26. D.-A. Koch, in his otherwise perspicacious treatment of pre-Pauline exegetical traditions, seems to overlook this evidence ("Beobachtungen zum christologischen Schriftgebrauch in den vorpaulinischen Gemeinden," *ZNW* 71 [1980]: 174-91; *Schrift als Zeuge*, 232-56).

The Hermeneutical Logic of Messianic Psalm Reading

Donald Juel, in his important book *Messianic Exegesis,* has hypothesized that Ps 89 is the missing link in New Testament Christology; although the text is never cited explicitly in the New Testament, it provides, according to Juel, the rationale for identifying the passion psalms as messianic: "The Christ speaks of his own sufferings in vv. 50-51 [of Ps 89], which may suggest that the 'I' in other laments is likewise the Christ."[27]

Juel's proposal is conjectural, but it seeks to grapple with an important issue rarely addressed by commentators: Why did the earliest church read the psalms as the Messiah's prayer book? Unfortunately, Juel's suggestion is not directly warranted by any evidence in the New Testament: one might say that the New Testament writers would have been delighted with Juel's reading of this psalm if they had thought of it. Surely, however, if Ps 89 had been the *source* of the idea that the Messiah was to suffer, or the original warrant for reading the royal lament psalms as Christ's words, some citation of it would appear somewhere in the New Testament. Juel's proposal focuses too narrowly on Ps 89, and it underestimates the scope of the early church's typological hermeneutic. In what follows I shall offer a sketch of another explanation.[28]

The earliest Christians (and here we are speaking, necessarily, of Jewish Christians) did not need to find an isolated sentence (like Ps 89:51) that spoke of the χριστός as the target of the scorn of God's enemies, because they read all the promises of an eternal kingdom for David and his seed typologically. Israel's historical experience had falsified a purely immanent literal reading of the texts; the line of David had in fact lost the throne, and Israel's enemies had in fact seized power. Thus, the promise that God would raise up David's seed and establish his kingdom forever (e.g., 2 Sam 7:12-14; Ps 89:3-4) *had* to be read as having reference to an eschatological future.

How, then, would the royal lament psalms be understood? They would be construed — by many Jews, not only by Christians — as paradigmatic for Israel's corporate national sufferings in the present time, and their

27. D. Juel, *Messianic Exegesis: Christological Interpretation of the Old Testament in Early Christianity* (Philadelphia: Fortress, 1988), 109.

28. Of course, the scope of this essay does not permit a full development and defense of the ideas presented here. For now, I shall be content with the attempt to show that Rom 15 is illuminated by these proposals.

characteristic triumphant conclusions would be read as pointers to God's eschatological restoration of Israel. Thus "David" in these psalms becomes a symbol for the whole people and — at the same time — a prefiguration of the future Anointed One (ὁ Χριστὸς) who will be the heir of the promises and the restorer of the throne. The shape of such an expectation is delineated clearly in the *Psalms of Solomon*, especially *Pss Sol* 17 and 18; the choice of the "psalm" genre for these outcries of national hope is testimony to the eschatological mode in which the canonical psalms would have been interpreted in the first century C.E.[29] The distinctive hermeneutical move of early Christianity was to see the sufferings of Israel in these psalms (or, to say the same thing differently, the sufferings of the king who represents Israel) as having been accomplished in an eschatologically definitive way by Jesus on the cross, *and* to see the vindication of Israel accomplished proleptically in his resurrection.[30] Thus, the movement of the royal lament psalms from suffering to triumph is correlated hermeneutically with the story of Jesus' death and resurrection. All of this lies behind the apparently strange uses of the psalms that we have surveyed above.

Paul's Use of the Exegetical Tradition

I have been contending that the christological reading of the psalms, including the image of Christ as the praying voice in these texts, is pre-Pauline. We must consider, in conclusion, what Paul is *doing* in Rom 15 with this traditional trope.

The citation of Ps 69:9 in Rom 15:3 occurs at the climax of Paul's careful response to the pastoral problem posed by the tension between the powerful and the powerless. The powerful are called upon to forgo their prerogatives and to please the neighbor in the interest of building up the

---

29. On the dating of the *Psalms of Solomon*, see R. B. Wright's introductory survey in *OTP* 2:640-41.

30. My thinking about this matter has been clarified and influenced by several essays of N. T. Wright; see esp. "Jesus, Israel and the Cross," in *SBLSP* (1985), 75-95; and Wright, "Adam, Israel and the Messiah" and "ΧΡΙΣΤΟΣ as 'Messiah' in Paul," both in Wright, *The Climax of the Covenant* (Edinburgh: T. & T. Clark, 1991), 18-40 and 41-55 respectively. Unlike Wright, I am not fully convinced that Jesus understood his own death in these terms; as an account of the earliest development of Christology in Jewish Christianity, however, Wright's proposals are highly persuasive.

community (vv. 1-2); this act of pleasing the other rather than oneself is warranted by the example of Christ, exemplified in the psalm quotation. The connection between the exhortation and its warrant is a bit imprecise, but Paul's point seems to be simply that Christ endured suffering and blame *vicariously:* he was innocent but incurred reproaches. Thus, the powerful, rather than pleasing themselves, should likewise be willing to suffer if necessary for the sake of others.[31]

The aptness of the quotation would be enhanced for readers who remembered its immediate context in Ps 69:6ff.:

> Do not let those who wait for [ὑπομένοντες; cf. ὑπομονή in
>   Rom 15:5-6] you be put to shame [αἰσχυνθείησαν;
>   cf. Rom 1:16; 5:5; 9:33; 10:11] because of me,
> O Lord, Lord of the powers [κύριε τῶν δυνάμεων].
> Do not let those who seek you be dishonored because of me,
>   O God of Israel.

This is an example of the allusive technique called metalepsis, which is pervasive in Paul;[32] the most telling elements of Paul's subtext are suppressed in his overt citation. Anyone who hears Ps 69 as the prayer of Christ would immediately realize the relevance of these petitions to the counsel that Paul is offering the Romans: the Messiah who prays such a prayer in the midst of suffering is a powerful model for the other-regarding conduct that Paul is urging. Paul wants the Roman Christians to echo the prayer of the Messiah by saying, in effect, "Do not let one for whom Christ died be put to shame because of me" (cf. Rom 14:15). (The sense ascribed to the psalm in this interpretation is hardly what historical criticism would regard as the original meaning of the text. Paul, however, was not deterred by such constraints.)

Against this background we can more adequately understand the function of the *"hermeneutischer Lehrsatz"* in Rom 15:4, which Keck finds so contextually intrusive that he deems it an interpolation.[33] In the hypothetical pre-Pauline tradition, as we have reconstructed it, the christo-

---

31. Cf. D. Worley, "He Was Willing," *ResQ* 18 (1975): 9: "The same attitude of desiring to please another instead of self is isolated by Paul as the disposition necessary in the relationship of the weak and strong brother."

32. For definition and examples, see Hays, *Echoes,* 20, 87-88, and passim.

33. Keck, "Romans 15:4."

logical interpretation of the royal lament psalms would have served either apologetic arguments (How can the crucified Jesus be confessed to be the Messiah? In what way was his death κατὰ τὰς γραφάς?) or reflections about soteriology (How is Jesus' death and resurrection salvific for others?). Paul, however, is making a very different application of the tradition. He is not just claiming that the death of Jesus fulfills Scripture; instead, he is holding up the image of the Jesus who died for others as *a paradigm for Christian obedience*. This is why he has to pause to justify his *hortatory* use of the image of Christ in Ps 69.[34] These things are written, he proposes, not merely to offer theological explanations about how God's redemptive purpose worked out in Jesus but also for our instruction (διδασκαλία), our training in the disciplines and character qualities appropriate to those who are now in Christ. Consequently, those who perceive the figure of Christ "pre-written" in the scriptural portrayal of the Righteous Sufferer should find themselves in turn instructed by and conformed to his example.

The Scriptures kindle and sustain *hope* (Rom 15:4). How? By placing human life in a christological and eschatological framework. The life pattern of suffering for others, defined by the Christ in Paul's reading of Ps 69, is possible only for those who hope in God's ultimate vindication. One must have hope to live sacrificially as Jesus did, even in the midst of conflict and suffering, trusting that God wills the community's eschatological unity (vv. 5-6). According to Rom 15:4-6, then, the purpose of Scripture — and the lament psalms are particularly in view here — is to provide a christologically grounded model of steadfastness to sustain hope in the midst of adversity, so that members of the community can continue to act for the edification of others even in the midst of opposition and temporary disunity.[35] Although the word "hope" does not appear in Ps 69 (but cf. the content of vv. 30-36), it echoes continually throughout the lament psalms. The voice that prays Ps 22, for example, invokes the example of the patriarchs: ἐπὶ σοὶ ἤλπισαν καὶ οὐ κατῃσχύνθησαν (cf. Rom 5:5).

Thus it is not true, as Keck asserts, that "there is no substantial connection between v. 3 and v. 4" of Rom 15.[36] The connection is subtle but material. It depends upon seeing two things: (1) for Paul, Ps 69 gives an ac-

---

34. So, rightly, Käsemann, *Romans*, 382.

35. Keck's objection ("Romans 15:4," 131) that "the original readers of Romans 15" would find a word of encouragement in the midst of suffering to be inappropriate to their situation is surprising, in light of Rom 5:3-5 and 8:18-39.

36. Keck, "Romans 15:4," 126.

count of ὁ Χριστός as example; and (2) Paul's *hortatory* use of the messianic interpretation of the psalm is a novel adaptation of the tradition. Paul can assume that his readers will share his assumption that it is Jesus Christ who prays the psalm; however, he cannot assume that they will automatically discern in Christ's words a pattern for their own lives; hence, the need for the *Lehrsatz* of verse 4.

Keck is correct, however, in his observation that "the scope of the subject matter [in v. 4] overshoots what is required, but it is appropriate to a self-contained precept which has been inserted."[37] It is entirely possible that Rom 15:4 is a previously formulated hermeneutical maxim that Paul cites to justify his didactic use of a psalm acknowledged to be messianic. (Cf. the closely analogous hermeneutical formulations in Rom 4:23-25, 1 Cor 9:9b-10, and 1 Cor 10:11.) This would hardly be the only case where Paul supports a highly particular pastoral dictum by appealing to a fundamental and general theological warrant. That is indeed his normal way of reasoning theologically about pastoral problems.

The prayer of Rom 15:5-6 concludes Paul's specific admonitions concerning the powerful and the powerless, and it envisions the community at Rome as a prefiguration of the eschatological community in which all with one voice glorify the God and Father of the Lord Jesus Christ. This image of a united community praising God then provides the transition to the letter's rhetorical climax in verses 7-13, moving beyond the immediate problem of factions at Rome to the larger issue of Jew-Gentile unity that has been the letter's great theme. Once again Paul drives home his point with Scripture quotations, and once again we find him treating the words of a psalm as the words of Christ. Although space precludes an analysis of all four quotations in Rom 15:9-12, it will be useful to consider in particular the use Paul makes of Ps 18 in the first quotation of this series.

When Paul cites Ps 18:49 (17:50 LXX) in Rom 15:9, the image of Christ praising God among the Gentiles must be interpreted not as an isolated proof text about Gentiles but as an allusion to the narrative of the psalm as a whole: "David" praises God for delivering him from death and Sheol (vv. 4-6) and from his enemies. The final verses of the psalm (vv. 46-50) are particularly provocative when read in the christological framework that I have sketched here:[38]

37. Keck, "Romans 15:4," 129.
38. The translation given here follows Ps 17:47-51 LXX.

The Lord lives [ζῇ κύριος]! And blessed is my God.
And let the God of my salvation be exalted [ὑψωθήτω],
The God who gives vengeance to me
And subjects [ὑποτάξας; cf. Ps 8:7] peoples under me,
Who delivers me from my angry enemies.
From those who rise up against me you will exalt [ὑψώσεις] me,
From the unrighteous man you will deliver me.
Therefore I will confess you among the Gentiles, Lord,
And I will sing to your name,
Magnifying[39] the salvation [τὰς σωτηρίας] of his king
And doing mercy [ποιῶν ἔλεος; cf. ὑπὲρ ἐλέους in Rom 15:9a]
    for his Messiah [τῷ Χριστῷ αὐτοῦ],
For David and for his seed [τῷ Δαυιδ καὶ τῷ σπέρματι αὐτοῦ] forever.

How would Paul have read the final sentence of this psalm? Are "his king" and "his Messiah" one and the same? Or are they to be distinguished from one another, in parallelism with "David and his seed"? The difficulty of deciding is a reflection of the hermeneutical phenomenon I have been describing: early Christian exegesis fuses past King David with the future Messiah.[40] The point here is that Paul does not read the text, in Matthean fashion, as a "prediction" about the Messiah;[41] rather, the Messiah embodies Israel's destiny in such a way that David's songs can be read retrospectively as a prefiguration of the Messiah's sufferings and glorification. That is why Keck cannot be correct in attributing to Paul the interpretation of

39. The LXX creates syntactical confusion here: the participle μεγαλύνων is most naturally understood as modifying the subject of the verb in the previous clause ("I"), but ποιῶν, in the following parallel line, must be understood to modify the "you" (= God) of v. 49 or perhaps the vocative κύριε of v. 50.

40. Ps 18 has a long superscription (beginning with εἰς τὸ τέλος) identifying it as a psalm of "David the servant of the Lord" (τῷ παιδὶ κυρίου), which he spoke "on the day when the Lord delivered him out of the hand of all his enemies and out of the hand of Saul" — a cross-reference to 2 Sam 22:1. The remainder of 2 Sam 22 = Ps 18.

41. In Acts 2:25-36 Luke reads the words of Ps 16 not as words *of* the Messiah but as David's prophetic words *about* the Messiah. The logic of Peter's speech does not posit a typological interpretation of David; rather, it drives an argumentative wedge between David and the Messiah predicted by David's words. This observation may be further evidence of the late and secondary character of the Acts speeches; Paul and the earlier tradition seem to have operated with a typological hermeneutic of continuity rather than with a prediction-fulfillment model.

Ps 18 as "the pre-existent Christ's declaring in advance the purpose of his impending incarnation."[42] Instead, the psalm is David's song "on the day when the Lord delivered him from the hand of all his enemies"; when it is read as Christ's song, it must be read as postresurrection discourse, celebrating (proleptically?) the eschatological triumph of God.

It is no accident that this nexus of ideas fits perfectly into the argument that Paul is bringing to a climax in Rom 15:7-13. Paul cites the psalm's line about singing praise among the Gentiles to evoke the image of a suffering and vindicated Christ whose deliverance from death confirms God's faithfulness to Israel (cf. Rom 15:8) and establishes God's merciful sovereignty over the nations (Rom 15:9a). Significantly, the chain of four quotations in Rom 15:9-12 ends with an explicit pointer — this time from Isaiah — to a "shoot of Jesse" who will "rise up to rule the Gentiles." The evocation of Davidic messianic themes here creates an effective *inclusio* with the epistle's opening christological confession (1:2-4).[43]

Here again we see Paul moving from a traditional Jewish Christian interpretation of Ps 18 as a messianic utterance to his own pastoral application of the tradition. The Messiah, the seed of David who has been delivered by the hand of God from all his enemies, has won this victory — Paul contends — precisely for the purpose of "welcoming" Israel and Gentiles together, as shown in the psalm's concluding words of praise; *therefore,* Jew and Gentile, weak and strong, should also welcome one another for the glory of God, joining in the chorus of praise created by Paul's climactic florilegium.

Again, as in Rom 15:1-6, Paul's hermeneutical strategy transforms a traditional piece of christological apologetic into a warrant for unity and hope within the mixed community of faith. Thus, this finding reinforces my previously expressed view that Paul's hermeneutic is ecclesiocentric rather than christocentric; even where Paul cites a psalm traditionally read as the Messiah's own speech, he *employs* it hermeneutically in service of an ecclesially focused exhortation. Keck is right, then, to say that in the quota-

---

42. Keck, "Christology," 93.

43. Puzzling is C. K. Barrett's comment (*The Epistle to the Romans,* HNTC [New York: Harper and Row, 1957], 272) that "Paul in general shows no interest in the Davidic descent of Jesus and offers no exposition of it here." If Barrett means that Paul is not interested in the genealogy of Jesus (as in Matt 1:1-17), the point may be granted; however, the Davidic messiahship of Jesus is the crucial hermeneutical emphasis of the rhetorical climax of Paul's *peroratio* in Rom 15:7-13.

tion of Ps 18:49, "Paul's interest is not on the 'I' but on the rationale of the whole: through Christ the Gentiles join in the praise of God."[44]

It is doubtful, however, that we should assent to Keck's judgment that in Rom 15:7-13 "the Christ-event is interpreted by incorporating its messianic/Davidic dimensions into a wider context based on the meaning of the resurrection."[45] It would be more accurate to turn the matter around: the resurrection is interpreted by incorporating it into a hermeneutical framework provided by the messianic/Davidic tradition, which had long envisioned as its telos the universal scope of God's rule and — according to Paul's reading of the tradition — the uniting of all nations in praise of Israel's God. It is precisely this hermeneutical context which ensures that the salvation offered by God through Christ can never be apolitical, can never intend merely the religious conversion of individuals. Because Jesus is ὁ Χριστός, his resurrection signifies God's eschatological intention to create a messianic *community* of those who know themselves summoned to welcome one another, as the Messiah has welcomed them, for the glory of God. Thus, in Pauline hermeneutics the community that learns to recognize the voice of the Messiah in the Psalms will learn finally to join in his suffering and in his song.

Implications for the Formation of Early Christology

What are the broader implications of this study of Rom 15:3? I offer, in conclusion, a series of eight theses for further reflection.

1. The Davidic messiahship of Jesus is a significant aspect of Pauline Christology, at least at the presuppositional level. This is most clearly evident in Romans. Critical studies of Pauline Christology have seriously underestimated the importance of this element of Paul's thought about Jesus.

2. The conventional wisdom that *Christos* in Paul is a name, not a title, is seriously misleading.

3. The interpretation of the lament psalms as *prayers of the Messiah* is already a presupposition of the earliest stratum of New Testament tradition.

4. Thus, New Testament texts that develop a Christology on the basis

44. Keck, "Christology," 93.
45. Keck, "Christology," 93.

of typological correspondence with psalms are not necessarily late, secondary apologetic phenomena. The interpretation of Jesus' death and resurrection, as far back as we can trace it, grows organically out of the matrix of the psalms of the Righteous Sufferer. These psalms may be the "Scripture" to which the confessional formula of 1 Cor 15:3-4 refers.

5. Of course, the proclamation of a crucified Messiah entails a fundamental revisioning of the messianic hope; however, once one grants the hermeneutical premise that the Messiah is the praying voice of the Psalms, then the homology between the lament psalms and the passion story helps make sense out of the oxymoronic confession that the crucified Jesus is God's anointed.

6. The convention of reading the Psalms as prayers of the Messiah makes sense if and only if the Messiah is understood as representatively embodying the fate of the whole people Israel. (Many of the Psalms, even where they employ first-person singular discourse, are not strictly individual; they address the crisis of theodicy created by God's apparent abandonment of the covenant people.) For this earliest phase of Christian hermeneutics, Jesus carries the destiny of Israel.

7. One must at least ask whether the tradition of reading the Psalms as prayers of the Messiah is a Christian innovation, or whether it might already have been an interpretative assumption in some groups of pre-Christian Jewish interpreters.

8. Early Christianity must be understood as a hermeneutical transformation of Judaism. This last thesis is hardly controversial, but we feel its force acutely in light of the above reflections. If we want to understand the confessional formulations of the earliest Christians, we must continue to delve into their practices of scriptural interpretation, because Scripture — especially the Psalms — provided the matrix from which early Christology grew. Paul bears witness to the practice of reading the Psalms with an imagination converted by the death and resurrection of the *Christos*.

Apocalyptic Hermeneutics:
Habakkuk Proclaims "The Righteous One"

Introduction: Apocalyptic and Hermeneutics

J. Louis Martyn has made a signal contribution to Pauline scholarship by patiently reminding his colleagues that apocalyptic thought asserts its influence in Paul not only through images of resurrection and parousia but also through signs more subtle and pervasive: wherever Paul construes the present time as fundamentally transformed through God's invasive act of deliverance — which is to say everywhere — we find him employing apocalyptic categories.[1] The texture of Paul's carefully tailored language reveals that it has been cut from an apocalyptic bolt; to read him rightly we must read with sensibilities responsive to this texture. Such a reading shows that Galatians, despite its omission of references to a specific future eschatological scenario, must be understood as "a letter fully as apocalyptic as are the other Paulines,"[2] because it reveals the present as the time of "the dawn of God's New Creation."[3]

If Paul's temporal sensibilities are apocalyptic in character, the same must be said of his hermeneutics — his way of understanding the message of Scripture. Because all things have been (or will be) transformed by

---

1. Important articulations of this insight are to be found in Martyn's essay "Epistemology at the Turn of the Ages: 2 Corinthians 5.16," in *Christian History and Interpretation: Studies Presented to John Knox*, ed. W. R. Farmer, C. F. D. Moule, and R. R. Niebuhr (Cambridge: Cambridge University Press, 1967), 269-87, and in his more recent "Apocalyptic Antinomies in Paul's Letter to the Galatians," *NTS* 31 (1985): 410-24.

2. Martyn, "Antinomies," 420.

3. Martyn, "Antinomies," 417. See now also J. L. Martyn, *Galatians*, AB 33A (New York: Doubleday, 1997), 97-105.

God's redemptive action in Christ, Scripture must be read with new eyes.[4] The reader who stands at the turn of the ages can no longer believe that Scripture merely authorizes religion-as-usual for Israel; instead, it must promise the new creation. Scripture must adumbrate, for those who have eyes to see, the coming of eschatological transformation.[5]

This approach to Scripture has direct consequences for Paul's Christology. If Paul interprets Christ's death as "the apocalypse of his cross,"[6] signifying the death of the old cosmos and the birth of the new, and if that death took place "according to the Scriptures" (cf. 1 Cor 15:3), might we not expect to find Paul interpreting scriptural texts through a hermeneutic that would disclose the apocalyptic dimensions of Jesus' identity and mission? And, if that is so, might a careful investigation of Paul's christological language disclose hitherto unrecognized (or at least underemphasized) links with the messianic expectation and categories of early Jewish Christianity? Certainly Paul's initial presentation of Jesus in Galatians has a strongly apocalyptic shading: God "raised him from the dead" (1:1), and he is characterized as "Lord Jesus Christ who gave himself for our sins in order to deliver us from the present evil age" (1:3b-4a).[7] Paul's citation of these apocalyptic formulas in his letter opening is surely not haphazard; their construal of Jesus' death and resurrection as an event signaling eschatological deliverance from the power of an evil age must govern our reading of Paul's subsequent statements.

One of the striking things about Paul's use of Scripture is his apparent disinterest, in contrast to Matthew and later Christian apologists, in overt appeals to christological proofs based on the fulfillment of prophecy. Nonetheless, it will be the burden of this essay to argue that Paul does indeed presuppose certain apocalyptic traditions of christological exegesis, traditions he shared with many other first-century Jewish Christians.

Specifically, this essay will reexamine Paul's reading of Hab 2:4 by testing a pair of closely linked hypotheses: (1) that ὁ δίκαιος ("The Righteous One")

---

4. Martyn makes a similar point in "Epistemology at the Turn of the Ages," not only about "knowing Christ" but about knowing in general; the application of the argument to hermeneutical issues is both natural and necessary.

5. Cf. 2 Cor 3:14-17.

6. Martyn, "Antinomies," 421. "[T]hrough the whole of Galatians the focus of Paul's apocalyptic lies not on Christ's parousia but rather on his death" (420).

7. Martyn translates the final clause as: "so that he might snatch us out of the grasp of the present evil age." On this translation see Martyn, *Galatians*, 90-91.

was a standard epithet for the Messiah in early Jewish Christian circles, and (2) that Paul's citation (in Rom 1:17 and Gal 3:11) of Hab 2:4 (ὁ δίκαιος ἐκ πίστεως ζήσεται) presupposes an apocalyptic/messianic interpretation of that text. Each of these hypotheses has been proposed from time to time by various scholars,[8] though the second thesis remains a minority view and the first is rarely seen as a matter of much importance. I have argued elsewhere, on grounds of the internal logic of Paul's argument in Gal 3, that Paul did indeed understand ὁ δίκαιος as a messianic designation.[9] Martyn's delineation of the apocalyptic contours of Galatians now provides a new perspective from which the problem must be considered: we should inquire how Paul's apocalyptic hermeneutic would have shaped his understanding of Hab 2:4 (and vice versa). The present essay, then, will first survey several non-Pauline texts in which ὁ δίκαιος appears to be used as a messianic designation and then return to consider Paul's use of the Habakkuk citation in light of Martyn's insights, remembering that apocalyptic perceptions may be embedded in the language and between the lines of the text.

"The Righteous One" as Messianic Designation? Non-Pauline Texts

NT scholars have for some time recognized that several first-century texts refer to a "Righteous One" who is the eschatological agent of God.[10] A sur-

---

8. For (1), see especially H. Dechent, "Der 'Gerechte' — eine Bezeichnung für den Messias," *TSK* 100 (1927-28): 439-43; and H. J. Cadbury, "The Titles of Jesus in Acts," in F. J. Foakes-Jackson and K. Lake, *The Beginnings of Christianity, Part I: The Acts of the Apostles* (London: Macmillan, 1920-33), 5:354-75. For (2), see A. T. Hanson, *Studies in Paul's Technique and Theology* (London: SPCK, 1974), 39-45; L. T. Johnson, "Romans 3.21-26 and the Faith of Jesus," *CBQ* 44 (1982): 90; further references in R. B. Hays, *The Faith of Jesus Christ: The Narrative Substructure of Gal. 3.1–4.11*, 2nd ed. (Grand Rapids: Eerdmans, 2002), 137 n. 67. In support of both points, see especially D. A. Campbell, "Romans 1:17 — a *Crux Interpretum* for the πίστις Χριστοῦ Debate," *JBL* 113 (1994): 265-85.

9. Hays, *Faith of Jesus Christ*, 134-41, 179-81. Even some of the critics who have received my book most graciously have expressed skepticism about this aspect of the argument (e.g., C. Roetzel, *JAAR* 53 [1985]: 490: "I remain unconvinced that Hab. 2.4 is or was a messianic text"; cf. R. N. Longenecker, *Themelios* 10, no. 2 [1985]: 38; T. L. Donaldson, "The 'Curse of the Law' and the Inclusion of the Gentiles: Gal. 3.13-14," *NTS* 32 [1986]: 112 n. 78). Consequently, I trust that readers will not find it tedious of me to reexamine this same problem from a completely different angle.

10. In addition to the studies mentioned in n. 8 above, see also L. Ruppert, *Jesus als der*

vey of these familiar passages will show not only how widespread the "Righteous One" designation is but also how it gathers significations by echoing a variety of antecedent scriptural texts.

The Evidence of 1 Enoch

Outside the canon of Christian texts, *1 Enoch* provides the only generally acknowledged example of a Jewish document antedating or contemporary with the NT that employs "The Righteous One" as a title for a messianic figure. This single example is, however, a very important one for our present purposes.

In *1 En* 38 the visionary Enoch begins to recount his revealed wisdom by describing a scene of eschatological judgment:

> When the congregation of the righteous shall appear,
> sinners shall be judged for their sins,
> they shall be driven from the face of the earth,
> and when the Righteous One shall appear before the face
>   of the righteous,
> those elect ones, their deeds are hung upon the lord of the Spirits,
> he shall reveal light to the righteous and the elect who dwell
>   upon the earth. . . .
> When the secrets of the Righteous One are revealed,
> he shall judge the sinners,
> and the wicked ones will be driven from the presence of the
>   righteous and the elect.[11]

---

leidende Gerechte? (Stuttgart: KBW, 1972); and E. Franklin, *Christ the Lord* (London: SPCK, 1975), 62-63.

11. This and the following citations from *1 Enoch* are taken from the translation of E. Isaac, in J. H. Charlesworth, *The Old Testament Pseudepigrapha*, vol. 1 (Garden City, N.Y.: Doubleday, 1983). In 38:3 the older standard translation of R. H. Charles (*Apocrypha and Pseudepigrapha of the New Testament* [Oxford: Clarendon, 1913]) and the recent translation of M. A. Knibb (*The Ethiopic Book of Enoch* [Oxford: Clarendon, 1978]), following different manuscript evidence, read the plural "secrets of the righteous," and Knibb also opts for the plural in 39:6: "the chosen ones of righteousness and of faith." In the crucial passages in 38:2 and 53:6, however, the singular "Righteous One" is unambiguously attested.

Taken alone, this text could be understood simply as a portrayal of God's activity in the final judgment, and "the Righteous One" could be God himself. However, as the visionary description unfolds, the Righteous One is clearly identified with a figure distinct from God, "the Elect One of righteousness and of faith" (39:6; cf. Hab 2:4!), the instrument of God's judging and saving power, who is glorified by God (see especially *1 En* 61) and is also called "the Son of Man, to whom belongs righteousness and with whom righteousness dwells" (46:3; cf. 48:2; 62:5ff.). While the author of *1 Enoch* seems to prefer as a title "the Elect One," the epithets can be combined, as in 53:6: "the Righteous and Elect One." Although this Righteous One is apparently a human figure rather than an angelic heavenly being, he appears only at the eschatological judgment, having been "concealed" by God until that moment (62:7). He is said to be righteous primarily with respect to his role as executor of divine justice.

This portrayal of the Righteous One is confined to the Similitudes of Enoch (*1 En* 37–71) and does not appear elsewhere in the book. Since that portion of *1 Enoch* is not attested in the fragmentary manuscript evidence discovered at Qumran, J. T. Milik has raised the conjecture that this entire section of the book is a later Christian addition. Most scholars, however, continue to regard the Similitudes as a first-century Jewish text.[12] While a resolution of the problem of the date and origin of the Similitudes is of course important for many reasons, our present inquiry need not hinge upon the outcome of this debate. If — as is probable — this material is non-Christian, it provides evidence for the existence of a Jewish tradition that identified the expected eschatological deliverer as "the Righteous One." If, on the other hand, the Similitudes are ascribed to Christian authorship, they provide one more piece of evidence, in addition to the NT texts cited below, that Jewish Christians characteristically and distinctively applied this designation to Jesus.[13]

---

12. See J. C. Greenfield and M. E. Stone, "The Enochic Pentateuch and the Date of the Similitudes," *HTR* 70 (1977): 51-65; J. A. Fitzmyer, "Implications of the New Enoch Literature from Qumran," *TS* 38 (1977): 340-44; J. H. Charlesworth, "The SNTS Pseudepigrapha Seminars at Tübingen and Paris on the Books of Enoch," *NTS* 25 (1978-79): 315-23; M. A. Knibb, "The Date of the Parables of Enoch: A Critical Review," *NTS* 25 (1978-79): 345-59; C. L. Mearns, "Dating the Similitudes of Enoch," *NTS* 25 (1978-79): 360-69; D. W. Suter, *Tradition and Composition in the Parables of Enoch*, SBLDS 47 (Missoula, Mont.: Scholars, 1979), 11-33; M. Black, *The Book of Enoch or 1 Enoch: A New English Edition*, SVTP 7 (Leiden: Brill, 1985), see 181-88.

13. This way of formulating the matter assumes that Milik's late dating of the Simili-

The Evidence of Acts

Three passages in the Acts of the Apostles, all appearing in the speeches rather than in the narrative framework, refer directly to Jesus as "the Righteous One." Let us examine each in turn before drawing some conclusions.

In Peter's speech to the crowd in Solomon's portico, after the healing of a lame man, he declares that "The God of Abraham and of Isaac and of Jacob, the God of our fathers glorified his servant (παῖδα) Jesus, whom you delivered up (παρεδώκατε) and denied in the presence of Pilate, when he had decided to release him. But you denied the Holy and Righteous One (τὸν ἅγιον καὶ δίκαιον), and asked for a murderer to be granted to you, and killed the Author of Life, whom God raised from the dead" (3:13-15). The references here to a παῖς who was "delivered up" may echo the language of Isa 52:13–53:12 (cf. also Acts 3:18), though the point is much disputed. Whether or not Isaiah's figure of the suffering servant stands behind this language,[14] it is certainly clear that "the Holy and Righteous One" is Jesus the Messiah (3:18, 20), who suffered an unjust death (3:15, 18) but who has now been received into heaven until the time of universal eschatological restoration (3:21), which is prefigured palpably by the healing of the lame man before the eyes of these onlookers. Like the 1 Enoch texts, Peter's speech depicts the Righteous One as a glorified figure whose appearance will accompany the cosmic resolution of all things; unlike the 1 Enoch texts, Peter's speech associates the righteousness of the Righteous One with the theme of wrongful suffering and vindication through resurrection.

The phrase, in its next appearance, is given special emphasis by its placement in the climax of Stephen's speech before a hostile Sanhedrin. "You stiff-necked people, uncircumcised in heart and ears, you always resist the Holy Spirit. As your fathers did, so do you. Which of the prophets did not your fathers persecute? And they killed those who announced beforehand the coming of the Righteous One (τῆς ἐλεύσεως τοῦ δικαίου), whom you have now betrayed and murdered, you who received the Law as delivered by angels and did not keep it" (7:51-53). Here "the Righteous One" is used in an unmistakably titular fashion, and the term is presented in a strongly apocalyptic context: his "coming" was prophesied by a whole

---

tudes is incorrect and that, even if judged to come from Christian circles, the sort of Christianity they represent is strongly Jewish in character.

14. Cf. the discussion of 1 Pet 3:18 below.

series of Israel's prophets, and he is identified in 7:55-56 with "the Son of Man standing at the right hand of God" (cf. Dan 7:13-14; Ps 110:1). Here again, as in 3:13-15, the ascription of heavenly glory to the Righteous One is fused with the theme of his death as a martyr, which is of course paradigmatic for Stephen's own fate as enacted in this very scene.

Four matters call for attention here. (1) Stephen's reference to the ἔλευσις of the Righteous One may echo a well-established tradition of reading Hab 2:3-4 as a messianic prophecy.[15] None of the other texts usually read as messianic scriptural prophecies corresponds so closely to the terminology of 7:52 as does Hab 2:3-4. That Luke was familiar with such traditions may be indicated by his inclusion (without explanation) of the question of John the Baptist's disciples to Jesus: "Are you the Coming One (ὁ ἐρχόμενος), or shall we look for another?" (Luke 7:19; cf. Hab 2:3 LXX; Ps 117:26 LXX).[16] (2) The proximity of the terms "Righteous One" and "Son of Man" as titles for the same figure might suggest a common background for this passage and the *1 Enoch* texts discussed above. (3) In the narrative context of the story of Stephen's martyrdom, the reference to Jesus as ὁ δίκαιος in 7:52 can hardly fail to recall Luke's distinctive account of the words of the centurion at the cross in Luke 23:47: "Truly this man was δίκαιος." If we assume that Luke thought of ὁ δίκαιος as a recognizable designation for the Messiah, the story would exemplify Luke's characteristic fondness for dramatic irony: the centurion means no more than "this man was innocent," but his words bear testimony to a truth larger than he realizes, the truth known to Luke and the reader that Jesus is the Righteous One.[17] (4) There are several distant but cumulatively interesting connections between Acts 7:51-53 and Gal 3. Most compelling, of course, is the ref-

---

15. On this tradition see A. Strobel, *Untersuchungen zum eschatologischen Verzögerungsproblem auf Grund der spätjüdisch-urchristlichen Geschichte von Habakuk 2,2ff.*, NovTSup 2 (Leiden: Brill, 1961), especially his comments on the LXX (47-56). The position is supported also by D.-A. Koch, "Der Text von Hab 2.4b in der Septuaginta und im Neuen Testament," *ZNW* 76 (1985): 73 n. 25.

16. The title in Luke 7:19 (= Matt 11:3) might also be explained by appeal to Ps 117:26 (LXX); however, once ὁ ἐρχόμενος came to be understood as a messianic title, a midrashic link between the psalm text and Hab 2:3 would have been in any case virtually inevitable. For a full discussion arguing for Hab 2:3 as the background for the Gospel saying, see Strobel, *Verzögerungsproblem*, 265-77.

17. Lake and Cadbury comment that "the story gains point if *ho dikaios* was a familiar title of Jesus" and draw the inference that "*ho dikaios* is less likely to be original" than Mark's θεοῦ υἱός (in Foakes-Jackson and Lake, *Beginnings of Christianity*, 4:83).

erence in both texts to the tradition that the law was given through the angels (Acts 7:53: εἰς διαταγὰς ἀγγέλων; Gal 3:19: διαταγεὶς δι' ἀγγέλων). Furthermore, however, both texts refer to the prior scriptural announcement of the gospel (Acts 7:52; Gal 3:8), and both relate ὁ δίκαιος in some way to the material content of Christian proclamation (Acts 7:52; Gal 3:11). (I deliberately formulate this last observation in the most general way possible; for further discussion see below.)

The final use of ὁ δίκαιος as a title in Acts appears in Paul's speech before the Jerusalem crowd, as he recounts Ananias's words to him after his Damascus road experience: "The God of our fathers appointed you to know his will, to see the Righteous One (τὸν δίκαιον) and to hear a voice from his mouth; for you will be a witness for him to all men of what you have seen and heard" (Acts 22:14-15). Here, despite the absence of eschatological motifs, the context is apocalyptic in the sense that ὁ δίκαιος appears in a revelatory vision, and the vision entails a commissioning of the "seer" to bear witness concerning the ἀποκάλυψις. What did Paul learn about the Righteous One? We are told here only that he is identified with Jesus of Nazareth (22:8); the motifs of the Righteous One's suffering, death, resurrection, and eschatological judgment are not explicitly invoked. The "persecution" of Jesus mentioned here is actually a reference to Paul's persecution of Christians (22:4-5); the point is an important one, because it illustrates the strong sense of identification between the Messiah and his people, an identification crucial for the soteriological logic of early Christian proclamation.[18]

With these passages before us, let us draw together some conclusions about the epithet ὁ δίκαιος in Acts. The term occurs *only* in speeches addressed to Jewish audiences — indeed, only to Jewish audiences in Jerusalem — and in every case the term is used without explanation, as though its meaning were presumed to be self-evident to the hearers. Luke does not use this title in his redactional framework or in constructive christological formulations elsewhere; there is no reason to regard it as a Lukan theologoumenon. This does not mean, however, that the language of the speeches is "authentic" in the sense of giving a precise account of what Peter, Stephen, and Paul said on the occasions narrated by Luke. It would be a serious methodological error to assume, for example, that Acts 22:14 proves that Paul knew and used ὁ δίκαιος as a messianic title. What it does show is that

18. See the discussion in Hays, *Faith of Jesus Christ*, xxix-xxxiii, 210-18.

Luke, with his interest in historical verisimilitude, believed that ὁ δίκαιος was a messianic title that would have been used by first-generation Jewish Christian preachers in speaking to Jewish audiences about the Messiah.[19] Whether Luke is actually drawing upon traditional sources or whether he is freely composing these speeches after what he believed to be the style of early Jewish Christian proclamation is very difficult to say. In either case, however, these three passages in Acts bear witness to the high probability that "the Righteous One" was a conventional messianic designation in early Christianity, specifically in Jewish Christian circles. The term appears in these passages in direct association with apocalyptic motifs of resurrection and judgment, and it also highlights the awful injustice of Jesus' death. The use of the epithet in the speeches suggests allusions to Hab 2:3-4 and to Isa 53, as well as points of contact with circles of theological ideas found in *1 Enoch* on the one hand and in Galatians on the other.

Finally, one odd silence in Acts is worth pondering. Hegesippus reports that James (whom Paul calls "the brother of the Lord") was called "the Just" (δίκαιος) "by all men from the Lord's time to ours,"[20] and indeed the account there given of his martyrdom repeatedly refers to him as ὁ δίκαιος, as though it were virtually a proper name. For instance, the climax of the account runs as follows: "And a certain man among them, one of the laundrymen, took the club with which he used to beat out the clothes, and hit *the Just* on the head, and so he suffered martyrdom."[21] Lake and Cadbury, evidently embarrassed for theological reasons by the temerity of their own suggestion, venture the guess that the title "Righteous One" was originally applied to Jesus and later "inherited — if the phrase may be forgiven — by his brother James."[22] Strikingly, however, though James appears as a key character in Acts, sympathetically portrayed by Luke in the Apostolic Council of Acts 15, Luke never refers to him as ὁ δίκαιος or gives his readers any hint that he was known by such a title.[23] This omission

---

19. For a helpful discussion of Luke's technique in tailoring the speeches in Acts to fit the narrative setting, see B. R. Gaventa, "The Overthrown Enemy: Luke's Portrait of Paul," in SBLSP (1985), 439-49.

20. Cited in Eusebius, *Historia ecclesiastica* 2.23.4.

21. Eusebius, *Historia ecclesiastica* 2.23.18.

22. Lake and Cadbury, in Foakes-Jackson and Lake, *Beginnings of Christianity*, 4:104.

23. The same observation could be made of Paul's references to James in Gal 2:9, 12; Paul's reasons for not mentioning such an honorific title, even if it were known to him, would be fairly obvious.

seems surprising. Why is there no trace of the title applied to James in the NT, particularly in Acts?

There are really only two possibilities. (1) Luke knew of no such tradition about James. Hegesippus's claim that James was universally known as ὁ δίκαιος is one more embellishment in an account admittedly heavily embroidered with legendary hagiographic motifs. This source provides no reliable information about what James was actually called by his contemporaries. (2) Hegesippus's account is indeed reliable on this point at least, and Luke has suppressed the information for reasons that parallel Lake and Cadbury's embarrassment: ὁ δίκαιος is a title that rightly applies to Jesus alone. I think there are good reasons for preferring the first of these explanations: the tradition about this epithet as a designation for James is attested neither by any of the several NT writings that mention him, including most tellingly even the Epistle of James,²⁴ nor by Josephus (*Antiquities* 20.200). Even if the latter explanation that Luke has suppressed James's characteristic title is correct, however — indeed, *especially* if it is correct — Luke bears witness to a stream of early tradition that reserves the epithet ὁ δίκαιος for the eschatological deliverer, Jesus.

The Evidence of the Catholic Epistles

A number of references to a Righteous One also turn up in the Catholic Epistles, offering further evidence of the use of the term as a christological designation. The most significant of these references is found in 1 Pet 3:18: "For Christ also suffered for sins once for all, the Righteous One for the unrighteous (δίκαιος ὑπὲρ ἀδίκων)."²⁵ Here, citing what would appear to be a traditional confessional formula, 1 Peter represents the suffering of Jesus as paradigmatic for the conduct of Christians, who are exhorted to follow his example (cf. 2:21) by suffering for doing right (3:17). Interestingly, although the confessional formula itself stresses the vicarious effect of the Righteous One's suffering, the author of 1 Peter chooses to highlight its exemplary character. These different emphases, which might ap-

---

24. What motive would a pseudepigraphist have for omitting a title that would so forthrightly commend the putative author of his work?

25. The diversity of readings in the textual tradition for 3:18a has no bearing upon the use of δίκαιος in the formula.

pear disparate to modern critics, are evidently part of a single conceptual package for this author. The confessional formulation is almost certainly based upon Isa 53:10b-12 (LXX): "And the Lord wills . . . to justify a Righteous One (δικαιῶσαι δίκαιον) who serves many well, and he will bear their sins. For this reason he will inherit many (κηρονομήσει πολλούς) and he will divide the spoils of the strong, because his soul was handed over (παρεδόθη) to death, and he was reckoned among the lawless. And he bore the sins of many, and he was handed over on account of their sins (διὰ τὰς ἁμαρτίας αὐτῶν παρεδόθη)."[26] The close resemblance of 1 Pet 3:18 to Gal 1:4 ("Jesus Christ who gave himself for our sins") should be observed.[27] The explicitly redemptive aspect of the Righteous One's suffering is a theme that did not appear in the Acts passages, but the other motifs associated with this figure are similar to what we have seen already: he suffered unjustly, he was vindicated by God, and now is exalted in glory "at the right hand of God, with angels, authorities and powers subject to him" (3:22; again we may wonder whether there are echoes here of *1 Enoch*, as well as of Ps 110). The reference to the destruction of the earth by water in the time of Noah (3:20; cf. *1 En* 65–67) reminds us also that 1 Peter's exhortation to the endurance of suffering is from start to finish located in an apocalyptic perception of the present time as the hour of eschatological crisis (see especially 4:12-19).

The last passage cited contains a quotation that is of particular interest for our investigation: "If the righteous man (ὁ δίκαιος) is scarcely saved, where will the impious and sinner appear?" (4:18, quoting Prov 11:31 LXX). Should we interpret this occurrence of ὁ δίκαιος, in light of 3:18, as another reference to Jesus, or should we interpret the passage as a generic reference to "the righteous person," which is of course its original meaning in Proverbs? The parallel with 4:17b suggests that the latter exegesis is the correct one. Thus, this text demonstrates a significant point: 1 Peter (unlike Luke?) can use ὁ δίκαιος either as an epithet of Jesus or as a generic term, depending on context. The interpretation of Jesus as *paradigmatic* righteous person allows the transition between the two senses to be made easily. In short, while the allusive connection between Jesus as ὁ δίκαιος and the ser-

---

26. Douglas J. Moo unaccountably remarks that "*dikaios* is not used in Is. 53.11 LXX" (*The Old Testament in the Gospel Passion Narratives* [Sheffield: Almond, 1983], 158). This is simply an error.

27. It is also interesting to speculate about the conceptual connections between these formulations and Gal 3:13-14.

vant figure of Isaiah is more evident in 1 Peter than in Acts, the titular force of the expression is weaker.

A similar problem arises with regard to James 5:6: "You have condemned (κατεδικάσατε), you have killed the righteous one (τὸν δίκαιον); he does not resist you." Nothing in the context suggests a christological reading of the verse, which appears at the conclusion of a pronouncement of woe upon the rich for their oppression of the innocent (5:1-6). The passage does appear, however, to play off the themes and language of Wis 2:6-20: "Let us oppress the righteous poor man. . . . Let us lie in wait for the righteous man (τὸν δίκαιον), because he is inconvenient to us and opposes our actions. . . . Let us condemn (καταδικάσωμεν) him to a shameful death" (vv. 10, 12, 20). Once the allusion to Wis 2 is recognized, however, the interpretation of James 5:6 becomes more rather than less complicated. The nonresistance of the righteous one in James 5:6b has no obvious basis in Wis 2; where does this motif come from? It is difficult to believe that any early Christian could read Wis 2:10-20 without finding in it a prophetic prefiguration of the passion of Jesus:

> He professes to have knowledge of God,
> and calls himself a child (παῖδα) of the Lord. . . .
> he calls the last end of the righteous happy,
> and boasts that God is his father.
> Let us see if his words are true,
> and let us test what will happen at the end of his life;
> for if the righteous one (ὁ δίκαιος) is God's son (υἱὸς θεοῦ),[28]
> he will help him,
> and will deliver him from the hand of his adversaries.
>
> (2:13, 16b-18; cf. also 5:1-7)

The more inclined we are to find an allusion to Wis 2 in James 5:6, the more prepared we must be to entertain the possibility that even here ὁ δίκαιος is an oblique reference to Jesus and that the motif of nonresistance derives from the traditions about Jesus' passion. In that case James 5:6 would present a close analogy to 1 Pet 4:18: a generic use of ὁ δίκαιος with Jesus as prototype of the genre. It should be reiterated that this use of the

28. In passing, it is intriguing to note that this line in Wis 2:18 contains both of the epithets ascribed to Jesus by the different Synoptic accounts of the centurion's "confession" at the foot of the cross (Matt 27:54 = Mark 15:39; Luke 23:47).

term ὁ δίκαιος is cognate with but distinguishable from the titular use of the same term in *1 Enoch* and Acts.

Finally, three instances of δίκαιος in 1 John must be noted. In 1 John 2:1b we find a turn of phrase that looks similar to 1 Pet 3:18's use of the δίκαιος epithet: "If anyone should sin, we have a paraclete with the Father, Jesus Messiah Righteous One ('Ιησοῦν Χριστὸν δίκαιον);²⁹ and he is the expiation for our sins, and not for ours only but also for the sins of the whole world" (2:1b-2). As in 1 Peter, the Righteous One is presented as a figure who makes vicarious atonement for the unrighteous; the parenetic application, however, is slightly different here in two ways: Jesus the Righteous One is offered as reassurance for those who sin, and there is no specific reference to his exemplary *suffering*. His moral example is apparently of a more general type, as we see from the further references in 2:29 and 3:7b: "If you know that he is righteous (δίκαιος), you may be sure that everyone who does righteousness (δικαιοσύνην) is born of him. . . . Whoever does righteousness (δικαιοσύνην) is righteous (δίκαιος), as he is righteous (δίκαιος)." In these passages δίκαιος is arguably used merely as an ascriptive adjective, its titular character virtually dissipated, or whispered into the reader's ear only through the initial appearance of the term in 2:1. There is no explicit attempt to connect this designation of Jesus to prophetic Scriptures. Furthermore, the term does not function here as a unique title for an eschatological judge and deliverer; it is rather a characterization of Jesus who stands as moral paradigm for the community of faith. Those who abide in him (2:28) will participate in the manner of life that he exemplifies. Although the tradition of describing Jesus as "Righteous One" thus receives a distinctive Johannine interpretation, it is noteworthy that the eschatological horizon of this language is not entirely lost, as 2:28-29 demonstrates: those who abide in him and do righteousness are thereby enabled to stand with confidence before Jesus at his parousia.

The Evidence of Hebrews

Finally, the Letter to the Hebrews brings us back within hailing distance of Paul, because, like Paul, it quotes Hab 2. The importance of this citation is such that it merits careful attention.

29. The translation here is mine.

The writer of this λόγος παρακλήσεως (13:22), admonishing his readers to "hold fast the confession of our hope without wavering" (10:23) amidst adverse circumstances, invokes Habakkuk's prophecy as a part of his appeal for ὑπομονή:

> Therefore do not throw away your confidence (παρρησία; cf. 10:19), which has a great reward. For you have need of endurance, so that you may do the will of God and receive what is promised (τὴν ἐπαγγελίαν; cf. 10:23; Gal 3:14-22).

> For yet a little while,
> and the Coming One (ὁ ἐρχόμενος) shall come and shall not tarry;
> but my righteous one shall live by faith (ὁ δὲ δίκαιός μου ἐκ πίστεως ζήσεται),
> and if he shrinks back,
> my soul has no pleasure in him.

> But we are not of those who shrink back and are destroyed, but of those who have faith and keep their souls. (10:35-39)

The form of the Habakkuk citation here provides major clues to the interpretation assigned to it by the author of Hebrews. Though the text is close to the LXX, there are several key differences.[30] If the LXX is already "messianic" in its rendering of the passage,[31] Hebrews removes any possible ambiguity on this point by inserting the definite article ὁ before the participle ἐρχόμενος. "The Coming One" here is understood as a title, just as in Matt 11:3 = Luke 7:19. The most crucial emendation of the text, however, occurs in 10:38, where the author of Hebrews has inverted the order of Hab 2:4a and 2:4b,[32] thus forging a significant reinterpretation. As T. W. Manson recognized,[33] the LXX text contrasts two possible modes of action for the Coming One, who — it is affirmed — will not shrink back but will live ἐκ πίστεως; thus, the most natural reading of the LXX is to treat ὁ

---

30. Cf. the discussion of Koch, "Der Text von Hab. 2.4b," 75-78.

31. See the references in n. 15 above, and T. W. Manson, "The Argument from Prophecy," JTS 46 (1945): 133-34.

32. For a clear chart and discussion, see C. H. Dodd, *According to the Scriptures* (London: Nisbet, 1952), 50.

33. Manson, "The Argument from Prophecy," 134.

δίκαιος synonymously with ὁ ἐρχόμενος, as another ascription of the Messiah. The writer of Hebrews, however, motivated by a parenetic agenda, achieves a very different reading by transposing the clauses. In light of the assurance that a Coming One will come very soon, the key issue is the response of those who wait: Will it be characterized by faithful endurance or by apostasy?[34] The summarizing comment in 10:39 demonstrates the point clearly, lifting the terms πίστις and ὑποστολή out of Hab 2:4 as thematic catchwords that distinguish between the faithful members of the Christian community and the apostates. Thus, Heb 10:37-38 forces a nonmessianic interpretation of ὁ δίκαιος: "my righteous one" in this passage means "the faithful Christian believer during the present eschatological interval before the coming of the Coming One."

Thus, the interpretation of Hab 2:3-4 in Hebrews bears a striking formal similarity to the interpretation given at Qumran, as attested by 1QpHab. Because the Qumran interpreter is working from a Hebrew text rather than from the LXX, there is no trace of a messianic reading even in 2:3, which is understood as a comment on the delay of "the appointed time"; nonetheless, both Hebrews and 1QpHab understand the passage fundamentally as an exhortation to keep the faith during trials that accompany the delay of the end.

> *If it tarries, wait for it, for it shall surely come and not be late* (ii, 3b). Interpreted, this concerns the men of truth who keep the Law, whose hands shall not slacken in the service of truth when the final age is prolonged. For all the ages of God reach their appointed end as He determines for them in the mysteries of His wisdom. . . . [*But the righteous shall live by his faith*] (ii, 4b). Interpreted, this concerns all those who observe the Law in the House of Judah, whom God will deliver from the House of Judgment because of their suffering and because of their faith in the Teacher of Righteousness.[35]

The Qumran commentary identifies "the righteous one" (presumably following the singular reading of the Hebrew text as found in MT)[36] with "all

---

34. This observation also probably explains the transposition of μου in the text of Heb 10:38: if μου were left to modify πίστεως, as in the LXX, the hortatory force of the point articulated in 10:39 would be blunted.

35. 1QpHab 7.9–8.3, as translated by G. Vermes, *The Dead Sea Scrolls in English*, 2nd ed. (Harmondsworth: Penguin Books, 1975), 239.

36. The portion of the scroll containing this part of the text has been destroyed.

(plural) those who observe the Law" according to the interpretation of the Teacher of Righteousness. For Hebrews, of course, faithfulness is defined not by observing the Law but by adherence to the Christian confession; still, the parenetic construal of Hab 2:4 is much the same in both texts, and the "righteous one" of Habakkuk is interpreted in both places as the ideal type for steadfast obedience in the face of suffering.

If we ask ourselves, however, *who* exemplifies that ideal type for steadfast obedience in the Letter to the Hebrews, the answer is plain: Jesus, "who was faithful to the one that appointed him" (3:2), who as the "pioneer and perfecter of faith" (τῆς πίστεως ἀρχηγὸν καὶ τελειωτήν, 12:2) recapitulates and culminates the testimony of the whole cloud of faithful witnesses rhetorically summoned up in chapter 11. Perhaps more clearly than any other NT writing, Hebrews presents Jesus as the paradigm for the life of faith. Thus, although the Habakkuk citation in Heb 10:37-38 does not understand ὁ δίκαιος as a messianic title, it does project a vision of faithfulness for which Jesus is the prototype. Though the author of Hebrews does not think of Jesus as "the Righteous One," he could hardly think of a "righteous one" without thinking of Jesus. Consequently, the situation here is similar to the state of affairs already discussed above with reference to James 5:6: though the term ὁ δίκαιος is not a title, Jesus is the prototype who provides its material content.

One final observation casts further light on the apocalyptic hermeneutical context presupposed in Heb 10 for the reading of Hab 2:3-4. That this passage was widely discussed in formative Judaism and in early Christianity as a locus crucial for theological understanding of the delay of the end time has been amply documented by A. Strobel's extensive study of the history of interpretation of this text;[37] thus, it is no surprise to find the author of Hebrews employing it as part of a plea for eschatological ὑπομονή. However, the strongly apocalyptic coloring of the quotation is even more clearly visible in the light of a fact often noted but rarely pondered by commentators: the Habakkuk quotation is introduced in Heb 10:37 by a fragmentary allusion to Isa 26:20 LXX ("For yet a little while" [ἔτι γὰρ μικρὸν ὅσον ὅσον]). Of course, when linked syntactically with Hab 2:3, the adverbial phrase simply serves to stress the imminence of the coming of the Coming One, but a careful reader may recall the apocalyptic

---

37. Strobel, *Untersuchungen zum eschatologischen Verzögerungsproblem auf Grund der spätjüdisch-urchristlichen Geschichte von Habakuk 2,2ff.*

imagery of the original context in the LXX of Isaiah: "The dead shall rise, and those who are in the tombs shall be raised, and those who are in the earth shall rejoice. For the dew that comes from you is a healing for them, but the land of the ungodly shall fall. Walk, my people, go into your closets, shut your door, be hidden for a little while (μικρὸν ὅσον ὅσον) until the wrath of the Lord passes away. For behold, the Lord is bringing wrath from the holy place (or: Holy One? [ἀπὸ τοῦ ἁγίου]) upon those who dwell upon the earth" (Isa 26:19-21). Visions of wrath and resurrection, judgment upon the ungodly and warnings to God's people to lie low for the briefest of times to await the working of God's power — is the echo of Isaiah in Heb 10:37 a calculated evocation of these themes and images? If not, it is hard to imagine why the distinctive phrasing of Isa 26:20 should be employed. If so, the apocalyptic matrix within which Hab 2:3-4 was read by early Christians becomes more clearly evident.

Having completed our survey of texts that speak of an eschatological "righteous one," we may draw some conclusions. It is difficult to make the case that "Righteous One" was a fixed formal title for the Messiah in pre-Christian Judaism. (Of course, it is notoriously difficult to make out *any* case for what may have been believed or said about "the Messiah" in pre-Christian Judaism.) It is clear, however, that at least in some Christian circles there was an early convention of applying the epithet ὁ δίκαιος to Jesus. The evidence of Acts leads us to suppose that this convention may have been characteristic of Jewish Christian communities, and the evidence of *1 Enoch* makes it likely that non-Christian Jews also entertained the expectation of an eschatological Righteous One who would appear as judge in the end time to set things right. Expectations of this sort may well have been grounded in Hab 2:3-4, although the specifically messianic interpretation of this text must have arisen within communities that read the prophecy in the LXX translation rather than in the Hebrew.

The linkage of the Coming/Righteous One to the righteous sufferer of Isa 53 is surely a distinctive Christian exegetical development. Once the linkage was made, however, several consequences followed: (1) the Isaiah text (and perhaps Wis 2 as well) was used apologetically to defend the innocence of Jesus and to argue the culpability of his executioners, as we see in the Acts speeches; (2) the suffering of the Righteous One was interpreted as making vicarious atonement for sin, as in 1 Peter and 1 John; (3) the Righteous One's suffering was interpreted as paradigmatic for steadfast obedience to God (= πίστις) in the time of eschatological adversity, as in 1 Peter, Hebrews, and perhaps James. The ideas of (2) and (3) are very closely connected, because both presuppose an identification between the Righteous One and his people — indeed, the identification is so complete that it seems at times to posit an ontological bonding, as becomes apparent in texts like 1 John 2:29 and Hebrews (passim).

All of these texts, with the possible exception of *1 Enoch,* are to be dated slightly later than the Pauline epistles, but the motif of the Righteous One appears in formulations that may be traditional and therefore early. This is especially true of the relevant passages in Acts and 1 Peter. The conflated citation of Isa 26:20 and Hab 2:3-4 in Heb 10:37-38 may also presuppose an existing exegetical tradition. The evidence, both within the NT itself and in the subsequent history of interpretation, makes it unlikely that the titular use of ὁ δίκαιος in relation to Jesus is a late theological development; if anything, the evidence runs the other direction. "The Righteous One" appears to be a designation accorded to Jesus within earliest apocalyptic Jewish Christianity but subsequently abandoned by the church, presumably because it was neither distinctive enough (cf. the discussion above of the application of the same title to James)[38] nor adequately expressive of the exalted metaphysical claims that Christians wanted to make about Jesus. Insofar as the designation continues to be ascribed to Jesus in the later Catholic Epistles, it is moving away from its apocalyptic point of origin and toward an emphasis on Jesus as good moral example, though the apocalyptic connotations are never entirely surrendered in the NT.

The Righteous One in Paul

In light of these reflections, we may approach Paul's two explicit citations of Hab 2:4 and ask how this text must have looked to him through the lenses of early Christian traditions and of his own apocalyptic hermeneutic. I leave Gal 3:11 for last because it is by far the more difficult of the two cases.

38. Cadbury ("Titles of Jesus," 364 n. 2) also points out parallels such as the Athenian statesman Aristides the Just and the use of Justus as a common Latin surname (cf. Acts 1:23; 18:7; Col 4:11).

Romans 1:17

That Paul's citation of Hab 2:4 in Rom 1:17 appears in an apocalyptic theological context should require no labored demonstration. The Habakkuk text is adduced in support of Paul's proclamation that the righteousness of God is being revealed (ἀποκαλύπτεται) in the gospel; furthermore, this revelation of the righteousness of God is accompanied by the revelation of God's wrath (1:18-32) and impending eschatological judgment (cf. 2:1-11). Thus, the programmatic declaration of 1:16-17 stands as the keynote of a gospel written in an apocalyptic key.[39]

The language used in this declaration echoes numerous passages in the Psalms and Isaiah that promise a future eschatological consummation in which God's salvific intervention on behalf of Israel will bring all nations to worship Israel's God. A particularly clear example, prefiguring almost all the key terms of Rom 1:16-17, is to be found in Ps 97:2 (LXX): "The Lord has made known his salvation (σωτήριον); in the presence of the nations (ἐθνῶν) he has revealed (ἀπεκάλυψεν) his righteousness (δικαιοσύνην)." (Cf. also Isa 51:4-5; 52:10.) Though Paul does not refer explicitly to these scriptural passages, his use of their language suggests that his gospel must be understood as the fulfillment of the hope to which they point: that God's righteousness will be revealed in an act of deliverance for the Jews first and also for the Gentiles.[40] This claim stands as the foundation of the apologetic edifice constructed by the rest of the letter, which argues vigorously that God's righteousness is confirmed, not compromised, by his act of deliverance through Jesus Christ (cf. 3:5-26).[41]

How, in this context, does the citation of Hab 2:4 serve to support the argument? Amidst all the controversy since the Reformation about how the expression ὁ δίκαιος ἐκ πίστεως ζήσεται should be interpreted, parties on all sides of the debate have been surprisingly content to assume that Paul employs the passage as a proof text with complete disregard for its

---

39. This point stands even if Ernst Käsemann is wrong about δικαιοσύνη θεοῦ as a technical term in apocalyptic theological discourse.

40. These observations also suggest that "the righteousness of God" in Romans should be understood first of all in relation to the background of this language in Isaiah and the Psalms. Cf. R. B. Hays, "Psalm 143 and the Logic of Romans 3," *JBL* 99 (1980): 107-15 (reprinted in the present volume); see also Hays, "Justification," in *ABD* 3:1129-32.

41. For a fuller discussion, see R. B. Hays, *Echoes of Scripture in the Letters of Paul* (New Haven: Yale University Press, 1989), 34-83.

original setting in Habakkuk's prophecy. When we realize, however, that Paul is setting out in Romans to address the question of God's faithfulness to the covenant with Israel, the aptness of the quotation from Habakkuk immediately stands forth. In Habakkuk the passage Paul quotes comes as the nub of God's answer to the prophet's complaint (Hab 2:1) against the apparent injustice of God's ways. How can God allow the wicked to oppress the righteous (1:13; cf. 1:2-4)? Has God abandoned his people? Whatever else Hab 2:4 might be construed to mean, it is a response to the problem of theodicy, an implicit assertion of God's righteousness. The faithful community is enjoined to wait with patience for that which they do not yet see: the appearing of God's justice. This hope God will not disappoint.

Unlike 1QpHab and Hebrews, however, Paul does not appeal to the Habakkuk text in service of an exhortation to patience. Instead, he treats the passage as a prophecy now fulfilled in the revelation of the gospel. The manifestation of the righteousness of God is present reality, not merely future hope. Just as it is written (καθὼς γέγραπται) that the righteous one will live by faith, so now indeed the righteousness of God is being revealed ἐκ πίστεως εἰς πίστιν. The gospel of God was "pre-announced" through prophets in holy writings (1:2), and now the prophesied eschatological deliverance has come/is coming to pass in such a way that the correlation between prophetic word and present reality undergirds the assertion of God's righteousness. In short, Paul is claiming that Habakkuk's hope has at last received its answer through a revelation ἐκ πίστεως.

It is not hard to understand such a claim if we recall that the LXX of Hab 2:3-4 was messianic in character. It promised a Coming One, and the whole weight of Christian proclamation declared that Jesus was precisely that long-expected figure. Thus, it is entirely probable that Paul's apocalyptic exegesis of Habakkuk would have recognized in the prophecy a promise about the coming of Jesus Christ. As C. H. Dodd remarked, Paul's use of the quotation is most readily intelligible if "he drew upon a tradition which already recognized the passage from Habakkuk as a *testimonium* to the coming of Christ."[42]

But what about ὁ δίκαιος? Is there any indication that Paul understood this term as a messianic designation? Or is it more likely that, like the writer of Hebrews, he read the Habakkuk passage as apocalyptic without construing ὁ δίκαιος as a direct reference to Jesus? Unfortunately, the com-

---

42. Dodd, *According to the Scriptures*, 51.

pressed formulaic character of Rom 1:17 makes this question impossible to answer definitively. The best that can be done within the compass of this essay is to suggest briefly three factors that might favor a "messianic" interpretation of Rom 1:17. (Readers can supply the counterarguments for themselves.)

1. What sense does it make to say, as the syntax of Rom 1:17 requires us to do, that God's saving righteousness is revealed *out of* faith (ἐκ πίστεως)? Surely it would be peculiar to suppose that the human (Christian) disposition of faith toward God should be itself the source out of which God's eschatological righteousness is now revealed in a new way. Paul has been so interpreted in some theological traditions, but the oddness of the interpretation must be marked. Have not Jews always had faith in God? Would not Paul's sentence make better sense if he meant that through the πίστις of Jesus the Righteous One, the righteousness of God is now revealed to those who believe (εἰς πίστιν)? (After all, in Rom 3:25-26 Paul says God put *Jesus* forward as a demonstration of his [God's] righteousness; this looks very much like an explication of the sense in which Hab 2:4 can be construed as a confirmation of Paul's claim [1:17] that the righteousness of God is revealed in the gospel.) Since I have contended elsewhere that the logic of the argumentation in Rom 3:21-26 requires this interpretation of "the faith of Jesus Christ,"[43] I will not try the reader's patience by repeating that argument here.

2. Paul's account of the mechanism of salvation in Rom 5:18-19, in an antithetical parallelism to the consequences of Adam's disobedience, asserts that Jesus' "righteous deed" (δικαίωμα, in contrast to Adam's παράπτωμα) has resulted in the "righteousness of life" (cf. Hab 2:4) for all and that many shall be constituted righteous (δίκαιοι) through *Jesus'* obedience. "Righteous One" is not used as an epithet of Jesus in this very dense passage, but the certain allusion in 5:19 to Isa 53:11 suggests that Paul is drawing here on a tradition that describes Jesus as the δίκαιος whose righteousness is vicariously efficacious for "many."[44]

3. The other NT texts considered in this essay (pp. 124-36) suggest that Paul lived and wrote in a world of discourse — i.e., early Jewish Christianity — where ὁ δίκαιος was a common designation for Jesus. If that is so, Paul might presuppose the christological exegesis of Hab 2:4 without com-

---

43. Hays, *Faith of Jesus Christ*, 156-61.
44. On Rom 5:18-19, see especially the discussion of Johnson, "Faith of Jesus," 87-90.

menting on it, just as he presupposes without comment the christological exegesis of Ps 69 in Rom 15:3. On the other hand, if he held some idiosyncratic interpretation of the text (such as "the one who is righteous-through-faith-not-through-works shall live"), he would certainly run the risk of being severely misunderstood in quoting the phrase to an unfamiliar Christian congregation at Rome with no more explanation than he offers in Rom 1.

None of these considerations is entirely compelling, but the strongly apocalyptic theological context of Rom 1 creates at least a presumption in favor of the messianic exegesis of Hab 2:4 as the interpretation that would have been most readily at hand for Paul and that makes the best sense out of the letter's argument. It remains to be seen whether a similar claim can be made in relation to Gal 3:11.

Galatians 3:11

With the aid of the observations above about the apocalyptic theology of Romans, we may identify four apocalyptic motifs in Galatians that are especially pertinent to the interpretation of Gal 3:11 in its context.[45]

1. As in his letter to the Romans, Paul contends in Galatians that the Scripture promises the inclusion of the Gentiles among God's people (3:8-9) and that the present empirical phenomenon of the Gentiles' receiving of the gospel constitutes the eschatological fulfillment of that promise (3:14). The (Christian) faith of the Gentiles is not merely a broadening of Israel's religious constituency; rather, it is an apocalyptic sign, a phenomenon that bears witness to the presence of the new age (3:23-29).[46] (That is one of the reasons behind Paul's bitter opposition to the efforts of others to turn the Galatians into Jewish proselytes: that would turn the calendar back by erasing the apocalyptic sign.)

2. The presence of the Spirit in the community (3:3-5) is also a sign of the new age, a fulfillment of the eschatological promise (3:14; 4:6).

3. The Spirit is the source of *life* (5:25), not just ordinary human existence but an eschatological life to/with God, a life lived in the power of the

---

45. Cf. the motifs enumerated by Martyn, "Antinomies," 416-18.

46. Cf. Donaldson, "Curse," 94-112, for a helpful discussion of the centrality of this theme within Paul's theological reflection.

new age through participation in the death of Christ (2:19-20). Paul construes the ζήσεται of Hab 2:4 as a reference to this eschatological life (cf. Rom 1:16-17), and he is sure that the Law, contrary to its self-advertisement (Lev 18:5; Gal 3:12), has no power to give such life (3:21).

4. All these apocalyptic blessings (faith, Spirit, life) are made available only at one appointed time (3:23; 4:4) and only to One, namely, "the Seed to whom it was promised" (3:19). The "Seed," Paul insists, is Christ alone (3:16), and others receive the abundance of eschatological blessing only "in Christ" (3:14), i.e., as a result of participation in him (3:26-29). For Paul Christ is the one to whom God's promise is made and in whom it is fulfilled.

In light of this configuration of apocalyptic themes, which constitute the foundation and framework of Paul's argument in Galatians, we may repeat one simple question: Who is ὁ δίκαιος? When Paul, operating out of this sort of apocalyptic intellectual matrix, read Hab 2:3-4 in the LXX, a text that already carried apocalyptic/messianic resonances for Jews of his time, how did he understand it? My contention is that he understood it as a messianic prophecy, just as he understood — in a way quite startling to us — Gen 17:8 as messianic prophecy (Gal 3:16). This sort of divinatory reading is a direct and natural consequence of the apostle's apocalyptic hermeneutical perspective: those who have experienced the apocalypse of the Son of God now find the veil taken away from Scripture so that they can perceive its witness to him, including its witness to him as the Coming/Righteous One.

There is one very simple test of this proposal: read through Gal 3:10-18 with the working hypothesis that ὁ δίκαιος = Χριστὸς Ἰησοῦς = τὸ σπέρμα. Does Paul's exegetical argument make more or less sense on the basis of the hypothesis?

We remain much more in the dark than we would like to be. If Paul has in mind a messianic interpretation of Hab 2:4, why does he not say so more clearly, as he does in the case of Gen 17:8? There can be no definitive answer, of course, but we would do well to bear in mind a salutary reminder of Strobel: the way Paul introduces the quotation in 3:11 (δῆλον) presupposes that his readers know all about it already,[47] a presupposition that appears entirely reasonable in light of Strobel's evidence about the status of Hab 2:3-4 as a locus classicus in Jewish apocalyptic traditions. Rather than having to explain the meaning of the quotation, Paul can use

---

47. Strobel, *Verzögerungsproblem*, 191.

it to argue a point. A similar observation could be made about the way he uses the same text in Rom 1:17: he appears to be citing a famous text that serves at once as rubric and clincher of his argument.

These reflections about the possibility that Paul understood Hab 2:4 as an apocalyptic *testimonium* to the coming of an eschatological deliverer are of course not probative in their force; they represent a first attempt to think through some of the implications of Martyn's deft and provocative placement of Galatians into an apocalyptic theological context.[48] Whether these suggestions about the interpretation of Rom 1:17 and Gal 3:11 find favor or not, a larger task lies before us as we take up Martyn's challenge to allow Galatians "to play its own role in showing us precisely what the nature of Paul's apocalyptic was."[49] The task is to seek an understanding of the way in which Paul's reading of *Scripture* unfolds apocalyptic perceptions of world and text.

48. One of the hazards of becoming an esteemed scholar for whom Festschriften are written is that all the contributors seek to attribute their divers schemes and notions to the influence of the honoree. Let it be said, therefore, that Lou is hereby absolved of responsibility for anything harebrained herein and gratefully thanked for the true and useful things that I have learned from him.

49. Martyn, "Antinomies," 412.

The Role of Scripture
in Paul's Ethics

The Problem

How does Scripture function in Paul's ethics? We might expect it to play a major role in his moral teaching, for he writes in Rom 15:4: "For whatever was written in former days was written for our instruction (εἰς τὴν ἡμετέραν διδασκαλίαν), so that by steadfastness and by the encouragement of the scriptures (διὰ τῆς παρακλήσεως τῶν γραφῶν) we might have hope." Here the biblical writings are portrayed as a fundamental source of instruction (διδασκαλία) and moral exhortation (παράκλησις). Such a view of the texts is hardly surprising for one who called himself a "Hebrew of Hebrews" (Phil 3:5) and distinguished himself among his contemporaries by his zeal for "the traditions of [his] ancestors" (Gal 1:14). The Scriptures of Israel were embedded deeply in his bones. Recent studies of Paul's thought have increasingly recognized the major role played by Scripture[1] in constituting his imaginative world.[2]

---

1. Paul characteristically uses the term "Scripture" (ἡ γραφή) to refer to Israel's sacred texts. He never uses the expression "Old Testament." His single use of the term "old covenant" (ἡ παλαιὰ διαθήκη, 2 Cor 3:14) refers not to the canon of Scripture as a whole but specifically to the Mosaic Law. The term "Hebrew Bible," also never used by Paul, is confusing and inappropriate since Paul, writing in Greek to Greek-speaking readers, normally quotes the LXX rather than translating the Hebrew text.

2. I have argued this position extensively in *Echoes of Scripture in the Letters of Paul* (New Haven: Yale University Press, 1989). See also D. A. Koch, *Die Schrift als Zeuge des Evangeliums: Untersuchungen zur Verwendung und zum Verständnis der Schrift bei Paulus*, BHT 69 (Tübingen: J. C. B. Mohr [Paul Siebeck], 1986); Christopher D. Stanley, *Paul and the Language of Scripture: Citation Technique in the Pauline Epistles and Contemporary Litera-*

Yet when we consider Paul's actual use of Scripture in shaping his *ethical* arguments, the evidence appears to be remarkably slight; Paul's own practice of moral teaching does not self-evidently exemplify the didactic role ascribed to Scripture in the programmatic statement of Rom 15:4. Paul is reluctant to treat Scripture as a rule book. Indeed, he explicitly argues that various requirements of the Torah are not binding for his Gentile churches: circumcision (1 Cor 7:17-20; Gal 5:2-6), food laws (Rom 14:1-4, 14, 20), and probably the Sabbath (Rom 14:5; Gal 4:9-11). The Law, he says, was a παιδαγωγός whose commission was valid and necessary until faith came, but now, since the resurrection of Jesus, the Law is no longer necessary (Gal 3:23-25). Thus, when he is confronted with various problems of conduct in his churches (e.g., divorce, eating idol meat), he does not settle them in a rabbinic fashion by seeking to apply Torah casuistically. For example, in dealing with the issue of divorce in 1 Cor 7:10-16, he makes no reference to Deut 24:1-4, the Pentateuchal passage that was the focus of rabbinic discussions of the topic. The omission is perhaps not surprising, since Deuteronomy permits divorce, while Paul is seeking to restrict it.

Victor Furnish, after surveying a number of passages in which Paul does cite Scripture in his ethical arguments, summarizes the situation aptly:

> It is noteworthy that Paul never quotes the Old Testament *in extenso* for the purpose of developing a pattern of conduct. Except for a few instances in which a catena of passages from several different scriptural contexts is assembled, the citations are always brief. Moreover, and even of greater significance, they are never casuistically interpreted or elaborated. . . . There is no evidence which indicates that the apostle regarded [the Old Testament] as in any sense a source book for detailed moral instruction or even a manual of ethical norms.[3]

---

ture, SNTSMS 69 (Cambridge: Cambridge University Press, 1992); J. W. Aageson, *Written Also for Our Sake: Paul and the Art of Biblical Interpretation* (Louisville: Westminster/John Knox, 1993); C. A. Evans and J. A. Sanders, eds., *Paul and the Scriptures of Israel*, JSNTSup 83 (Sheffield: JSOT Press, 1993); R. H. Bell, *Provoked to Jealousy: The Origin and Purpose of the Jealousy Motif in Romans 9–11*, WUNT 2, ser. 63 (Tübingen: J. C. B. Mohr [Paul Siebeck], 1994); F. Wilk, *Die Bedeutung des Jesajabuches für Paulus*, FRLANT 179 (Göttingen: Vandenhoeck & Ruprecht, 1998); J. R. Wagner, *Heralds of the Good News: Isaiah and Paul "In Concert" in the Letter to the Romans*, NovTSup 101 (Leiden: Brill, 2002); F. Watson, *Paul and the Hermeneutics of Faith* (London: T. & T. Clark, 2004).

3. V. P. Furnish, *Theology and Ethics in Paul* (Nashville: Abingdon, 1968), 33. More re-

Instead, Paul seeks to commend his normative moral teachings on the basis of the gospel itself: right behavior is understood as "the fruit of the Spirit" (Gal 5:22-23), the natural outflow of the new life in Christ. Moral judgment becomes a matter not of obeying a written law but of discerning God's will in the new apocalyptic situation: "I appeal to you therefore, brothers and sisters, by the mercies of God, to present your bodies as a living sacrifice, holy and acceptable to God, which is your spiritual worship. Do not be conformed to this age (τῷ αἰῶνι τούτῳ), but be transformed by the renewing of your minds, so that you may discern what is the will of God — what is good and acceptable and perfect" (Rom 12:1-2).

Thus, many scholars have argued, Scripture becomes de facto irrelevant — or at least a minor factor — for Pauline ethics.[4] Andreas Lindemann, for example, declares: "[Paulus] versteht aber das Alte Testament, seine Bibel, gerade nicht mehr als Tora in eigentlichen Sinne; sie ist ihm nicht mehr die Quelle der Weisungen Gottes für das Verhalten der Menschen, soweit sie Christen sind."[5] Can this be correct? If so, how could Paul write Rom 15:4?[6] Or again, what are we to make of 1 Cor 10:11, which comments on the fate of Israel's wilderness generation? "These things happened to them typologically (τυπικῶς), and they were written down for our instruction (ἐγράφη δὲ πρὸς νουθεσίαν ἡμῶν), upon whom the ends of the ages have met." Here Paul regards the written scriptural witness as a word for the instruction of his own community, a word intended by God

---

cently P. J. Tomson (*Paul and the Jewish Law: Halakha in the Letters of the Apostle to the Gentiles*, CRINT III/1 [Assen and Maastricht: Van Gorcum; Minneapolis: Fortress, 1990]) has argued, to the contrary, that Paul's ethical teaching is deeply grounded in rabbinic traditions of halakic scriptural interpretation.

4. For an impressive roster of scholars who take this position, see the summary of B. S. Rosner, *Paul, Scripture, and Ethics: A Study of 1 Corinthians 5–7*, AGJU 22 (Leiden: Brill, 1994), 3-9.

5. "Paul, however, no longer understands the Old Testament, his Bible, as Torah in the proper sense; it is for him no longer the source of the directions of God for the behavior of human beings, insofar as they are Christians." A. Lindemann, "Die biblischen Toragebote und die paulinische Ethik," in *Studien zum Text und der Ethik des Neuen Testaments: Festschrift zum 80. Geburtstag von Heinrich Greeven,* ed. W. Schrage (Berlin: De Gruyter, 1986), 242-65, quotation from 263-64.

6. One solution to this problem is offered by L. E. Keck ("Romans 15:4 — an Interpolation?" in *Faith and History: Essays in Honor of Paul W. Meyer,* ed. J. T. Carroll, C. H. Cosgrove, and E. E. Johnson [Atlanta: Scholars, 1991], 125-36), who has argued that Paul did *not* write it: Keck proposes that the verse is a post-Pauline gloss.

precisely for the eschatological moment in which apostle and church now find themselves. The ethical import of this word for the situation Paul is addressing is very clear: the community is to flee from association with idols (10:14) and to beware of overconfident presumption upon the grace of God (10:12). In such a case, we see Paul appealing to Scripture very directly as a basis for ethical admonition to the church.

Clearly, a fresh look at the problem is needed. Lindemann and others are right that Paul does not use Scripture as the rabbis did, yet there are numerous indications in Paul's letters that the Scripture somehow shapes his moral vision.[7] The conclusions drawn by Furnish in his discussion of the problem suggest a promising way forward:

> In fact, Paul's use of the Old Testament in his ethical teaching is not to be radically differentiated from his use of the Old Testament overall. In connection with ethical admonition and instruction, as elsewhere, an important presupposition is that the Old Testament is scriptural witness to the history of God's dealings with his people, his claim upon them, and his promises concerning their future. . . . While the Old Testament, then, is not a "source" for Paul's ethical instruction in a narrow sense, it is a source for it in a more basic way. . . . The Old Testament is not a source for his ethical teaching in that it provides him rules, aphorisms, maxims, and proverbs. Rather, it is a source for his ethical teaching in that it provides him with a perspective from which he interprets the whole event of God's act in Christ, and the concomitant and consequent claim God makes on the believer.[8]

Although Furnish does not develop this programmatic claim in detail, his basic insight merits fuller reflection: to understand the role of Scripture in Paul's ethics, we must widen our field of vision and consider the way in which Scripture renders a "world" for Paul, the way in which his symbolic universe is constituted by a particular reading of Israel's sacred texts.

I propose that we think about this problem by considering five ways in

7. The work of Rosner, for example (*Paul, Scripture, and Ethics*), traces some of the ways Paul's teaching in 1 Cor 5–7 presupposes and alludes to biblical texts. See my review in *WTJ* 58 (1996): 313-16.

8. Furnish, *Theology and Ethics*, 34, 42. The present essay is dedicated to Victor Furnish with gratitude for his collegial support, as well as for his careful and generative work on Pauline ethics.

which Scripture informs Paul's ethics. Our treatment of these five aspects will move from the most global to the most particular roles played by the biblical texts in shaping Paul's moral world.

Some Functions of Scripture in Pauline Ethics

Scripture as Narrative Framework for Community Identity

Paul reads Scripture in light of a narrative hermeneutic as a grand story of election and promise, the story of δικαιοσύνη θεοῦ, God's covenant faithfulness reaching out to reclaim a fallen and broken humanity.[9] That is why his use of Scripture highlights the story of Abraham (the patriarch to whom God's universal promise was made), the climactic chapters of Deuteronomy (which promise covenant renewal and restoration of the people), and above all the prophetic passages known to us as Deutero-Isaiah (which promise the revelation of God's salvation to all flesh, the Jew first and then also all nations). The church is called to find its identity and mission within this epic story stretching from Adam to Abraham to Moses to Isaiah to Christ to the saints in Paul's own historical moment.

"What time is it?" "What is God doing in the world?" "What is our vocation as God's people?" These are the questions Paul asks and answers on the basis of Scripture. A particularly powerful illustration of this way of reading Scripture is found in 2 Cor 5:17–6:2:

> So if anyone is in Christ, there is a new creation: everything old has passed away; see, everything has become new! All this is from God, who reconciled us to himself through Christ, and has given us the ministry of reconciliation; that is, in Christ God was reconciling the world to himself, not counting their trespasses against them, and entrusting the message of reconciliation to us. So we are ambassadors for Christ, since God is making his appeal through us; we entreat you on behalf of Christ, be reconciled to God. For our sake he made him to be sin who knew no sin, so that in him we might become the righteousness of God. As we work together with him, we urge you also not to accept the grace of God in vain. For he says,

9. For fuller development and defense of these themes see Hays, *Echoes,* especially 156-64.

> "At an acceptable time I have listened to you,
> and on a day of salvation I have helped you."

See, now is the acceptable time; see, now is the day of salvation!

What time is it? Now is the day of salvation announced by Isaiah (Isa 49:8), the time in which the Servant of the Lord will both raise up the tribes of Jacob and extend God's salvation to the ends of the earth (Isa 49:6). *What is God doing in the world?* God is reconciling the world to himself and actualizing the new creation that Isaiah prophesied (Isa 43:18-19; 65:17-25; 66:22-23). *What is our vocation as God's people?* Our vocation is to embody the message of reconciliation by *becoming* the righteousness of God (δικαιοσύνη θεοῦ). That is to say, the vocation of the community is to become a visible manifestation of God's reconciling covenant love in the world.[10] Such a description of the community's identity has wide-ranging implications for ethics, even though Paul does not spell them out fully at this point in 2 Corinthians. He does, however, in the apostolic self-description that follows immediately in 6:3-10, offer some hint of what it might mean to model the new creation in a world still hostile to God: hardships, suffering, and conformity to the example of Jesus.

Thus, Scripture provides an overarching proleptic vision of God's design to redeem the world and situates the community of believers within the unfolding story of this dramatic redemption. Every word of ethical guidance that Paul gives to his churches finds its ultimate warrant in this narrative framework. If ethical judgments are inseparable from foundational construals of communal identity, then any consideration of Pauline ethics must attend to the way in which Paul's understanding of the church's vocation is rooted in his reading of Scripture.

Scripture as Call to Righteousness and Love

Paul's vision of the church's identity carries with it the axiomatic conviction that the people of God are called to be a holy people whose conduct conforms to the will of God (cf. 1 Cor 1:2). Equally axiomatic for Paul is the conviction that the Law — which is "holy and righteous and good" (Rom

---

10. On δικαιοσύνη θεοῦ as covenant language, see R. B. Hays, "Justification," in *ABD* 3:1129-33.

7:12) — positively discloses God's will. Consequently, in several places Paul offers sweeping summary statements that construe the Law in global fashion as a mandate for righteousness and/or love. "Owe no one anything, except to love one another; for the one who loves another has fulfilled the Law. The commandments 'You shall not commit adultery; You shall not murder; You shall not steal; You shall not covet' [Exod 20:13-17; Deut 5:17-21]; and any other commandment, are summed up in this word, 'You shall love your neighbor as yourself' [Lev 19:18]. Love does no wrong to a neighbor; therefore, love is the fulfilling of the Law" (Rom 13:8-10). Here Paul cites Lev 19:18 as a summation of the content of the moral precepts of the Decalogue, thereby elaborating more fully what he meant in Gal 5:14 by saying, "For the whole Law is summed up in a single commandment, 'You shall love your neighbor as yourself.'" It has often been observed that this appeal to Lev 19:18 as an encapsulation of Torah is formally similar to the teaching of Rabbi Hillel: "What is hateful to you, do not do to your neighbor" (*b. Šabbat* 31a).[11] Our particular concern here, however, is not only to notice that Paul's strategy of summing up the Law has parallels among his Jewish contemporaries but also to observe that he accomplishes this summation by citing another biblical text, interpreting Scripture by means of Scripture.[12] The hermeneutical reconfiguration of the Law is achieved not through appeal to the teaching of Jesus or to some other normative consideration but through a rereading of Scripture itself.

One remarkable feature of this global construal of the Law is that it allows Paul to contend that Christians can "fulfill" the Law without actually observing all the particular practices it requires. This conviction — surely strange to Jews who shared Paul's own prior Pharisaic beliefs — underlies 1 Cor 7:19: "Circumcision is nothing, and uncircumcision is nothing; but what matters is keeping the commandments of God." Since circumcision *was* one of the commandments of God, this affirmation can only have

---

11. On Paul's use of Lev 19:18, see V. P. Furnish, *The Love Command in the New Testament* (Nashville: Abingdon, 1972), 94, 97, 102-4, 107-11; W. Schrage, *Die konkreten Einzelgebote in der paulinischen Paränese* (Gütersloh: Gütersloher Verlagshaus, Gerd Mohn, 1961), 97-100, 249-71; A. Nissen, *Gott und der Nächste im antiken Judentum: Untersuchungen zum Doppelgebot der Liebe,* WUNT 15 (Tübingen: J. C. B. Mohr [Paul Siebeck], 1974).

12. Whether Paul's singling out of Lev 19:18 was original with him or he was dependent on early Christian tradition, perhaps going back to Jesus himself (cf. Mark 12:28-34 par.), is a question that need not concern us here. See J. D. G. Dunn, *Romans 9–16,* WBC 38B (Dallas: Word, 1988), 779.

seemed bizarre and scandalous to Paul's Jewish contemporaries. Paul, however, had undergone a conversion of the imagination in his reading of Scripture that allowed him to see Gentiles in Christ as fulfilling what the Law requires. This is made explicit in Rom 2:26-29a:

> So, if those who are uncircumcised keep the requirements of the Law (τὰ δικαιώματα τοῦ νόμου), will not their uncircumcision be regarded as circumcision? Then those who by nature are uncircumcised (= Gentiles) but who keep the Law will condemn you that have the written code and circumcision but break the Law. For a person is not a Jew who is one in appearance, nor is circumcision a matter of appearance in the flesh. Rather, the (real) Jew is one who is one inwardly, and (real) circumcision is circumcision of the heart in the spirit, not in letter.

The interpretative move here is the same one Paul makes in Phil 3:2-3 in his warning against Judaizers who "mutilate the flesh": "For it is *we* who are the circumcision, who worship in the Spirit of God and boast in Christ Jesus and have no confidence in the flesh." In both cases, rather than conceding that the honorific term περιτομή ("circumcision" — understood as a designation for God's elect) can be restricted to the Jewish people, Paul metaphorizes the term and claims it for the members of the new community that trusts in Jesus Christ. Even if they are physically uncircumcised, they nonetheless manifest the kind of obedience from the heart that the Law commands. This is not merely an arbitrary hermeneutical sleight of hand: it is based, as the Rom 2 passage shows, on the biblical image of the "circumcision of the heart," which Paul finds prominently in Deuteronomy. Particularly important is Deut 30:6, which depicts the circumcision of the heart as God's gracious act of covenant renewal: "The Lord your God will circumcise your heart and the heart of your descendants, so that you will love the Lord your God with all your heart and with all your soul, in order that you may live" (cf. also Deut 10:16). If God has chosen now to circumcise the hearts of Gentile believers, as Paul maintains, that means they must be full participants in the covenant community.

All of this is set forth strikingly in Rom 8:3-4: "For God has done what the Law, weakened by the flesh, could not do: by sending his own Son in the likeness of sinful flesh and as a sin-offering,[13] he condemned sin in the

---

13. On this translation see N. T. Wright, *The Climax of the Covenant: Christ and the Law in Pauline Theology* (Minneapolis: Fortress, 1991), 220-25.

flesh, *so that the just requirement of the Law* (τὸ δικαίωμα τοῦ νόμου: cf. Rom 2:26) *might be fulfilled in us,* who walk not according to the flesh but according to the Spirit." The general mandate to fulfill the Law by walking in love is, on Paul's reading, to be found in Scripture itself. Thus, at a high level of generality Scripture both commands and prefigures a certain "ethic," a way of life dedicated to God's service. Those in Christ — whether Jews or Gentiles — who walk in the Spirit now fulfill what the Law requires, a life animated by the love of God.

Scripture as Implicit Source of Particular Norms

Of course, such a general mandate requires further behavioral specification. When Paul speaks of Gentiles fulfilling the Law, he is making certain assumptions about the sort of moral conduct that is pleasing to God. He assumes, as Rom 13:8-10 indicates, that adultery, murder, theft, and covetousness are contrary to loving the neighbor and that "fulfilling the law" implicitly requires obedience to the commandments of the Decalogue. We see here, however, only the tip of the iceberg: Paul assumes without supporting argumentation a whole network of moral judgments and norms whose source lies ultimately in Israel's Law.[14] These assumptions, rarely raised to the level of conscious reflection, appear offhandedly in Paul's occasional vice lists. "Now the works of the flesh are obvious: fornication, impurity, licentiousness, idolatry, sorcery, enmities, strife, jealousy, anger, quarrels, dissensions, factions, envy, drunkenness, carousing, and things like these. I am warning you, as I warned you before: those who do such things will not inherit the kingdom of God" (Gal 5:19-21). Paul makes no attempt to derive his condemnation of these behaviors explicitly from Scripture; he regards their negative character as self-evident (φανερά). Nor can every item in the vice list be traced to a particular Old Testament commandment. Nonetheless, some of the items are clear violations of biblical teaching: fornication, impurity, idolatry, sorcery. In such lists, even though Paul does not bother to draw clear distinctions between biblical norms and general

14. See W. Schrage, *The Ethics of the New Testament* (Philadelphia: Fortress, 1988), 205: "There are instances where Paul as it were instinctively and without further justification presupposes certain conclusions deriving from Jewish thought based on the Torah."

commonsense moral standards, it is clear that Scripture has played a role in shaping his vision of the moral life.

Paul summons those who have become members of the Christian community to live a new kind of life, leaving behind immoral conduct that formerly characterized their existence: "Do you not know that wrongdoers will not inherit the kingdom of God? Do not be deceived! Fornicators, idolaters, adulterers, male prostitutes (μαλακοί), sodomites (ἀρσενοκοῖται), thieves, the greedy, drunkards, revilers, robbers — none of these will inherit the kingdom of God. And this is what some of you used to be. But you were washed, you were sanctified . . . in the name of the Lord Jesus Christ and in the Spirit of our God" (1 Cor 6:9-11). The similarity of this list to that of Gal 5:19-21 is obvious, but the addition of μαλακοί and particularly of ἀρσενοκοῖται provides an interesting example of the "background" function of Scripture in Pauline ethics. Paul assumes a negative evaluation of same-sex intercourse that is rooted in distinctively Jewish attitudes which in turn depend upon the OT Law. Indeed, as Robin Scroggs has proposed, the term ἀρσενοκοῖται — not previously attested in Greek sources — is almost certainly a coinage derived from the language of Lev 18:22, 20:13 LXX.[15] Paul feels no need here, however, to cite chapter and verse or to make an ethical *argument* against homosexual acts. The Torah's condemnation of such behavior has become thoroughly diffused in Jewish culture and moral attitudes; Paul simply assumes his readers will share this moral judgment, just as he expects they will not need to be persuaded that stealing is wrong.

Similar assumptions underlie Paul's most extensively developed vice list in Rom 1:18-32, in which he depicts the plight of humanity in rebellion against their Creator.[16] The biblical subtexts here are manifold and complex: the condemnation of idolatry shows significant indebtedness to the Wisdom of Solomon (especially 12:23–14:31), but the idea that faithless humans have "exchanged" the glory of God for idolatrous images (Rom 1:18-23) draws upon Ps 106:20 ("They exchanged the glory of God/for the image of an ox that eats grass") and Jer 2:11:

> Has a nation changed its gods,
> even though they are no gods?

---

15. R. Scroggs, *The New Testament and Homosexuality* (Philadelphia: Fortress, 1983), 106-8.

16. For fuller discussion see R. B. Hays, "Relations Natural and Unnatural," *JRE* 14, no. 1 (1986): 184-215.

> But my people have changed their glory
> for something that does not profit.

This root sin of idolatrous rejection of the one true God leads humanity into a range of horrifying behavior, as God "gives them up" to follow their own devices and desires (Rom 1:24-32). Once again, Paul does not seek to adduce specific scriptural warrants for his condemnation of this catalogue of offenses; a negative judgment is assumed as part of the fabric of moral discourse. Yet there is no question that this fabric is woven with many threads drawn from Israel's Scripture.[17]

Scripture as Paradigmatic Narrative

Beyond specific norms and commandments, however, Scripture functions also in Paul's thought as a source of narratives that provide broader paradigms — examples of behavior, either positive or negative — for the life of the church. This is most evident in the passages where Paul explicitly reads the stories of Israel as prefiguring the experience of the church in his own day. I have contended in *Echoes of Scripture in the Letters of Paul* that this typological reading strategy — an ecclesiocentric hermeneutic for reading the OT — is pervasive in Paul's letters.[18] The identity of the community is shaped by its identification with Israel.

Writing to a predominantly Gentile church at Corinth, Paul addresses them in a way that includes them within Israel's story and simultaneously reconfigures Israel's story in the light of the church's practices: "I do not want you to be ignorant, brothers and sisters, that our fathers (οἱ πατέρες ἡμῶν) were all under the cloud, and all passed through the sea, and all were baptized into Moses in the cloud and in the sea, and all ate the same spiritual food, and all drank the same spiritual drink. For they drank from the spiritual rock that followed them, and the rock was Christ" (1 Cor 10:1-4).

---

17. I do not mean to deny that Paul drew his moral judgments also from other sources, including Greco-Roman philosophical traditions. See, for example, Furnish, *Theology and Ethics*, 44-51; H. D. Betz, *Galatians*, Hermeneia (Philadelphia: Fortress, 1979), passim; J. Paul Sampley, *Walking between the Times: Paul's Moral Reasoning* (Minneapolis: Fortress, 1991), 94-98. The point is rather that Scripture is part of the mix, that the taken-for-granted account of righteousness and unrighteousness that Paul presupposes as normative is influenced in countless important ways by the moral world of Israel's Scripture.

18. Hays, *Echoes*, 84-121.

The Gentile Corinthians are to recognize Israel's wilderness generation as "our fathers," and the story of their wanderings and misfortunes is now to be read as a prefiguration of the situation of the church. Even the supernatural spiritual events whereby God delivered Israel from captivity and preserved them in the desert could not serve as unconditional guarantees of God's favor; so, too, the Corinthians should not rely exclusively on baptism and the Lord's Supper as foolproof claims on God's grace.

The only biblical text actually quoted in 1 Cor 10:1-22 is a narrative description of the golden calf incident: "The people sat down to eat and drink, and they rose up to play" (Exod 32:6, quoted in 1 Cor 10:7). This single citation, however, evokes the larger story of Israel in the wilderness, and Paul follows it up with allusions to incidents described in Num 14:26-35, 25:1-9, 26:62, 21:5-9, and 16:41-50 (1 Cor 10:8-10). Paul uses each of these incidents in a hortatory fashion to warn the Corinthians against certain behavior: idolatry, sexual immorality, putting Christ to the test, and murmuring against God. In short, Paul uses the story of Israel here as a negative paradigm illustrating both rebellious behavior and its dire consequences.[19] The Corinthians should recognize themselves in the mirror of the biblical narrative and modify their behavior accordingly. If they fail to heed the warning, if they continue to flirt with idolatry by carelessly eating idol meat, they will be reenacting Israel's faithlessness. Paul subtly underscores the point by concluding the unit with a rhetorical question that echoes the Song of Moses (Deut 32): "Or are we provoking the Lord to jealousy (παραζηλοῦμεν)? Are we stronger than he?" (1 Cor 10:22). The full force of the question comes clear only when we recall the Deuteronomy text:

> They made him jealous with strange gods,
> with abhorrent things they provoked him.
> They sacrificed to demons, not God [cf. 1 Cor 10:20]. . . .
> The LORD saw it, and was jealous (ἐζήλωσεν);
> he spurned his sons and daughters.
> He said: I will hide my face from them. . . .

19. Paul's deft way of retelling the wilderness story, however, will not allow for a supersessionist interpretation: Israel had Christ (v. 4) and the sacraments (vv. 1-4), and the church faces the same testing they did (vv. 12-13). Thus, the church is not in a superior position, despite their privileged eschatological vantage point (v. 11). Indeed, the rhetoric of Paul's typological reading seeks to lead the Corinthians to see themselves in the *same* situation as Israel in the desert. See Hays, *Echoes*, 91-104.

They made me jealous (παρεζήλωσαν) with what is no god,
   provoked me with their idols.

(Deut 32:16-17a, 19-20a, 21a)[20]

Since the account of Israel's misadventures was written down "to instruct us, upon whom the ends of the ages have come" (1 Cor 10:11), the Corinthians should learn the lesson from the biblical story and shun "the table of demons" (10:21).

It is noteworthy that Paul argues the point here not by quoting commandments but by retelling the story and encouraging his readers to hear the resonances between the scriptural narrative and the contemporary problem. This passage in 1 Cor 10 is the most extensively developed illustration of this style of ethical argument in Paul's letters, but one could adduce numerous other examples. Paul reads Scripture as a vast network of typological prefigurations of himself and his communities. This allows him to use the scriptural stories as paradigms for his own mission (e.g., Rom 10:14-17; 11:1-6; Gal 1:15) and for the actions he wants these communities to perform (e.g., Gal 4:21–5:1; 2 Cor 8:7-15).[21]

A special case of this strategy of reading scriptural narratives as ethical paradigms is Paul's use of the figure of Jesus — *as prefigured in Scripture* — as a pattern for imitation.[22] Paul sees in Scripture the story of Jesus Christ as the servant who suffers and relinquishes power for the sake of others. The clearest example is found in Rom 15:1-13, where Paul exhorts the strong to accept the weak for the sake of building up the community, in accordance with the example of Christ. The character of Christ's action is then explained by a quotation of Ps 69:9: "For Christ did not please himself; but, as it is written, 'The insults of those who insult you have fallen on me'" (Rom 15:3). Paul goes on to suggest in verses 7-13 that Christ's welcoming of Jews and Gentiles alike is also prefigured in a string of scriptural passages: Ps 18:49, Deut 32:43, Ps 117:1, and Isa 11:10.[23] In light of this action of Christ, the Christians at Rome are exhorted to "Welcome one another . . . for the glory of God" (Rom 15:7).

20. This is the NRSV translation. Greek insertions demonstrate how the LXX rendered the pertinent words.

21. See discussion of these passages in Hays, *Echoes*, 111-18, 88-91.

22. On the importance of the *imitatio Christi* as a motif in Pauline ethics, see Furnish, *Theology and Ethics*, 217-23.

23. Note once again that Deut 32 shows up in a climactic summary.

One striking feature of this passage — the rhetorical summation of the letter to the Romans — is its portrayal of Christ as the speaker in the first-person quotations from the Psalms (Rom 15:3, 9). I have argued elsewhere[24] that the device of understanding the Messiah as the praying voice in the royal lament psalms was a widespread hermeneutical convention in early Christianity, and that Paul's distinctive adaptation of that tradition here in Rom 15 is to interpret this motif in a *hortatory* (rather than apologetic) manner. In other words, Paul takes the suffering righteous figure of the Psalms as a pattern for the conduct of the church: "the community that learns to recognize the voice of the Messiah in the Psalms will learn finally to join in his suffering and in his song."[25] Once again, we see that Paul's fundamental reading of Scripture — in this case, the christological interpretation of the Psalter — yields a narrative that becomes paradigmatic for his ethical vision for the community.

Scripture as Specific Word Addressed to the Community

Finally, we may consider a number of passages in which Paul reads Scripture as a word of God spoken immediately to the situation of his community. What I have in mind here is not merely general moral advice that would apply always and everywhere, such as Rom 12:19-21, which quotes Deut 32:35 and Prov 25:21-22: "Beloved, never avenge yourselves, but leave room for the wrath of God; for it is written, '"Vengeance is mine, I will repay," says the Lord' [Deut 32:35]. No, 'if your enemies are hungry, feed them; if they are thirsty, give them something to drink; for by doing this you will heap burning coals on their heads' [Prov 25:21-22]. Do not be overcome by evil, but overcome evil with good." There is a sense in which this teaching of Scripture is addressed to the church, but the address is of a very general character. The appeal to Proverbs shows that Paul is drawing on a stock of generalizable moral wisdom in the service of parenesis. To be sure, the force of such wisdom is enhanced for the early church by the teaching and example of Jesus, but there is no clear indication in the text of

24. R. B. Hays, "Christ Prays the Psalms: Paul's Use of an Early Christian Exegetical Convention," in *The Future of Christology: Essays in Honor of Leander E. Keck*, ed. A. J. Malherbe and W. A. Meeks (Minneapolis: Fortress, 1993), 122-36; reprinted in the present volume (pp. 101-18).

25. Hays, "Christ Prays the Psalms," 136 (117 in the present volume).

Romans that Paul regards this moral counsel as distinctively pertinent to the situation of the Roman Christians.

In other cases, however, Paul hears the word of Scripture as a word on target, a word spoken directly for the guidance of his churches, "on whom the ends of the ages have come." Probably the citation of Deut 25:4 in 1 Cor 9:8-12 fits this category: "For it is written in the Law of Moses, 'You shall not muzzle an ox while it is treading out the grain.' Is it for oxen that God is concerned? Or does he not speak entirely for our sake (δι' ἡμᾶς πάντως)? It was indeed written for our sake. . . . If we have sown spiritual good among you, is it too much if we reap your material benefits?" The Law's commandment not to muzzle a threshing ox was written for the sake of the church, and its real referent is Paul and his apostolic colleagues. The hidden meaning of this law is that Paul as an apostle has the right to expect financial support from his churches.

Sometimes the word may be even more sharply targeted to the specific situation, as in Gal 4:30. What does Scripture say? Scripture (ἡ γραφή), virtually personified as a character, an intermediary spokesperson for God, addresses the Galatians directly, commanding them to "drive out the slavewoman and her son" (Gen 21:10), a command which, in light of Paul's allegorization of the Sarah-Hagar story, means that the Galatians are to expel the Jewish Christian preachers of circumcision from their community.[26]

Not always, however, is the command of Scripture directed to a single action. In the opening chapters of 1 Corinthians Paul repeatedly calls upon his readers to hear the word of Scripture as a *character-shaping* message that speaks precisely to the conflicts dividing the Corinthian church. Paul's first explicit quotation from Scripture in 1 Corinthians is adduced in support of his assertion that the word of the cross is, paradoxically, the power of God:

> For the word of the cross is foolishness to those who are perishing, but to us who are being saved it is the power of God. For it is written,
>
> > "I will destroy the wisdom of the wise,
> > and the discernment of the discerning I will thwart."
> >   (1 Cor 1:18-19)

---

26. For discussion of the passage, see Hays, *Echoes*, 111-18. For a different interpretation, see S. Eastman, "'Cast Out the Slavewoman and Her Son': The Dynamics of Exclusion and Inclusion in Galatians 4:30," *JSNT* (forthcoming).

This citation from Isa 29:14 is a pointed word of warning directed to those at Corinth who pride themselves on being σοφοί. Indeed, the metaleptically suppressed echo of the wider Isaiah context should rebound on the prideful Corinthians with particular force:

> The Lord said:
> Because these people draw near with their *mouths*
> and honor me with their *lips,*
> while their hearts are far from me,
> and their worship of me is a human commandment learned by rote;
> so I will again do amazing things with this people,
> shocking and amazing.
> The wisdom of their wise shall perish,
> and the discernment of their discerning shall be hidden.
>
> (Isa 29:13-14)

The Corinthians who glory in their speech gifts and their knowledge (cf. 1 Cor 1:5) are to hear themselves challenged directly by the word of Isaianic judgment that Paul adduces.

This is made even more explicit at the end of chapter 1 by Paul's next citation: Christ is said to have become "wisdom for us from God, and righteousness and sanctification and redemption, in order that, as it is written, *'Let the one who boasts boast in the Lord'*" (1:30-31). God has chosen to reverse normal human standards of valuation, overturning wisdom and power and privilege, in order to remove all possible ground for human boasting (1:20-29). Thus, there can be no ground for boasting at all except for boasting in the Lord — that is, giving God praise for what he has done through the cross. The quotation that forbids boasting is usually thought to be derived loosely from Jer 9:22-23, a passage that occurs at the conclusion of a harsh judgment oracle against the unfaithful people of God.[27] An equally good case, however, can be made for hearing in 1 Cor 1:31 a citation of 1 Kgdms 2:10 LXX (= 1 Sam 2:10), the conclusion of Hannah's song of praise to God for overturning human power and raising up the poor and needy.[28]

---

27. For a perceptive discussion of the rhetorical and theological implications of this intertextual link, see G. R. O'Day, "Jeremiah 9:22-23 and 1 Cor 1:26-31: A Study in Intertextuality," *JBL* 109 (1990): 259-67.

28. J. R. Wagner, "'Not beyond the Things Which Are Written': A Call to Boast Only in the Lord (1 Cor 4.6)," *NTS* 44 (1998): 279-87.

(Cf. also 1 Kgdms 2:3: "Do not boast [μὴ καυχᾶσθε], and do not utter high things; let not high-sounding words come out of your mouth, for the Lord is a God of knowledge, and God prepares his own designs.") In either case, regardless of the precise source, Paul's citation is to be heard by the Corinthians as a word spoken directly to them, calling them to humility and changed behavior.

The same themes are sounded again in 1 Cor 3:18-23, this time discouraging boasting in any particular apostles. The texts cited here are different (Job 5:12-13 and Ps 93:11 LXX), but the aim of these citations, as explained in 1 Cor 3:21, is to recall the concerns of the first chapter of the letter: "so that no one might *boast* (καυχάσθω) in human beings."

In light of these observations, we should conclude that the somewhat obscure comment of 1 Cor 4:6 refers back to these particular Scripture quotations: "I have applied all this to Apollos and myself for your benefit, brothers and sisters, so that you may learn through us the meaning of the saying 'Nothing beyond what is written,' so that none of you will be puffed up against one another." Paul has spoken of his own relationship to Apollos in chapter 3 of the letter in order to illustrate what it would mean to be constrained by the scriptural mandate to boast only in the Lord, not in human gifts or personalities. The Corinthians should heed the scriptural admonition against boasting as God's word directly to them and their situation.

A final example, also taken from 1 Corinthians, is Paul's deft use in 5:13 of the recurrent Deuteronomic refrain, "Drive out the evil person from among you." Here in 1 Corinthians the directive stands — unmarked as a biblical quotation — at the conclusion of Paul's instructions to the Corinthian church to expel the man involved in a sexual relationship with his father's wife. Of course, in the context of Deuteronomy this command is aimed at preserving the purity of Israel as a covenant community. Thus, by addressing the Gentile Corinthians as though they were members of Israel's covenant community, Paul makes a subtle theological point: the command of God to Israel applies to them not just by analogy but directly, because they really have been grafted into the people of God (cf. Rom 11:17-24). This command (ἐξαρεῖς τὸν πονηρὸν ἐξ ὑμῶν αὐτῶν, or its near equivalent) appears some nine times in Deuteronomy, prescribing the death penalty for conduct that would lead Israel into idolatry or impurity: Deut 13:5; 17:7, 12; 19:19; 21:21; 22:21, 22, 24; 24:7.[29] The situation closest to the Co-

---

29. Paul changes the LXX's *future* active *indicative* second-person *singular* form of the

rinthian case is the one treated in Deut 22:22: "If a man is caught lying with the wife of another man, both of them shall die, the man who lay with the woman as well as the woman. So you shall purge the evil from Israel." This section of the text (Deut 22:13-30) provides legislation dealing with various sexual offenses, culminating in verse 30 with a prohibition directly pertinent to the case of the Corinthian offender: "A man shall not marry his father's wife, thereby violating his father's rights." Although Deuteronomy does not explicitly prescribe a penalty for this case, it seems highly probable that Paul, thinking of this passage in relation to the problem at Corinth, simply appropriated the exclusion formula from the near context in Deut 22:22.[30]

In any case, the point is that Paul reads the Deuteronomy text as a word addressed directly to the Corinthians. They are called by Scripture to exercise community discipline by expelling the perpetrator of a form of sexual immorality (πορνεία) that is not found "even among the Gentiles" (1 Cor 5:1). They are to purify the community.

This example brings us full circle: the pertinence of this direct command to a Gentile church depends upon Paul's assumption of a grand framing narrative (see under "Scripture as Narrative Framework for Community Identity" above). The covenant command of Deuteronomy can be heard as the word of God for the Gentile Corinthians only because God has acted to reconcile the world to himself and thereby bring them into "the Israel of God" (cf. Gal 6:16). Within that overarching story, Scripture provides the symbolic vocabulary for Pauline ethics. Paul's rereading of Scripture in light of God's reconciling work in Christ produces fresh imaginative configurations, calling on his Jewish contemporaries to read the text in surprising ways and his Gentile converts to read their lives anew within the story of Scripture. The generative power of this hermeneutical strategy is suggested by the remarkable metaphor that Paul articulates in

---

verb (ἐξαρεῖς) into an *aorist* active *imperative* second-person *plural* (ἐξάρατε). This has the effect of rendering the LXX expression (which follows the LXX's tendency to use the future in place of the imperative) into more idiomatic Greek usage; at the same time, the change to second-person *plural* more clearly emphasizes the church's communal responsibility to exercise discipline in this case.

30. My treatment of this passage in *Echoes* (97) refers only to Deut 17:7, which is the parallel noted in the margin of the Nestle-Aland text. Further study of the text has persuaded me that the echo of Deut 22:22 is of greater importance for understanding Paul's use of the formula in 1 Cor 5:13.

1 Cor 5:6-8: the church itself becomes the Passover bread, which must be purified by removal of the "old leaven of malice and evil," and Christ becomes the paschal lamb sacrificed to signify and celebrate the community's passage out of bondage into freedom. Because this sacrifice has already been made, the community's ethical action of purification through community discipline is now crucial so that the feast may be celebrated rightly. Such a "use" of the OT in ethical reflection goes far beyond reading the text as a rule book and suggests that the community of the new creation must discover the will of God through boldly imaginative readings of the old story.

Conclusion

Our survey has shown that Scripture plays a major role in shaping Paul's moral vision. When we understand the meaning of "ethics" to include all the factors that shape a community's ethos and identity, we see that Scripture is crucial for Pauline ethics in a variety of ways. It provides the overarching narrative framework for the moral life, calls the community to aspire to love and righteousness, underwrites an implicit conception of the conduct that is pleasing to God, tells stories that model both negatively and positively the meaning of faithfulness, and speaks specific words of challenge and direction to the community.

Paul calls his churches to live within the world story told by Scripture. They are to find their identity there as God's covenant people, bearing the message of reconciliation to the world and manifesting the righteousness of God through loving, self-sacrificial conduct that fulfills the Law. Working out the specific behavior associated with this vision requires Spirit-led discernment and the transformation of the community's life. But Paul was convinced that the Spirit would lead his churches to become more discerning readers of Scripture, to hear themselves addressed directly by Scripture, and to shape their lives accordingly.

Paul's bold hermeneutical example may lead us in turn to reflect afresh on what it would mean for Scripture to shape our communities. If we followed Paul's lead, we would immerse ourselves in Scripture and ask how our lives fit into the ongoing story of God's reconciliation of the world through Jesus Christ. Ethics would not be a matter of casuistry, not a matter of reasoning through rules and principles, but of hearing the word of God and responding in imaginative freedom to embody God's righteousness. To do that with integrity, of course, we would have to undergo a conversion of the imagination: we would have to believe that "whatever was written in former days was written for our instruction" and that we are those "upon whom the ends of the ages have come." The challenge of Pauline ethics to the church is to take these claims seriously and to put them into action.

On the Rebound:
A Response to Critiques of
Echoes of Scripture in the Letters of Paul

The Society of Biblical Literature program unit on Scripture in Early Judaism and Christianity devoted a session in 1990 to the discussion of my then newly published book *Echoes of Scripture in the Letters of Paul*. Critical responses were offered by Craig A. Evans, James A. Sanders, William Scott Green, and J. Christiaan Beker, followed by my reply and by group discussion. These essays were subsequently gathered and published in Craig A. Evans and James A. Sanders, eds., *Paul and the Scriptures of Israel*, JSNTSup 83 (Sheffield: JSOT Press, 1993). The essay that follows here is my reply, originally published on pages 70-96 of that volume. I have edited it slightly to make my comments followable for readers who have not first read the critiques, but I have not sought to remove the marks of the essay's genesis in an occasional and dialogical setting. The questions raised and discussed in that forum have continued to feature prominently in discussions of *Echoes of Scripture in the Letters of Paul*; therefore, I hope my response on that occasion will be of more general interest to students of Paul's interpretation of Israel's Scripture. I want to record once again my gratitude to Professors Evans and Sanders for organizing this conversation about my work.

It is a distinct honor to have my work given a careful reading by Craig A. Evans, James A. Sanders, William Scott Green, and J. Christiaan Beker. I have found their responses instructive, and I am grateful for the opportunity to carry forward the discussion initiated by *Echoes of Scripture in the Letters of Paul*. The book was conceived not as a definitive treatment of its topic but as a probe, an attempt to pose some new questions about familiar but intractable texts. Consequently, it is fitting for the conversation to continue. I welcome the opportunity to respond to the discerning critiques of my colleagues.

Response to Craig A. Evans

Craig Evans has rightly focused attention on my plea for greater care in our use of the terms "midrash" and "typology"; the latter is — as Evans puts it — "not so much a *method* of exegesis as it is a *presupposition* underlying the Jewish and Christian understanding of Scripture," and the former is not so much a *literary form* as an *activity*, whose hermeneutical strategies and results require close investigation in each actual instance. I am pleased that Evans finds my cautionary words apt. His substantive response to my interpretations demonstrates the value of pushing beyond these labels to consider in more careful detail how Paul reads Scripture.

Evans raises two important matters for discussion, both of which I take to be friendly suggestions for further development of my proposals. First, Paul the apostle does not come as a *tabula rasa* to the reading of Scripture; he interprets within a Jewish hermeneutical tradition. "Paul has heard more than Scripture itself; he has heard Scripture as it had been interpreted in late antiquity." Thus, "it would be more accurate to speak of the echoes of interpreted Scripture in the letters of Paul." (Sanders makes a similar point; see further discussion below.) Second, Evans suggests that Paul's revisionary interpretations that subvert Israel's favored status before God are less startling than my discussion would make them appear: Paul is practicing a "hermeneutics of prophetic criticism" already well developed in Israel's classical prophets.

The first of these points is the weightier challenge to the working method of *Echoes*. The phenomena of intertextuality in Paul are more complex, Evans contends, than my interpretations allow. His example offers a useful illustration: the reference in Rom 10:7 to a "descent into the abyss" must be understood as an echo of *Targum Neofiti* Deut 30:13. (Or perhaps the echo is not of the Targum itself but rather of an interpretative tradition attested independently by the Targum; I assume that Evans means the latter.) In this case we must reckon with at least a four-part polyphony: Deuteronomy (as mediated through the LXX), Baruch, Neofiti, and Paul.

This example is useful for several reasons. As Evans notes, my interpretation of the passage had already drawn attention to the importance of the Baruch passage as a middle term between Deut 30 and Rom 10: the traditional identification of Torah with Wisdom allows Paul, presupposing a Wisdom Christology, to interpret "the word" of Deuteronomy as a figurative pointer to Christ.[1] Thus, Evans and I have no disagreement in principle about the necessity of discerning multilayered intertextual echoes. Indeed, Evans's challenge allows me to reiterate a point perhaps insufficiently emphasized in the book: my discussion of Paul's intertextual hermeneutics in no way forecloses the possibility of extrabiblical echoes and influences in Paul's letters. I have no stake in arguing for an unmediated encounter between Paul and Scripture. (The methodological difficulty, of course, is to know how to distinguish between traditions already known to Paul and those that emerged later, either independently or even in reaction against Paul's exegesis.) Whether the nonscriptural echoes come from Greco-Roman culture or from the traditions of Jewish biblical interpretation, Paul's discourse is performed within the linguistic symphony (or cacophony, as the case may be) of his culture. As critical listeners, we can identify some of the major parts in the score, but none of us at this historical distance can hope to recover all the resonances that a competent listener contemporary with Paul would have heard. We do the best we can.

So where do Evans and I differ? I had proposed that the "abyss" motif in Rom 10:7 is derived from texts like Sir 24:5, which speaks of Wisdom making the circuit of the vault of heaven and walking in the depths of the abyss. This still seems to me a valid reading, in view of the close affinities between Sir 24:5 and *Bar* 3:29-30. Evans, however, has offered a more compelling suggestion — a clearer echo — by pointing to *Targum Neofiti*, where the "abyss" motif is explicitly employed in the interpretation of Deut 30:12-13. It seems entirely likely that Paul knew (or presupposed that his readers knew) this tradition.[2]

In this instance Evans has offered a better reading because he is a more competent hearer; that is, he brings to the hearing of Romans an ear tuned to a tradition that was not "in the ear" for me. His reference to the Targum

---

1. This suggestion is not of course original; my discussion was significantly informed by M. J. Suggs, "'The Word Is Near You': Romans 10.6-10 within the Purpose of the Letter," in *Christian History and Interpretation: Studies Presented to John Knox*, ed. W. R. Farmer, C. F. D. Moule, and R. R. Niebuhr (Cambridge: Cambridge University Press, 1967), 289-312.

2. This is a case where the evidence of Paul's letters might help to confirm the early dating of a Targum tradition.

enriches our hearing of the text of Romans without invalidating my identification of Sirach as one overtone also present here. Now we have at least five parts in the polyphony.

This is exactly the sort of complex reading urged upon us by the example of John Hollander, whose work on literary echo was catalytic for my study of Paul: in *The Figure of Echo* Hollander seeks to trace how motifs and images are passed along through literary traditions in such a way that they gather significations through time. For example, in the invocation of book III of *Paradise Lost* Milton coins a simile comparing his own poetic activity to the singing of a nightingale: ". . . as the wakeful Bird/Sings darkling, and in shadiest Covert hid/Tunes her nocturnal note. . . ." Keats in "Ode to a Nightingale" subliminally evokes Milton's language, but transmutes it so that he, the poet, now *listens* "darkling" rather than sings. Thomas Hardy, in turn, in "The Darkling Thrush," evokes both Milton and Keats in such a way that the effect of his poem depends on the hearer's aural memory of both predecessors and recognition of the tension between them.[3] The discerning reader will hear the different voices at play. I welcome Evans's contribution to a similarly nuanced hearing of Rom 10.

On the other hand, I am skeptical of Evans's further proposal that Paul was drawn to the Deuteronomy text because he knew the tradition that Jesus had compared himself to Jonah (Matt 12:40) and because *Targum Neofiti* Deut 30:13 also refers to Jonah's descent into the abyss. This is not impossible, of course, but I see no evidence for it in the text, and Evans's contribution to our understanding of Rom 10 hardly requires this speculation. This seems to me an instance of what I called the "vanishing point" problem: "As we move farther away from overt citation, the source recedes into the discursive distance, the intertextual relations become less determinate, and the demand placed on the reader's listening powers grows greater. As we near the vanishing point of the echo, it inevitably becomes difficult to decide whether we are really hearing an echo at all, or whether we are only conjuring things out of the murmurings of our own imaginations."[4]

The important point here is that I have no fundamental disagreement

---

3. See J. Hollander, *The Figure of Echo: A Mode of Allusion in Milton and After* (Berkeley: University of California Press, 1981), 89-91.

4. R. B. Hays, *Echoes of Scripture in the Letters of Paul* (New Haven and London: Yale University Press, 1989), 23.

with Evans about the proper method to employ in our efforts to read Paul. Evans calls us to attend to certain traditions of scriptural interpretation within Judaism that might thicken our perception of Paul's readings of Scripture. I say that is a laudable goal, where appropriate evidence exists. I continue to insist, however, that the work of interpretation must include careful attention to the manner in which *Paul puts his own distinctive spin on the inherited traditions.* In the case of Deut 30:12-13, the Targum explicitly understands the passage as a reference to the commandments of the Mosaic law. Paul, by identifying the "word" with Christ, reads the reference to bringing the word up "from the abyss" as an ironic reference to Christ's resurrection. So, even if Paul is hearing Deuteronomy "as it had been interpreted in late antiquity" by the Targum tradition, he is at the same time also reading it through his own distinctive hermeneutical filter.

Evans's other point about the "hermeneutics of prophetic criticism" is one that I am happy to acknowledge. He cites the example of Isa 28:21, in which the prophet recalls the Lord's aid of King David in victories at Mount Perazim and in the valley of Gibeon, only to declare that God will now do the "alien work" of fighting *against* Jerusalem. This powerful instance could of course be multiplied: one thinks, for example, of the way Amos's oracles against the nations culminate dramatically in revisionary oracles of judgment against Judah and Israel (Amos 2:4–3:2): "You only have I known of all the families of earth; therefore I will punish you for all your iniquities." So, yes, as Evans indicates, "the Pauline hermeneutic is in fact a biblical hermeneutic."[5] Clarification is necessary, however, on three points.

First, it should be emphasized that Evans's comment supports, rather than challenges, my argument. In the final chapter of *Echoes,* where I sum up my conclusions about Pauline hermeneutics, I observe that Deuteronomy and Isaiah in particular are Paul's hermeneutical precursors: he has adopted their device of reading the history of God's past dealings with Israel as "a prefiguration of a larger eschatological design." Thus, Paul's "reading strategy extends a typological trajectory begun already in the texts themselves."[6] This remark is made precisely with reference to the dia-

---

5. For elaboration of Evans's point, see his helpful article "Paul and the Hermeneutics of 'True Prophecy': A Study of Romans 9–11," *Bib* 65 (1984): 560-70. I regret that this essay had not come to my attention when I was writing *Echoes.*

6. Hays, *Echoes,* 164.

lectic of judgment and salvation that appears in Paul's precursors as well as in Romans. Consequently, I find it puzzling when Evans writes that "apparently Hays has not fully realized . . . that this kind of deconstruction, or scandalous inversion, was frequently practiced by Israel's classical prophets." One who has written, as I have, that "Deuteronomy 32 contains Romans *in nuce*"[7] hardly needs to be pressed to admit that Paul's hermeneutic is biblical. One suspects that Evans, by concentrating his remarks on my analysis of Romans in chapter 2 of *Echoes,* may have given insufficient weight to my conclusions in the book's final chapter.

Second, Paul's hermeneutic is selective: from among various canonical models, he adopts the highly dialectical hermeneutic of judgment and salvation that appears in Deuteronomy and Isaiah, rather than — for instance — the straightforwardly triumphalist ideology of 2 Sam 7. This dialectical hermeneutic is, to be sure, homologous with the kerygma of the cross. Indeed, one might put it the other way around: the kerygma of the cross becomes the hermeneutical lens through which Paul refocuses the classical hermeneutics of prophetic criticism. It is precisely in this respect that Paul's reading of Scripture differs dramatically from many other Jewish traditions of scriptural interpretation: one could scarcely find a construal of Isaiah more dissonant with Pauline hermeneutics than the Isaiah Targum.

Finally, Paul's gospel transposes the hermeneutics of prophetic criticism into a new key by proclaiming God's embrace of Gentiles on the same terms as Israel (i.e., through the grace of Jesus Christ), οὐ γάρ ἐστιν διαστολή (Rom 3:22). One may contend — as Paul did — that this message was already latent in Scripture and/or in the very logic of monotheism,[8] but at the same time it must be acknowledged that no Jew before Paul, so far as we are able to tell, drew the same conclusions from the prophetic texts that Paul drew. Paul's Gentile mission creates a new hermeneutical context within which the classical prophetic hermeneutic is *metaphorically reconfigured.* That reconfiguration is what I mean to emphasize when I say Paul "*extends* a typological *trajectory* begun already in the texts them-

---

7. Hays, *Echoes,* 164.

8. The point is elegantly put by J. A. Sanders, *Torah and Canon* (Philadelphia: Fortress, 1972), 87: "For the prophets were true monotheists, and nothing they said so stressed their monotheism as the idea that God was free enough of his chosen people to transform them in the crucible of destitution into a community whose members could themselves be free of every institution [scil. 'Law'] which in his providence he might give them."

selves": Paul's hermeneutic is *analogous* to the prophetic hermeneutic, not a simple continuation of it.[9]

Response to James A. Sanders

James A. Sanders helpfully places *Echoes* within the discipline of biblical studies, recognizing it as a counterproposal both to the sort of New Testament scholarship that reads the New Testament "synchronically only in terms of its Hellenistic context" and to Michael Fishbane's exclusion of the New Testament from the continuing stream of Israel's "inner-Biblical interpretation." Sanders's own sensitivity to "the canonical process" also disposes him favorably toward my emphasis on the power of texts to engender unforeseen interpretations that may transcend the original authorial intention and historical setting. The book "succeeds remarkably well," in his judgment, in holding together in creative tension the various possible loci for the hermeneutical event.

While I am grateful for Sanders's gracious and discerning remarks, I find it necessary to qualify his suggestion that "whether [Hays] as its author intended it or not, he does indeed deal throughout the book with aspects of the canonical process." This sentence can be accepted as an account of my book, rather than as an account of what Sanders believes I should have written, only if one emphasizes the word "aspects." Unlike Sanders, I am not engaged in tracing the *"process"* of tradition and canon formation; herein lies a significant distinction between my project and his desideratum. My study of Paul as reader of Scripture might be employed in the larger project that Sanders envisions,[10] but my focus is on the "hermeneutical event" that occurs in Paul's applications of Scripture.

---

9. In this last point I find myself in agreement with Sanders, who speaks of "this *further* act of God in calling an unboundaried people through Christ" and perceives that this act "forces a re-reading of the old texts, both to affirm that God has once more acted in consonance with the record of previous divine work and to insist that every new chapter throws light on those that precede it." (I suspect that Evans would not find this emphasis on the newness of God's act in Christ and its hermeneutical consequences to be uncongenial, but he does not articulate it so clearly as Sanders.)

10. Indeed, I describe my inquiry into Paul's use of Scripture — largely conducted without reference to the diachronic trajectories that Sanders emphasizes — as "a valid and necessary (even if preliminary) task" (*Echoes*, 11).

Thus, I aim at a deep reading of a single text (or handful of Pauline texts) rather than at a comparative or developmental treatment of motifs "from inception within the Tanak itself . . . through the Septuagint and her daughters, Dead Sea Scrolls, Apocrypha, Pseudepigrapha, Philo, Josephus, Tannaitic Literature and the Vulgate." Sanders's question about the history of the canonical process is both important and interesting, but it is not quite mine. My approach and Sanders's are complementary; still, it is important not to confuse one with the other.

While I am quibbling with Sanders's characterization of my work, I should also note that he misreads my comparison of Rom 10:5-10 to *Baba Meṣi'a* 59b. Sanders cites a passage from page 3 of *Echoes* in which I set the two interpretations of Deut 30:12-14 in opposition to one another, and then objects that the *B. Meṣ.* passage "can be read in just the same way, that is, Scripture's 'right' interpretation is not in some *tavnit* (Idea or Form) in heaven . . . it is in the hands of succeeding generations of interpreters who read and re-read scripture out of ever-changing community needs." Sanders's point is certainly correct, but I find it a puzzling objection to my treatment of the passage, since I say substantially the same thing on the page following the one Sanders cites: "Both sides . . . presuppose the legitimacy of innovative readings that disclose truth previously latent in Scripture. . . . [T]he rabbis gain leverage on the text by appealing to majority opinion within an interpretive community. The rabbinic story, therefore, exposes the quest for hermeneutical closure as an illusion. Texts will always demand and generate new interpretation, as this halakhic dispute demonstrates."[11] It seems to me that Sanders has reacted against a provisional formulation in the middle of my unfolding comparison without following the comparison through to its conclusion. Thus, contrary to his suggestion that we might have a difference of opinion here regarding the character of rabbinic hermeneutics, I think in fact that we do not.

The most significant, in my judgment, of Sanders's constructive responses to *Echoes* is his insistence that Paul's hermeneutic is not ecclesiocentric, as I had argued, but theocentric. It is *God* who promises to circumcise the hearts of his people, *God* who kills and makes alive, *God* who keeps faith with the promises of Israel; in short, God, not the church, is the center and protagonist of Scripture as Paul reads it. Sanders's point is very well taken, and the letter to the Romans is eloquent testimony for his case. I am

---

11. Hays, *Echoes*, 4.

content, then, to accept this word of correction and say that Paul's hermeneutic is, in an important sense, theocentric.

What then of the considerable body of evidence that led me to identify an ecclesiocentric hermeneutic in Paul?[12] That evidence still stands and must be granted its force, as Sanders is willing to do. Perhaps we need a new term, such as "ecclesiotelic." Granting that Scripture tells the story of *God's* activity, we must say in the same breath that God's activity is directed toward the formation of a *people*.[13] God reveals himself precisely through his activity of choosing and saving Israel.[14] It is then impossible to speak of a theocentric hermeneutic without simultaneously recognizing that the God disclosed through Scripture read theocentrically is the God whose activity drives toward the creation of the eschatological ἐκκλησία; likewise, it is impossible to speak of an ecclesiocentric hermeneutic without recognizing that the ἐκκλησία disclosed through Scripture read ecclesiocentrically has its life only in and through the merciful action of the one God.

Perhaps the difficulty lies in the spatial metaphor of "center." If Paul's theological hermeneutic is fundamentally narrative in character — as both Sanders and I have argued elsewhere[15] — then it is artificial to single out one motif as the "center" of everything else. The distinctive character of the hermeneutic can be displayed only in its capacity to incorporate all of the community's experience into the *story* of God's redemptive righteousness.

So far I think Sanders and I would agree. But is it correct to describe Paul's hermeneutic as "argument . . . from theological history"? Here caution is necessary. The history in question, the history of God's dealings with Israel, is always read by Paul retrospectively through the lens of God's act of reconciling the world to himself through the death of Jesus

12. See Hays, *Echoes*, 84-121. My aim in choosing the deliberately provocative term "ecclesiocentric" was to call attention to Paul's relative lack of interest in christological prophecy-fulfillment schemes, in contrast to Matthew and John.

13. Cf. the emphasis placed by N. T. Wright on monotheism and election as the fundamental twin organizing themes of Pauline theology, in "Putting Paul Together Again," in *Pauline Theology* I, ed. J. Bassler (Minneapolis: Fortress, 1991), 183-211.

14. Indeed, if we join Karl Barth in confessing that God is the one whose being is known only in his act, then the God revealed in Scripture is not thinkable apart from his covenant people Israel.

15. See, e.g., J. A. Sanders, "Torah and Christ," *Int* 29 (1975): 372-90; R. B. Hays, *The Faith of Jesus Christ: The Narrative Substructure of Galatians 3.1–4.11*, 2nd ed. (Grand Rapids: Eerdmans, 2002); Hays, "Crucified with Christ," in *Pauline Theology* I, 227-46.

Christ. The "pattern of divine activity" that Paul discerns in Scripture is not a simple one that can be read off the surface of the text; it appears only through the dialectical encounter between Scripture and gospel in the missionary situation in which Paul finds himself. Furthermore, for Paul ἡ γραφή is not simply the source for constructing a historical outline of God's past activity; rather, Scripture addresses the community in the present directly.[16]

In all this I suspect that Sanders and I are in reasonably close agreement. I am concerned only that his emphasis on categories such as "process" and "history" might lead to an underestimation of the dramatic discontinuities introduced by Paul's revisionary readings of Scripture,[17] and to a simultaneous underestimation of the metaphorical aspects of his reading strategies. The test of such concerns, of course, can be conducted only in the detailed exegesis of particular texts; consequently, I gladly anticipate the continuation of this collegial discussion.

Response to William Scott Green

The sorts of questions posed by William Scott Green are not susceptible to adjudication at the exegetical level. Green poses fundamental questions about the theoretical underpinnings of my work and about the way in which my own theological commitments may color, or even determine, the results of my analysis. I am grateful to him for posing the issues in such an incisive fashion. To formulate an adequate answer to his astute methodological challenge, I would have to write another book. For the present, however, I offer a brief response to three closely related points: (1) the character of intertextual analysis as a critical method; (2) the relation between literary and theological analysis of Paul's letters; and (3) the issue of my critical stance *within* the tradition I am seeking to explicate.

1. Green regards what he calls my "minimalist notion of intertextuality" as problematic, because I fail to take on board the ideological baggage carried by most recent literary critics who use the buzzword. "The larger

---

16. For extended discussion of this, see Hays, *Echoes*, 154-78.

17. For a strong word of warning against the assumption of simple linear continuities between Scripture and Paul's theology, see J. L. Martyn, "Events in Galatia: Modified Covenantal Nomism versus God's Invasion of the Cosmos in the Singular Gospel: A Response to J. D. G. Dunn and B. R. Gaventa," in *Pauline Theology* I, 160-79.

purpose of intertextual analysis," Green asserts, "is to undergird and underscore an ideological position about the fluidity of textual meaning." Since Green cites no authority for his pronouncement, I can only assume that he has in mind the work of poststructuralist semiotic theorists such as Roland Barthes and Julia Kristeva,[18] or perhaps Harold Bloom's theorizing about "misreading."[19] While I am well aware of the philosophical context in which these theorists employ intertextual analysis, I fail to see why my interest in intertextual echo should compel me to accept their ideological framework. As I argued in a long footnote in *Echoes,* the literary-critical operation of tracing the meaning effects created by Paul's intertextual figurations is "in principle neutral with regard to metatheories about language and truth."[20] In fact, one possible outcome of analyzing intertextual phenomena would be to demonstrate the persistence of certain semantic constraints imposed by precursor texts on their later interpreters; if so, the method could disclose not only "the fluidity of textual meaning" but also, if I might turn the trope again, its solidity. In fact, that is one of the findings of my analysis in *Echoes:* the scriptural texts keep imposing at least part of their original sense on Paul's argument, even if only subliminally, even when Paul is trying to employ them for new purposes. That is what I mean when I propose in the book's final chapter, using Thomas M. Greene's typology, that Paul's hermeneutic is "dialectical."[21]

As Green correctly notes, the major theoretical influences on my working method are John Hollander and Thomas Greene — and Michael Fishbane should be duly noted as well. None of these critics espouses the ideological perspective that William Scott Green believes to be the necessary concomitant of intertextual analysis. I thought I had made all this reasonably clear in *Echoes* from the moment in chapter 1 where I first introduced the term "intertextuality."[22]

Similarly, contrary to Green's statement, my use of the synonymous terms "metalepsis" and "transumption" is dependent neither on Harold Bloom nor on his student Herbert Marks but directly on Hollander. The distinction is important, because Hollander's usage of these terms is rooted in his extensive historical account of the definition of this trope by

18. For bibliographic citations see Hays, *Echoes,* 198 n. 50.
19. For discussion and bibliographic references, see Hays, *Echoes,* 16-19 and 199 n. 58.
20. Hays, *Echoes,* 227 n. 60.
21. Hays, *Echoes,* 173-78.
22. Hays, *Echoes,* 14-21.

ancient and medieval rhetoricians.[23] One of the stated purposes of Hollander's long appendix on this terminology is to *distinguish* his usage from Bloom's idiosyncratic appropriation of it.

One other matter concerning the definition of intertextuality requires comment. When Green asserts that "intertextuality really is the reader's work, not the writer's,"[24] he seems to abolish by fiat one side of the dialectical interaction that occurs in Paul's wrestling with Scripture and again in our wrestling with Paul. If Green means to suggest that my work, despite its "historically-descriptive-sounding phrases," actually reveals *only* my own creativity in discovering intertextual correspondences and that such discoveries can be attributed neither to Paul nor to the reading experience of his original readers, then Paul falls mute. His reading of Scripture contributes nothing to the phenomena of intertextual echo; the echoes are only inside our heads. (Can one read Joyce's *Ulysses* and suppose that the Homeric intertextual resonances are only the product of the reader's ingenuity? Can we read Dante without supposing that he intended to echo Virgil?) Apparently, however, Green does not go so far as to endorse this sort of hermeneutical solipsism; he deems my discussions of scriptural echo to be "responsible, disciplined, well within the range of textual plausibility and imaginative possibility." Thus, his comment that "intertextuality really is the reader's work" must be taken as a cautionary note, rather than as an embargo on the importation of authorial meaning.

In any case, Green finds fault with my work because, despite my focus on intertextual allusion, I fail to fall in line with the currently fashionable skepticism about the stability of meaning in texts. I can only respond that I am indeed operating with a notion of intertextuality that is "minimal" by Green's canons, and that I have chosen consciously to do so. If Green should insist on denying me permission to use the term "intertextuality" (since my work does not properly reverence its "larger purpose"), I will surrender it with a shrug. Nothing is at stake for me in the use of the term.

2. Green asks, penetratingly, "Even if we grant . . . the book's claim that in Paul's writing Scripture and gospel are in tensive and dialectical relationship, does it follow that the literary is co-essential with the theological? Does a literary relationship between two texts necessarily imply a

---

23. "Appendix: The Trope of Transumption," in Hollander, *The Figure of Echo*, 133-49.
24. For a similar critique, see the review of *Echoes* by D. B. Martin in *Modern Theology* 7 (1991): 291-92.

theological one?" The specific matter at issue here is the question of supersessionism: Does Paul's theology annihilate Torah and replace it with a new religion?[25]

Green correctly states that my book seeks to show that Paul's theology is *not* supersessionist. More significantly, he correctly poses the issue by asking whether "the literary is co-essential with the theological." Green rightly perceives that the argumentation of *Echoes* moves from a description of the complex literary linkages between Paul's letters and Scripture to an assertion of a corresponding theological coherence. From Green's point of view, this assertion is problematic, both materially and methodologically.

Green argues[26] as follows: because, for Paul, Scripture's "narrative of election and promise . . . is completed by something outside Scripture" (the death and resurrection of Jesus), Paul's position is theologically discontinuous with Scripture, no matter how many literary allusions and echoes Paul may create. In other words (mine, not his), Green would describe Paul's hermeneutic — using Thomas Greene's typology again — as *heuristic:* Paul evokes the symbolic world of Scripture precisely to reconfigure it systematically into his own symbolic world.

The complaint is as old as Paul's letters themselves. The letter to the Romans in particular bears witness to Paul's vigorous debate with his contemporaries over precisely these issues. Paul insists that his gospel, despite its evident revisionary relation to Israel's Law, stands nonetheless in an authentic relation of continuity with it. "But now, apart from Law, God's righteousness has been revealed — though it is attested [μαρτυρουμένη] by the Law and the prophets — God's righteousness, revealed through the

---

25. Incidentally, when Green says that "the charge of supersessionism" was "made in various ways by Harnack, Bultmann, and Herbert Marks," his formulation is slightly misleading, because it suggests that these critics *disapproved* of supersessionism. In fact, Harnack and Bultmann were enthusiastic Christian supersessionists seeking to enlist Paul in support of their position. Marks is a very different case: his Paul is "a dogmatist affirming the priority of his own conceptions by imposing them on the earlier tradition." But that makes Paul a "strong misreader," which is, in Marks's critical universe, a *good* thing to be; Marks is actually defending Paul against Bloom's judgment that he is a weak conventional reader.

26. To be precise, I should note that Green casts his remarks in the interrogative mode: "Does this not mean that . . ." For the sake of simplicity, I have taken the liberty of treating Green's rhetorical question as though it were an assertion. I do not believe I have thereby misrepresented his position.

faithfulness of Jesus Christ, for all who believe. . . . Do we then abolish the Law through this faith? By no means! On the contrary, we confirm the Law" (Rom 3:21-22, 31). Should Paul's claim be credited, or should we share Green's dubiety? About one point Green is certainly correct: the mere presence of scriptural citations, allusions, and echoes in Paul's discourse cannot settle the question. If that were the burden of my argument in *Echoes*, Green's skepticism would be fully warranted.

In fact, however, my argument is far less simple than Green makes it sound. Everything rides on the *character* of the intertextual relation between Paul's writing and what was written in Israel's Scripture. If, as I have tried at some length to show, the intertextual relation is genuinely *dialectical*, if Scripture really does retain its own voice and power to challenge and shape Paul's unfolding discourse, then indeed Paul's stance is not supersessionist, at least not as that term is ordinarily understood. But the determination of whether Scripture's voice continues to be heard rather than suppressed is, in significant measure, a literary judgment about how the text's tropes work. Thus, if the literary is not coessential with the theological, it is at least organically fused.

A truly supersessionist Christian theology would steamroller the scriptural text, flatten it onto the pavement to "prepare the way of the Lord [Jesus]." A nonsupersessionist theology will necessarily grapple in a more anguished and loving way with Scripture. The difference will manifest itself not only in the "bottom-line" theological position but also in the specific dialogical character of the literary nexus between old text and new. Thus, in response to Green's question, I would say yes, there is *some* correlation between the literary relation of two texts and their theological relation. The correlation is not one-to-one identity; nonetheless, intertextual literary linkages both reflect and create theological convictions.

3. Finally, Green accuses me of "doing the text's work for it," of becoming the tool manipulated by Paul's rhetoric. Because my "minimalist notion of intertextuality" is insufficiently suspicious of Paul's readings, my analysis "loses its critical force and falls into mere descriptiveness," with the result that the book "reinforces just what [Paul's] letters want hearers and readers to apprehend: that Christian teaching is 'grounded . . . in' Israel's Scripture rather than imposed upon it." In short, the book functions, albeit subtly, as a piece of Christian theology. Thus — the final jab — the argument of *Echoes* is "less an analysis of religion than a specimen of it." A specimen!

And when I am formulated, sprawling on a pin,
When I am pinned and wriggling on the wall,
Then how should I begin?

Green is exactly right: my book is written ἐκ πίστεως εἰς πίστιν. It is consciously and explicitly an attempt to write a work of scholarly analysis that seeks to do what my last chapter says Christian thinkers and writers should do: to take Paul as a hermeneutical model. In the closing pages of the book I suggest, inter alia, that "If we learned from Paul how to read Scripture, we would read it in the service of proclamation."[27]

Thus, I take Green's critique as unintended praise, confirmation that I accomplished what I set out to do. If my book "reinforces just what [Paul's] letters want hearers and readers to apprehend," then it has served faithfully as an instrument of the word. (I note with interest that Green chides me for precisely the same things that Sanders lauds: "appreciating Scripture not only as historically generated literature but also as canon.") To say that the book is a "specimen" of religion is to say, in the putatively value-neutral argot of the "religious studies" academic subculture, that it stands in confessional continuity with its subject matter, that it carries forward Paul's theological trajectory. If so, this is — for me — cause to rejoice.

Still, I find the dichotomy disturbing: Why are the confessional and the analytical deemed antithetical? Does a scholar's hermeneutical stance within a particular faith tradition preclude critical reflection about that tradition?[28] On the contrary, I would suggest that *Echoes* seeks to enact a mode of sympathetic reading that may be possible only for interpreters who know the tradition and its struggles from the inside.[29] By reflecting the text's message faithfully, but in a slightly new idiom, this kind of reading tries to make the text come alive for readers who otherwise would not be able to hear it. That is not the only thing scholarly analysis can or should do, but it is surely one legitimate aim of study. Does Green want to foreclose such readings?

27. Hays, *Echoes*, 184.
28. For an eloquent rebuttal to such assumptions, see R. L. Wilken, "Who Will Speak *for* the Religious Traditions?" *JAAR* 57 (1989): 699-717.
29. In the infelicitous, but perhaps useful, terminology current in anthropology, the book's account of Pauline hermeneutics is "emic" rather than "etic."

Response to J. Christiaan Beker

As I turn to J. Christiaan Beker's critique of *Echoes,* I find myself back on familiar terrain. Beker's most pressing questions address the exegesis of particular texts; his criticisms are not about the propriety of a theological reading of Paul but about the theological contours of the reading I have given. His challenges are particularly important for me to answer, because they express the sorts of objections that many traditional New Testament critics might have to my book. Beker divides his response into three sections: literary-critical and historical questions, exegetical issues, and theological questions. I shall consider briefly the first category of questions before discussing in more detail the exegetical and theological concerns.

Literary-Critical and Historical Questions

What are the constraints, Beker wants to know, on imaginative freedom, both Paul's and mine? There are two distinct questions here, I think: What constraints limit our critical assertions about the presence and significance of scriptural echoes in Paul's writings, and what constraints limit our own constructive theological uses of biblical texts? I have already answered both questions in *Echoes* as well as I know how.

Regarding the first question, I refer my colleague to pages 29-33, where I propound seven tests for assessing the possible presence of particular echoes in Paul's letters. Beker may not find the criteria proposed in my seven tests to be sufficient, but it is hard to see how they are less clear than Fishbane's; if anything, my criteria are more extensive and nuanced.[30] (These seven tests are further explained in my essay "'Who Has Believed Our Message?' Paul's Reading of Isaiah," pp. 34-44 in the present volume.)

Regarding the second question, I have offered three hermeneutical constraints on pages 190-91: our creative interpretations of Scripture must affirm that God remains faithful to the promises made to Israel, must confess the death and resurrection of Jesus as the decisive manifestation of God's righteousness, and must drive toward shaping the community of

---

30. I agree with Beker that Gail O'Day's "Jeremiah 9.22-23 and 1 Corinthians 1.26-31: A Study of Intertextuality" (*JBL* 109 [1990]: 259-67) is a splendid example of fruitful intertextual analysis.

readers into a community that embodies the love of God as shown forth in Christ. Beker cites this passage in a footnote, but — mysteriously — he seems to think it proposes that "echoes" themselves somehow serve as constraints on hermeneutical whimsy. I urge him to go back and read these pages again.

Likewise, I think Beker has simply misunderstood my treatment of Job 19:25-26 in relation to Phil 1:19. I cite the passage as a limiting case, a possible echo so faint that it has no semantic significance. It is employed as an illustration of the sort of echo I do *not* intend to discuss in the book.[31] I am forced to conclude that Beker was not reading very carefully at this point.

More weighty is Beker's question about the "communication-structure" in Paul's allusive uses of Scripture, its persuasive value for his readers. If these letters are pastoral communications addressing contingent situations, as Beker rightly insists, how effective are Paul's indirect echoes of a text that his readers, mostly Gentile converts, may not know very well in the first place? The question is an important one. The answer is that the effectiveness of Paul's communication strategy varies with different situations and with different readers/hearers. Each case must be considered individually. It would be wrong to assume that Paul was always a consummate communicator. The evidence suggests otherwise: he was trying, with mixed results, to resocialize his converts into a new symbolic world that was still in process of formation even in his own mind. There were some successes, some failures. Often it appears that his readers found him baffling. One reason for their incomprehension may have been that he was not able to fill in all the gaps left for his hearers by his allusive references to Scripture; he may have been consistently presupposing knowledge he ought not to have presupposed.

The basic point, however, is this: the fact that Paul was trying to communicate in contingent situations does *not* mean that he could not have used allusive echoes in his letters. When they are understood, allusions are potent strategies of communication. On the other hand, many uses of echoes and allusions are unpremeditated, subconscious; they are grasped consciously, even by their author, only sometimes.

Beker also remarks that he would have expected a more detailed discussion of "pesher and midrashic methods." Of course, we can hardly assume that Paul's original audience would have been acquainted with such

---

31. Hays, *Echoes*, 23-24.

methods. Beker's point is that midrashic exegesis selects proof texts without evoking the wider context of that citation. Actually, I doubt the adequacy of this characterization of the midrashists' use of Scripture,[32] but in any case, Paul's own hermeneutical practices are sufficiently different from theirs to demand independent investigation. (I note with some satisfaction that Green, whose own expertise is in the field of formative Judaism, endorsed my methodological decision to explicate Paul's readings of Scripture without using formal categories derived from rabbinic midrash.)[33]

Exegetical Issues

Beker's exegetical critique identifies four loci for discussion.

1. He challenges my declaration that "Deuteronomy 32 contains Romans *in nuce*." He notes that "the overall scheme of Deuteronomy 32 does not seem to apply to *all of Romans*, but only to the movement of Romans 9–11." This strikes me as an odd objection coming from Beker, who has published an article arguing persuasively that God's faithfulness to Israel is the central theme not only of chapters 9–11 but also of the letter as a whole.[34] Indeed, according to Beker, Rom 11:32 is "the climax and crown of Paul's argument."[35] If the contingent character of Romans appears most clearly in Rom 9–11, then whatever governs the movement of these three chapters is surely to be deemed generative for the entire epistle.

Consequently, Beker's protest that there are only three explicit citations of Deut 32 in Romans misses the point: Paul's meditation on the mystery of Israel's election, rejection, and restoration finds its theological genesis in Deuteronomy. The importance of Deut 32 is shown not only by explicit citations, but also by allusions in Rom 9:14 and 11:11-14. Beker quotes me — without citing a reference — as claiming that Deut 32 is present as a "pervasive echo" in Romans, but I cannot find any such statement

---

32. See D. Boyarin, *Intertextuality and the Reading of Midrash* (Bloomington: Indiana University Press, 1990) on the allusive character of the biblical references in rabbinic midrash.

33. Hays, *Echoes*, 10-14. Green's written response passes over this matter without comment; his agreement with my approach emerged in a group discussion.

34. Beker, "The Faithfulness of God and the Priority of Israel in Paul's Letter to the Romans," *HTR* 79 (1986): 10-16.

35. Beker, "The Faithfulness of God," 14.

in my text. My suggestion, rather, is that Deut 32 is generative, not that it is pervasive. To say that Deut 32 contains Romans *in nuce* is to say that Deuteronomy is to Romans as the acorn is to the oak tree.

Let me try to put the point another way: Deuteronomy provides a fundamental theological resource for Paul's attempt to explain the puzzling experience of his own missionary activity. Gentiles believe, Jews do not. What is happening here? Deuteronomy offers Paul not only the explanatory narrative pattern (covenant election, Israel's unfaithfulness, God's judgment, followed by God's ultimate gracious act of reconciliation/new creation), but also the "jealousy" theory, based on Deut 32:21, as an explanation for God's surprising decision to bring many Gentiles to salvation before reclaiming unfaithful Israel.

This is not to deny the comparable generativity of other scriptural sources. Genesis, Psalms, and Isaiah appear in Paul with regularity, and, as Beker notes, Hab 2:4 is given a place of special importance in the rhetorical structure of Romans. One might note, however, against Beker, that Habakkuk is quoted only *once* in Romans. How then, using Beker's criterion of frequency of citation, can it be claimed to be "*the* crucial Old Testament text for Paul"?[36]

2. Beker questions whether intertextual scriptural echo actually is as pervasive in Romans as I have claimed: "a superficial glance at the letter shows that, whereas scriptural references abound in chs. 1–4 and 9–11, they are almost completely absent in the crucial chs. 5–8 and sharply reduced in chs. 12–14, in order to reappear in the conclusion of the letter in ch. 15." The operative word here is "superficial."

One implication of my work is that we cannot confine our investigation of Pauline intertextuality to passages in which there is an explicit quotation (καθὼς γέγραπται) of a source. In fact, if we look not just for citations but for allusions to Old Testament figures and motifs, it is not difficult to show that the chapters Beker singles out contain fundamental features that would be incomprehensible apart from their relation to Old Testament subtexts. In Rom 5 we have Moses and — especially — Adam as key figures whose identity and stories are treated by Paul as *déjà lu;* furthermore, Rom 5:19 echoes Isa 53:11 artfully. In Rom 7 we find a complex analysis of the impact of the commandments of the Mosaic Torah on those who hear it, with Exod 20:17/Deut 5:21 taken as a paradigmatic illustration

---

36. See further discussion of Rom 10:6, below.

(Rom 7:7). In Rom 8 we find several pivotal scriptural allusions: the sin offering (8:3),[37] τὸ δικαίωμα τοῦ νόμου (8:4), the fallen creation subjected to decay (8:20-21), the echo of Abraham's offering of Isaac (Gen 22:12, 16: "did not spare his own son") in Rom 8:32, the citation of Ps 44 in Rom 8:36, and the many echoes of Isa 50 in the surrounding verses.[38]

I have cited here only the most obvious evidence in Rom 5–8. Does Beker really want to maintain that references to Scripture are "almost completely absent" in these chapters? Such a position can be maintained only by focusing narrowly on direct quotations and ignoring the Scripture-laden language that Paul employs in his own discourse. To be sure, Paul is not arguing *about* the interpretation of particular biblical texts in these chapters, as he is in other parts of the letter. But I never claimed that he was. Again, Beker's criticism simply suggests to me that he has misunderstood my discussion.

A book that begins with the assertion that the gospel was "promised beforehand through [the] prophets in holy Scriptures" (Rom 1:2) and concludes its train of argument with the glad affirmation that "whatever was written in former days was written for our instruction, so that by steadfastness and by the encouragement of the Scriptures we might have hope" (15:4) — with at least fifty-one direct Scripture quotations and dozens more allusions in between — can surely be claimed to be pervasively concerned with Scripture and its interpretation.[39] Can this be a controversial claim? As Paul might say, "I am astonished!"

Beker also contests my description of Rom 15:1-13 as the climax of the letter, claiming instead that 15:14-21 should be read as the climax. I believe that an analysis of the letter's rhetorical structure will support my view, but there is insufficient space here to set forth the argument. I note that my analysis is in agreement with J. D. G. Dunn, who treats 15:7-13 as a "concluding summary . . . intended to round off the body of the letter."[40]

---

37. See now the compelling argument of N. T. Wright that περὶ ἁμαρτίας in its context in Rom 8:3 must be a metaphorical reference to the Torah's offering for unwilling sin: *The Climax of the Covenant* (Edinburgh: T. & T. Clark, 1991), 220-25.

38. I have discussed the biblical texture of Rom 8:31-39 in *Echoes*, 57-63.

39. I leave aside the matter of Rom 16:26, which might not be an original part of the letter. Even if this is a conclusion added by a later editor, it shows that the letter was understood at a very early date as fundamentally concerned with the role of "prophetic writings" in making the gospel known.

40. Dunn, *Romans 9–16*, WBC 38B (Dallas: Word, 1988), 844.

3. Still arguing that Scripture does not play a constitutive role in Paul's thought, Beker contends, following the lead of Adolf von Harnack, that Paul cites Scripture only when he is forced into it by the contingency of refuting Judaizing opponents. (One might well doubt whether this is an appropriate description of the use of Scripture in Romans, but I let that pass for now.) The evidence for this position is supposed to be that Paul rarely cites Scripture in Philippians, 1 Thessalonians, and Philemon.

One of the last places I would have expected to find Chris Beker is in alliance with Harnack! Surely Beker's own programmatic case for the apocalyptic character of Pauline theology would be far better served by acknowledging the biblical roots of Paul's proclamation of the universal triumph of God than by attributing Paul's use of Scripture to purely contingent factors. I am, consequently, puzzled by Beker's decision to pursue this line of argument.

In any case, 1 Corinthians stands as the decisive refutation of the Harnack/Beker position. Here, where there is no "Judaizing" problem, Paul repeatedly employs biblical citations (e.g., 1:19; 1:31; 2:16; 3:19-20; 5:13; 6:16; 9:9; 10:7; 14:21, 25; 15:32; 15:54-55) and allusions, and he unreflectively addresses his Gentile converts as part of the covenant community (see especially 5:13; 10:1; 12:2).[41] In none of these cases is Paul arguing *about* the interpretation of Scripture or contending that some "Judaizing" tendency is to be rejected; rather, he simply takes Scripture as an authoritative or illuminating warrant in his argumentation. Furthermore, he assumes that his readers will acknowledge the force of such arguments.

It is noteworthy that the three letters claimed to show that Paul uses Scripture "only when the contingent situation forces him to do so" (Beker) are the three shortest of the letters generally acknowledged to be authentic. Thus, the absence of explicit citation is not so striking as it might be in a longer letter. In any case, the diction of these letters continues to reflect Paul's immersion in the language of Scripture. As I have noted elsewhere,[42] there are a number of biblical allusions in these letters: for example, Phil 1:19/Job 13:16; Phil 2:10-11/Isa 45:23; 1 Thess 3:9/Ps 115:3 LXX; 1 Thess 3:13/Zech 14:5 (?); 1 Thess 5:8/Isa 59:17.

---

41. For discussion of this rhetorical strategy in 1 Corinthians, see Hays, *Echoes*, 91-104. Now see also my essay "The Conversion of the Imagination," in the present volume (pp. 1-24).

42. Hays, *Echoes*, 195 n. 16; R. B. Hays, "Crucified with Christ," in *Pauline Theology* I, 246.

Even more peculiar is Beker's suggestion that the deutero-Pauline and Pastoral Epistles ought to be taken as evidence that Scripture was not crucial for Paul, because they rarely cite Scripture. Are we to conclude, Beker asks, "that Paul's pupils completely misunderstood him"? This argument can cut both ways. It is usually alleged that Paul's pupils did indeed misunderstand him, or at least that they developed the traditions of his teaching in directions quite foreign to the distinctive character of his own thought. That is how these later epistles are usually distinguished from the "authentic" ones. Why then should we find it surprising that second- or third-generation followers should have allowed Scripture to recede to a more peripheral position? That might be one more theological litmus test applied in conjunction with others (e.g., eschatology, ecclesiology) to demonstrate the inauthenticity of these letters. Surely this argument backfires on Beker.

4. Finally, we come to the matter of the exegesis of Rom 10. Beker correctly identifies this as a crucial text for my enterprise, and his remarks make it evident that we are in substantive disagreement about its proper interpretation. The passage is, on any showing, a very difficult one. A full discussion of the problems is impossible within the scope of this essay; I offer here only a response to some of Beker's specific criticisms. I am surprised that Beker describes my manner of argumentation as "apodictic." My claim that "Rom. 10.5 and 10.6 must not stand in antithesis to one another"[43] is not arbitrary: it is based on the evidence adduced in the foregoing paragraph (note that my sentence begins with a "therefore"), which Beker apparently overlooks. I shall restate the salient points: the whole argument of Romans insists repeatedly that the Law bears witness to the righteousness of God (3:21), and that the gospel of righteousness through faith confirms rather than abolishes the Law (3:31). The appeal to the story of Abraham (Rom 4) functions to support the claim that the law (i.e., Scripture) calls its hearers to receive righteousness through faith. "The mind set on the flesh" (τὸ φρόνημα τῆς σαρκός) does not submit to the Law of God (τῷ γὰρ νόμῳ τοῦ θεοῦ οὐχ ὑποτάσσεται — 8:7); this is synonymous with Paul's lament that his kinfolk κατὰ σάρκα have not submitted to the righteousness of God (τῇ δικαιοσύνῃ τοῦ θεοῦ οὐχ ὑπετάγησαν — 10:3). Those, however, who walk κατὰ πνεῦμα now fulfill τὸ δικαίωμα τοῦ νόμου (8:4); that is why Paul can affirm — based on the empirical evidence of his Gentile mission — that Christ is τέλος νόμου. "The sum and sub-

43. Hays, *Echoes*, 76.

stance of Torah . . . is righteousness through faith."[44] Otherwise, what possible function does the γάρ in 10:4 have? It would appear that, if Paul had meant what Beker proposes, he should have written ἀλλά instead.

In view of these considerations, I am amazed by Beker's assertion, on the basis of Rom 3:9-20, that "the argument in Romans . . . has already determined — *before* we read ch. 10 — that the νόμος, embodied in Lev. 18.5, can *only* [emphasis added] condemn us." Rather, I would suggest, this Reformation-era construal of Romans is so firmly fixed in Beker's mind before he reads chapter 10 that he ignores Paul's massive effort to assign a far more positive revelatory function to the Torah. As I propose in an important footnote, the burden of proof lies strongly on Beker and other interpreters who read τέλος as "termination."[45] The strength of the interpretation of τέλος as "goal, aim" is underscored by the convincing studies of Badenas and Meyer, cited in that note.[46]

To be sure, this means that Paul is interpreting Lev 18:5 in Romans in a way different from his negative construal of it in Gal 3:12. That is one of the difficulties for my interpretation of the passage. Nevertheless, I would suggest that this shift in the reading of Lev 18:5 is consistent with the larger shift between Paul's relentlessly negative treatment of the Law in Galatians and his more dialectical interpretation of it in Romans.

When Beker notes that "Paul underscores — contrary to Deuteronomy — πίστις and not the *miṣwoth* of the Torah," I would agree, with the important qualification that *Paul* himself does not at all think that his emphasis on πίστις is contrary to Deuteronomy. Indeed, he finds in Deuteronomy a decisive witness for ἡ ἐκ πίστεως δικαιοσύνη. This surprising revisionary reading, I have argued, is made possible in part by the hermeneutical focusing of Deut 32, in which God (in Moses' song) condemns Israel as "a perverse generation, sons in whom there is no πίστις" (Deut 32:20).[47]

Rom 10:5-10 remains a vexing passage because Paul so daringly coopts the voice of Moses. Paul's rhetorical strategy is one of revision rather than rejection. Despite our discomfort about his reading, we cannot es-

---

44. Hays, *Echoes*, 76.

45. Hays, *Echoes*, 208 n. 83.

46. In addition to the references cited in Hays, *Echoes*, 208 n. 83, see also C. T. Rhyne, *Faith Establishes the Law*, SBLDS 55 (Chico, Calif.: Scholars, 1981), and G. N. Davies, *Faith and Obedience in Romans*, JSNTSup 39 (Sheffield: JSOT Press, 1990), 185-204.

47. For discussion see Hays, *Echoes*, 82-83.

cape acknowledging that Paul is subjecting Deuteronomy to a hermeneutical transformation that makes the Law bear witness to the gospel. The Reformation reading of the passage (defended by Beker), on the other hand, plays down the hermeneutical scandal by factoring law and gospel out into the very antithesis that Paul (in Romans) is determined to preclude.

Theological Questions

Beker's first theological question is an outgrowth of his last exegetical one: Does my reading of Paul underestimate the discontinuity between "Israel and Christianity, that is, between law and gospel"?[48] Certainly this issue of continuity versus discontinuity is one of the central issues raised by my book. Beker acknowledges that my argument is an important "corrective to the views of Martin Luther and Rudolf Bultmann"; reciprocally, I will acknowledge that my work might occasionally overstate the case for continuity. If so, I have done so in the effort to redress what I perceive to be a drastic imbalance in the literature of the discipline. The task for all of us who seek to interpret Paul is to do justice to both aspects of his thought: he insists on the one hand that the gospel of Jesus Christ is a decisive and radically new manifestation of God's saving power and, at the same time, that this manifestation is fully consistent with — and adumbrated by — God's past gracious dealing with his people Israel. I think Beker and I are generally in agreement about this; the disagreements go back to matters of the exegesis of particular passages.

Secondly, Beker questions my description of Paul's hermeneutic as "ecclesiocentric." The question has two prongs. Beker asks, first, whether an ecclesiocentric hermeneutic can be separated from a christocentric one, since Paul understands the church as σῶμα Χριστοῦ. Here, as with regard to Beker's first theological question, I believe that whatever disagreements may exist are matters of emphasis. Many readers of *Echoes* seem to have reacted to my catchphrase "ecclesiocentric hermeneutics" without noting the conclusion of chapter 3:

---

48. This is the same issue raised, in slightly different terms, by William Scott Green's objection that I misconstrue literary intertextual linkage as theological continuity. See my discussion of this matter, above.

[C]hristology is the foundation on which his ecclesiocentric counter-readings are constructed . . . Gal. 3.29 finally unlocks the riddle of the relation between Paul's ecclesiocentric hermeneutic and his christological convictions. . . . [T]hese aspects of Pauline thought are complementary rather than contradictory: Paul's understanding of Jesus Christ as the one true heir of the promise to Abraham is the essential theological presupposition for his hermeneutical strategies, though these strategies are not in themselves christocentric.[49]

My emphasis on the ecclesiocentric character of Paul's hermeneutic is the result of seeking to ask in a disciplined manner, What is Paul actually *doing* with Scripture when he appeals to it in his arguments? The striking result of such an inquiry is to reveal the relative scarcity of christologically interpreted Old Testament passages in Paul. My explanation for this phenomenon is to propose that Paul's christological convictions belong to a foundational "substructure" of his thought; apart from his christological presuppositions, his ecclesiocentric (or, as I suggested above, *ecclesiotelic*) readings make no sense. To formulate the issue in these terms, however, still leaves room — and indeed, necessity — for a more careful study of the few passages in which Paul does interpret the scriptural text christologically (e.g., Rom 15:3).[50]

The second prong of Beker's question, however, precisely skewers my work: "How . . . is an ecclesiocentric hermeneutic related to Paul's apocalyptic perspective?" As I reread *Echoes* in light of Beker's complaint that my ecclesiocentric focus yields a reading of Paul as having a "realized eschatology," I must acknowledge the force of the objection. Most of my attention is given to the way in which past narratives find their meaning in the present reality of Paul's churches, to whom he proclaims, "Now is the day of salvation" (2 Cor 6:2). By identifying the apocalyptic context of Paul's ecclesiocentric hermeneutic, I intended to locate his interpretative activity within the "already/not yet" dialectic that pervades his thought, but in fact my discussion fails to do justice to the "not yet" pole.

To remedy this deficiency my analysis ought to place more emphasis on two key points. First, when Paul writes that the words of Scripture were

---

49. Hays, *Echoes*, 120-21. Cf. the exegesis of Gal 3 in my earlier work, *The Faith of Jesus Christ*; see especially 193-209, 225-35.

50. See my essay "Christ Prays the Psalms," pp. 101-18 in the present volume.

written "for our instruction, upon whom the ends of the ages have met" (1 Cor 10:11), he identifies the church as standing precisely at the temporal juncture in which the old age has lost its claim upon us but the new age is present only proleptically. That, in fact, is precisely the force of his use of the story of the exodus generation: let the one who thinks he stands (the "strong" in the Corinthian church) take heed lest he fall (1 Cor 10:12). The story is not over yet, and the church should imagine itself to be, analogously to Israel in the wilderness, a pilgrim people that has not yet arrived at its promised destination. Second, Rom 9–11 clearly underscores the provisional character of the experience of salvation in the church. Just as those who have received the firstfruits of the Spirit still groan and suffer along with the unredeemed creation (Rom 8:18-25), so the present community that confesses Jesus as Lord remains anomalous and incomplete, in anguish over Israel's unbelief until the eschatological consummation in which "all Israel shall be saved" (Rom 11:26). These "unrealized" aspects of Paul's eschatology must be acknowledged as integral to his hermeneutical perspective. I regret that my discussion did not illuminate this aspect of Paul's thought — which I myself consider of central importance for Pauline theology — more adequately.[51]

Beker's final theological question, however, seems to me to miss the mark. He accuses me of "imposing a Methodist hermeneutic on Paul," by which he means that "the Word is now fully fused with the gift of the Spirit" in such a way that the church "embodies the Spirit completely," with the result that written word loses its critical function, its "*overagainstness*' to the church." No doubt my insistence on the embodiment of the word in the real-world obedience of the faithful is influenced by my own Wesleyan heritage, but I categorically reject the charge that my interpretation of Paul leads to an abandonment of the critical function of the word over against the church. On the contrary, it seems to me that Paul conceives of the word as alive and dangerous, always at work to shape and transform the community in ways that could not have been predicted. That is the explicit import of my use of Thomas Greene's category of "dialectical imitation" to describe Paul's reading strategy: "two symbolic worlds are brought into collision so that each is vulnerable to criticism and

---

51. With regard to Beker's insistence that Paul's apocalyptic perspective has "a theocentric focus and climax," I refer the reader back to my response to Sanders's similar point, above.

interpretation by the other."[52] I argue that "Paul's allusive manner of using Scripture leaves enough silence for the voice of Scripture to answer back. . . . The word that Scripture speaks where Paul falls silent is a word that still has the power to contend against him."[53]

To follow Paul's example, then, as I have urged, would mean to stand with him in this life-or-death wrestling with the word, recognizing that all our claims about God's activity in our lives must be subjected to the scrutiny of Scripture and — simultaneously — that our readings of Scripture must always be subject to the test of enactment:[54] "No reading of Scripture can be legitimate, then, if it fails to shape the readers into a community that embodies the love of God as shown forth in Christ."[55] If Beker wants to call that a "Methodist hermeneutic," so be it. In such a hermeneutic, has the word lost its critical function? Μὴ γένοιτο. On the contrary, we uphold the word's critical function by upholding its living power.

Conclusion

Despite my emphatic rejoinder to Beker's final theological question, I deeply appreciate his asking it. This is precisely the sort of ultimate theological question that we exegetes ought to ask each other. That we do it so seldom is an indictment of our discipline. The present forum, however, has been an occasion for considering issues that matter profoundly. Our elder brother Paul would be pleased, I think, with the theological gravity of our debate. My thanks again to Evans, Sanders, Green, and Beker for their careful and provocative responses. May this round of discussion help us all to a better understanding of the way in which Paul heard Scripture and the ways in which the word is near also to us.

---

52. Hays, *Echoes,* 174.

53. Hays, *Echoes,* 177.

54. See G. Steiner's fine account of hermeneutics as "the enactment of answerable understanding" in *Real Presences* (Chicago: University of Chicago Press, 1989), 7-11.

55. Hays, *Echoes,* 191.

A Hermeneutic of Trust

The Protestant reformers of the sixteenth century proclaimed that God's word in Scripture must serve as the final judge of all human tradition and experience. Left to our own devices, we are capable of infinite self-deception, confusion, and evil. We therefore must turn to Scripture and submit ourselves to it, the Reformers insisted, to find our disorders rightly diagnosed and healed. Only through the biblical writers' testimony do we encounter the message of God's grace; only the revelation of Jesus Christ, disclosed uniquely and irreplaceably through the testimony of the evangelists and apostles, tells us the truth about the merciful God and our relationship to that God. Without this word which comes to us from outside ourselves, we are lost.

Clearly, the climate in which we read the Bible has changed drastically. Living as we do on this side of the Enlightenment, we cannot escape the intellectual impact of the great "masters of suspicion": Nietzsche, Marx, Freud, and more recently Foucault, along with other purveyors of "critical theory." These thinkers have sought to demystify language and to expose the ways in which our linguistic and cultural systems are constructed by ideologies that further the interests of those who hold power.

The Bible has not been exempt from such suspicious scrutiny. One need only consider the book display at the annual convention of the American Academy of Religion and the Society of Biblical Literature. Anyone who spends time browsing there will find the stalls flooded with books that apply a hermeneutic of suspicion to biblical texts. Some portray the apostolic witnesses less as revelatory witnesses to God's mercy than as oppressive promulgators of abusive images of God. For example, Elisabeth Schüssler Fiorenza writes that "a feminist critical hermeneutics of suspicion places a warning label on all biblical texts: *Caution! Could be dangerous to your health and survival.*"[1] I am not suggesting that suspicious interpreters categorically reject the Bible; most of them believe it can contain both liberating and oppressive messages. That is why they suggest that we must subject the Bible to ideological critique. Elsewhere Schüssler Fiorenza explains: "[N]o biblical patriarchal text that perpetuates violence against women, children, or 'slaves' should be accorded the status of divine revelation if we do not want to turn the God of the Bible into a God of violence. That does not mean that we cannot preach . . . on the household code texts of the New Testament. It only means that we must preach them critically in order to unmask them as texts promoting patriarchal violence."[2]

The moral passion of such statements is to be welcomed. Sadly, our common history is marked by epidemic violence, including violence against women, children, and the powerless. Certainly this violence is to be condemned, and one might hope that interpreters of the Bible would have good grounds for proclaiming such condemnation. The difficulty in which we find ourselves, however, is this: If the Bible itself — the revelatory, identity-defining text of the Christian community — is portrayed as oppressive, on what basis do we know God or relate to God? A corollary question has crucial implications for biblical interpretation: If the Bible is dangerous, on what ground do we stand in conducting a critique of Scripture that will render it less harmful?

For Schüssler Fiorenza the answer to the latter question is clear: a feminist critical hermeneutic "does not appeal to the Bible as its primary source but begins with women's own experience and vision of liberation."[3] *Experience* (of a certain sort) is treated as unambiguously revelatory, and the Bible is critically scrutinized in its light. Regrettably, many practitioners of the hermeneutics of suspicion — and by no means only feminist interpreters — are remarkably credulous about the claims of experience. As a result, they endlessly critique the biblical texts but rarely get around to hearing Scripture's critique of us, or hearing its message of grace.

1. Schüssler Fiorenza, "The Will to Choose or to Reject: Continuing Our Critical Work," in *Feminist Interpretation of the Bible,* ed. L. Russell (Philadelphia: Westminster, 1985), 130.

2. Schüssler Fiorenza, *Bread Not Stone: The Challenge of Feminist Biblical Interpretation* (Boston: Beacon Press, 1984), 145.

3. Schüssler Fiorenza, *Bread Not Stone,* 88.

While the hermeneutics of suspicion — rightly employed — occupies a proper place in any attempt to interpret the Bible for our time, I want to argue that *a hermeneutic of trust* is both necessary and primary. To get our bearings on the question of our fundamental attitude toward Scripture, I propose that we take our cue from the Reformers and return to Scripture itself.[4] If we attend carefully to Paul's treatment of trust and distrust in his letter to the Romans, the apostle may lead us to suspect our own suspicions.

This essay will proceed in four stages: (1) an examination of Paul's use of the term πίστις ("faith" or "trust") and its opposite, ἀπιστία (literally, "unfaith" or "distrust"), in Romans; (2) some observations about the relation between trust and atonement; (3) a discussion of Paul's *own* approach to Scripture interpretation as a model of the hermeneutic of trust; and (4) some theses about the practical implications of all this for our own practices of interpretation.

Ἀπιστία and Πίστις in Romans

According to Paul, those who stand in right relation to God are those who hear and trust what God has spoken. He laments Israel's tragic failure to do this. The name he gives that failure is ἀπιστία (Rom 3:3). The term refers both to the failure of the people of Israel to obey God's Torah and to their failure to trust God's covenant promises — and the two things are bound closely together. Their ἀπιστία has been brought into stark focus for Paul through their negative response to the proclaimed gospel of Jesus Christ. He addresses the problem explicitly in Rom 3:1-4: "Then what advantage has the Jew? Or what is the value of circumcision? Much, in every way. For in the first place they were entrusted (ἐπιστεύθησαν) with the oracles of God. What if some were unfaithful (ἠπίστησαν)? Their ἀπιστία doesn't nullify the πίστις of God, does it? By no means!" Paul's wordplay highlights the contrast between human infidelity and God's fidelity: God's faithfulness to Israel (πίστις) is declared to Israel through the word of promise ("the oracles of God"). But Israel, failing to trust that word, is

---

4. The Reformers were not naive or credulous readers: they were acutely suspicious of the ecclesiastical institutions that controlled interpretation in their time; however, it was their conviction that only a fresh reading of Scripture under the guidance of the Holy Spirit gave them critical leverage against these institutions.

guilty of unfaithfulness — ἀπιστία. We might well translate the word here as "distrust" or "suspicion." Rather than trusting the scriptural oracles of God (which in Paul's view point to Christ and the church), they have slid away into unfaithfulness, just like the Gentiles. (Cf. also 9:30-33.) Nonetheless, their unfaithfulness cannot negate the faithfulness of the God who has embraced them through the covenant promise spoken to them.

The paradoxical relation between Israel's unfaithfulness and the divine faithfulness creates the problem Paul wrestles with throughout the letter. His reflections on these issues culminate in chapter 11, where the theme of Israel's ἀπιστία arises once again in his metaphor of the olive branches broken off the tree: "They were broken off because of their ἀπιστία, but you stand only through πίστις. . . . But even these, if they do not persist in ἀπιστία, will be grafted in, for God has the power to graft them in again" (Rom 11:20, 23).

Earlier in the letter Paul depicted Abraham, in contrast to unfaithful Israel, as the figural type of trust in God:

> Hoping against hope, he trusted (ἐπίστευσεν) that he would become "the father of many nations," according to what was said, "So numerous shall your descendants be" [Gen 15:5]. He did not weaken in trust (πίστις) when he considered his own body, which was already as good as dead (for he was about a hundred years old), or when he considered the barrenness of Sarah's womb. No ἀπιστία made him waver concerning the promise of God, but he grew strong in trust (πίστις) as he gave glory to God, being fully convinced that God was able to do what he had promised. (Rom 4:18-21)

This passage is particularly interesting because Abraham's πίστις is interpreted explicitly as his *trust* in God's promise despite its incongruence with Abraham's own *experience* of sterility and frustration. Abraham might have had good reason to exercise a hermeneutic of suspicion toward the divine word that had promised him numerous descendants, for all the empirical evidence — his experience — seemed to disconfirm God's word. Yet he did not: "no ἀπιστία, no suspicion, made him waver." Abraham was not a simpleton who failed to see the tension between his experience and the word that God had spoken to him. He had to wrestle with doubts and — indeed — with the extinction of all human hope for normal progeny. This wrestling is clearer in the Genesis narrative, where Abraham openly questions God (see Gen 15:2-3; 16:1-16; 17:17-18; for Sarah's doubts see 18:12-15), than in Paul's brief summary. Nonetheless, according to Paul, Abraham discounted his own experience, rejected skepticism, and clung to the promise of God "who gives life to the dead and calls into existence the things that do not exist" (Rom 4:17); therefore, "it was reckoned to him as righteousness." Thus, Abraham becomes the prototype of the community of faith, which interprets all human experience through trust in God's word: in short, *Abraham exemplifies a hermeneutic of consent, a hermeneutic of trust.* (In this respect he is like Mary, who asks suspiciously, "How can this be?" but in the end submits herself to the word of promise: "Let it be with me according to your word" [Luke 1:34, 38].)

A trusting hermeneutic is essential for all who believe the word of the resurrection but still see the creation groaning in bondage to decay and do not yet see death made subject to God. The hermeneutics of trust turns out to be, on closer inspection, a hermeneutics of death and resurrection[5] — a way of seeing the whole world through the lens of the kerygma. Our reliance on God entails a death to common sense, and our trust is validated only by the resurrection.

Trust and Atonement

For Paul the theme of trust — πίστις — is also intimately related to the formation of right relations between God and humans. Another way of saying this is that for Paul the themes of trust and atonement are inseparable. But I must sound an important caveat here. We must not suppose that we can place ourselves in right relation to God through our own act of trust, as though faith were a meritorious work. Rather, Paul's argument is that covenant relationship is restored by God's initiative διὰ πίστεως Ἰησοῦ Χριστοῦ — through the faithfulness of Jesus Christ. Thus, for Paul trust and atonement are inextricably linked *in the person of Jesus Christ.*[6]

Paul's view of the relationship between trust and atonement is most compactly articulated in Rom 3. The argument goes like this:

5. I owe this observation to N. T. Wright (conversation on November 17, 1996). See now also R. B. Hays, "Reading Scripture in Light of the Resurrection," in *The Art of Reading Scripture,* ed. E. F. Davis and R. B. Hays (Grand Rapids: Eerdmans, 2003), 216-38.

6. See R. B. Hays, *The Faith of Jesus Christ: The Narrative Substructure of Gal 3:1–4:11,* 2nd ed. (Grand Rapids: Eerdmans, 2002).

1. Israel's ἀπιστία cannot nullify the faithfulness (πίστις) of God (3:3-6a).
2. Jews and Greeks alike are under the power of sin (3:9-18).
3. The Law holds the whole world accountable to God but has no power to *justify* those who are under the power of sin — to set them in right relation to God (3:19-20).
4. Therefore God's justice has been manifested apart from the Law through the faithfulness of Jesus Christ (3:21-22) — through his obedient, self-sacrificial death on the cross.[7]

Thus, according to Paul, God has overcome our ἀπιστία through a dramatic new act of πίστις — the πίστις of Jesus Christ, whom God "put forward" as a definitive demonstration (ἔνδειξις) of God's own covenant faithfulness (3:25). That is the meaning of "the righteousness of God" (3:21). Our relationship of trust with God is restored through the faith of Jesus Christ.

Those who receive this good news respond to it with trust. Their πίστις, which is prefigured in the Old Testament story of Abraham, becomes shaped by the pattern of Jesus' own faith-obedience. That is part of what Paul means when he says that those whom God calls are to be "conformed to the image of his Son" (Rom 8:29), and when he calls upon his readers to model themselves upon Christ Jesus who emptied himself and became obedient even unto death on a cross (Phil 2:5-13).

Thus, atonement for Paul is not merely the forgiveness of sins through a vicarious blood sacrifice. Atonement also entails the *transformation* of God's people into the image of Jesus Christ, who is the embodiment of trust in God. Because Jesus was faithful, we are both called and enabled to trust.

Paul's Own Interpretative Practice

Paul's understanding of *trust* not only characterizes his view of atonement but also shapes his hermeneutical theory and practice. Israel, he says, failed to trust the oracles of God (Rom 3:2-3), but he is determined that this error not be repeated in the interpretative practices of the new community of

---

7. Cf. Rom 5:19: "through the obedience of one man the many were constituted δίκαιοι [righteous]."

faith that is constituted by the trust of Jesus. With his mind remade by the gospel, Paul goes back to Scripture and reads it anew through a hermeneutic of trust.

Rereading Scripture from this new perspective was no less challenging a task for him than trusting God's promise was for Abraham. The actual *experience* of Paul's missionary preaching had created a serious difficulty, both for Paul and for the new community. As Paula Fredricksen has expressed it, among those who believed the gospel, there were "too many Gentiles, too few Jews, and no end in sight."[8] If God's purpose was to overcome Israel's ἀπιστία, what had gone wrong? Why did Israel persist in ἀπιστία even when it heard the proclamation of the heralds of good news?

In light of this crisis, Paul was driven back to Scripture. The promises of God to Israel must be true, he reasoned, because "the gifts and the call of God are irrevocable" (Rom 11:29). But how can this be true in light of his own *experience?* Jews refused to accept the good news, and God apparently had conferred grace upon those who had not even been seeking righteousness at all — the Gentiles. Scripture must be true, but how can this situation be understood?

The problem comes to a head, of course, in Rom 9–11. "I say then, has God abandoned his people?" (11:1). Paul's answer is a ringing μὴ γένοιτο, "No way!" Trusting that God had not abandoned Israel, he wrestled with Scripture and found his way to a powerful new reading of God's promises.

Rom 9–11 is a powerful example of the hermeneutic of trust in action. In these chapters Paul achieves a transformative rereading of Scripture through the lens of the conviction he articulated earlier in Rom 5:8: "God shows his love for us in that while we were yet sinners Christ died for us." This conviction, applied to the problem of Israel's ἀπιστία, leads Paul to discover in Scripture both the prefiguration of God's calling of the Gentiles ("Those who were not my people, I will call 'my people'" — 9:25, quoting Hos 2:25 [= Hos 2:23 in English translations]) and the prefiguration of his ultimate mercy on Israel ("'God has not abandoned his people,' whom he foreknew" — 11:2, quoting Ps 94:14).[9]

Thus, in Paul's fresh reading of Scripture the whole mysterious drama

---

8. Paula Fredricksen, "Judaism, the Circumcision of the Gentiles, and Apocalyptic Hope: Another Look at Galatians 1 and 2," *JTS* 42 (1991): 532-64.

9. Or again: "The deliverer will come from Zion; he will banish unfaithfulness from Jacob; and this will be my covenant with them when I take away their sins" — Rom 11:26-27, quoting Isa 59:20-21 and Isa 27:9, while alluding also to Jer 31:33-34.

of God's election of Israel, Israel's hardening, the incorporation of Gentiles into the people of God, and Israel's ultimate restoration is displayed as foretold *in Scripture itself* — but this foretelling can be recognized only when Scripture is read through the hermeneutic of trust. God's oracles and promises are interpreted anew, in ways no one could have foreseen, in light of the experience of grace through the death and resurrection of Jesus. At the same time, the church's experience in Paul's own historical moment is interpreted in light of Scripture, which leads Paul to warn Gentile believers against being wise in their own conceits (11:25a). Events are in God's hands. Gentiles have no reason to boast. This dialectical process through which experience is positively correlated with Scripture is possible only through the hermeneutics of trust.[10]

Reading Scripture with a Hermeneutic of Trust

What consequences follow from this analysis of Paul's hermeneutics for *our* work as interpreters of the word? At least three things can be said.

1. To read Scripture rightly we must *trust* the God who speaks through Scripture. As Schüssler Fiorenza rightly insists, this God is not a God of violence, not an abuser, not a deceiver. This God so passionately desires our safety and wholeness that he has given his own Son to die for us. "The one who did not spare his own Son but gave him up for us all, how will he not also graciously give us all things, along with him?" (Rom 8:32). Like Abraham, like Mary, like Jesus, like Paul, we stand before God with empty and open hands. That is the posture in which the reading of Scripture is rightly to be performed. Peter Stuhlmacher says something similar when he calls for a "hermeneutics of consent" *(Einverständnis):* a readiness to receive trustingly what a loving God desires to give us through the testimony of those who have preceded us in the faith.[11]

2. What, then, of the hermeneutics of suspicion? Is all questioning to be excluded, all critical reading banished? Μὴ γένοιτο. Asking necessary and difficult questions is not to be equated with ἀπιστία. When we read

---

10. For a much fuller discussion of Paul's strategies as an interpreter of Scripture, see R. B. Hays, *Echoes of Scripture in the Letters of Paul* (New Haven: Yale University Press, 1989).

11. P. Stuhlmacher, *Historical Criticism and Theological Interpretation of Scripture* (Philadelphia: Fortress, 1977).

Scripture through a hermeneutic of trust in God, we discover that we should indeed be suspicious: suspicious first of all of ourselves, because our own minds have been corrupted and shaped by the present evil age (Gal 1:4). Our minds must be transformed by grace, and that happens nowhere more powerfully than through reading Scripture receptively and trustingly with the aid of the Holy Spirit.

Reading receptively and trustingly does not mean accepting everything in the text at face value, as Paul's own critical sifting of the Torah demonstrates. Cases may arise in which we must acknowledge internal tensions within Scripture that require us to choose guidance from one biblical witness and to reject another. Because the witness of Scripture itself is neither simple nor univocal, the hermeneutics of trust is necessarily a matter of faithful struggle to hear and discern.[12] Consequently, we welcome the readings offered by feminists and other interpreters whose experience enables them to hear the biblical texts in new and challenging ways.

At the same time, we should be suspicious of the institutions that govern and shape interpretation. That means not only ecclesiastical institutions but also academic institutions. If our critical readings lead us away from trusting the grace of God in Jesus Christ, then something is amiss, and we would do well to interrogate the methods and presuppositions that have taught us to distance ourselves arrogantly or fearfully from the text and to miss Scripture's gracious word of promise.

3. My concern that distrust may impede our reading of the Bible leads me to my final point. The real work of interpretation is to *hear* the text. We must consider how to read and teach Scripture in a way that opens up its message, a way that both models and fosters trust in God. So much of the ideological critique that currently dominates the academy fails to achieve these ends. Scripture is critiqued but never *interpreted*. The critic *exposes* but never *exposits*. Thus the word itself recedes into the background, and we are left talking only about the politics of interpretation, having lost the capacity to *perform* interpretations.

Many of us in the academy are weary of these tactics of critical evasion. And perhaps the tide is beginning to turn. Frank Lentricchia, who

---

12. For an extended attempt to work out how Scripture might shape the community of faith, including situations in which we find internal tensions within the canon, see R. B. Hays, *The Moral Vision of the New Testament: Community, Cross, New Creation* (San Francisco: HarperSanFrancisco, 1996).

teaches English literature at Duke, has published a remarkable public recantation of his prior complicity with an approach to criticism that concentrates on literary *theory* and ignores *literature*. The piece, which appeared in *Lingua Franca*, was titled "Last Will and Testament of an Ex-Literary Critic."

Lentricchia, whose earlier work earned him the epithet "the Dirty Harry of literary theory," was the author of *Criticism and Social Change* (1983), which argued for reading all literature as "the most devious of rhetorical discourses (writing with political designs upon us all), either in opposition to or in complicity with the power in place."[13] But Lentricchia has grown impatient with having his own critical perspective parroted by graduate students who have no love of literature, no appreciation for the themes and content of great literature — indeed, who rarely read it at all because they are so enamored of "critical theory." So now Lentricchia repents publicly:

> Over the last ten years, I've pretty much stopped reading literary criticism, because most of it isn't literary. But criticism it is of a sort — the sort that stems from the sense that one is morally superior to the writers that one is supposedly describing. This posture is assumed when those writers represent the major islands of Western literary tradition, the central cultural engine — so it goes — of racism, poverty, sexism, homophobia, and imperialism: a cesspool that literary critics would expose for mankind's benefit. . . . It is impossible, this much is clear, to exaggerate the heroic self-inflation of academic literary criticism. . . . The fundamental, if only implied, message of much literary criticism is self-righteous, and it takes this form: "T. S. Eliot is a homophobe and I am not. Therefore, I am a better person than Eliot. Imitate me, not Eliot." To which the proper response is: "But T. S. Eliot could really write, and you can't. Tell us truly, is there no filth in your soul?"[14]

Lentricchia's question, "Tell us truly, is there no filth in your soul?" reaches back, perhaps unwittingly, to the deeper roots from which the Western literary imagination springs — an imaginative tradition that owes

---

13. Lentricchia, "Last Will and Testament of an Ex-Literary Critic," *Lingua Franca*, September/October 1996, 60.

14. Lentricchia, "Last Will and Testament," 60.

much to Paul's hermeneutic of trust in God and suspicion of ourselves. Precisely because there is filth in our own souls we come to the text of Scripture, expecting to find the hidden things of our hearts laid bare, and expecting to encounter there the God who loves us.

When I was an undergraduate at Yale University, students flocked to Professor Alvin Kernan's lecture courses on Shakespeare. Kernan's work predated the academy's current infatuation with ideological criticism. Even though it was the late 1960s and we were all living in an atmosphere charged with political suspicion and protest, none of this overtly impinged on Kernan's lectures. Kernan was not a flashy lecturer. What, then, was the draw?

He *loved* the texts. His teaching method — as I remember it — was simply to engage in reflective close readings of the Shakespeare tragedies and comedies, delineating their rich texture of image and metaphor and opening up their complex central themes — moral, philosophical, and religious. Often, Kernan would devote a significant part of his lecture time to reading the text aloud, not in any highly dramatic manner, but with sensitivity to the text's rhythms and semantic nuances. I would often sit in class thinking, "Oh! . . . I hadn't *heard* that in the text before." And I would leave the class pondering the problems Shakespeare addressed: love, betrayal, fidelity, sacrifice, death, and hope.

In Shakespeare's *Measure for Measure* the self-righteous villain Angelo pronounces a death sentence on Claudio, who is guilty of committing fornication. Claudio's sister Isabella comes to Angelo to plead for the life of her brother, but Angelo, who is trying to manipulate Isabella into bed with him, spurns her suit, saying,

> Your brother is a forfeit of the law,
> And you but waste your words.

Isabella's reply alludes to the great theme of Romans and calls upon the hypocritical judge Angelo to see his life anew in light of God's judgment and grace:

> Why, all the souls that were were forfeit once;
> And He that might the vantage best have took
> Found out the remedy. How would you be
> If He, which is the top of judgment, should

But judge you as you are? O, think on that;
And mercy then will breathe within your lips,
Like man new made.[15]

Isabella resists the oppressor by applying a hermeneutic of suspicion to his pose of righteousness and by appealing to a hermeneutic of trust in the biblical story of God's mercy. Isabella is a profound interpreter of Scripture. We should follow her example.

15. W. Shakespeare, *Measure for Measure* 2.2.

Index of Names

Index of Scripture and Other Ancient Literature